Hebrew Hammer

Hebrew Hammer

A Biography of Al Rosen,
All-Star Third Baseman

JOSEPH WANCHO

McFarland & Company, Inc., Publishers
Jefferson, North Carolina

This book has undergone peer review.

LIBRARY OF CONGRESS CATALOGUING-IN-PUBLICATION DATA

Names: Wancho, Joseph, author.
Title: Hebrew Hammer : a biography of Al Rosen, all-star third baseman /
    Joseph Wancho.
Description: Jefferson : McFarland & Company, Inc., Publishers, 2022 |
    Includes bibliographical references and index.
Identifiers: LCCN 2021058424 | ISBN 9781476681313
    (paperback : acid free paper) ∞
    ISBN 9781476643939 (ebook)
Subjects: LCSH: Rosen, Al. | Baseball players—United States—Biography. |
    Cleveland Indians (Baseball team)—History—20th century. | Baseball
    managers—United States—Biography. | BISAC: SPORTS & RECREATION /
    Baseball / History
Classification: LCC GV865.R68 W36 2022 | DDC 796.357092 [B]—dc23
LC record available at https://lccn.loc.gov/2021058424

BRITISH LIBRARY CATALOGUING DATA ARE AVAILABLE

ISBN (print) 978-1-4766-8131-3
ISBN (ebook) 978-1-4766-4393-9

Front cover: Al Rosen prepares to unleash his potent swing.
(National Baseball Hall of Fame and Museum, Cooperstown, New York)

Printed in the United States of America

McFarland & Company, Inc., Publishers
    Box 611, Jefferson, North Carolina 28640
    www.mcfarlandpub.com

In loving memory of my mother,
Kathleen A. Wancho (1934–2020).
Her favorite player as a young Tribe fan
was Al Rosen. That is partly the reason
why I wrote his biography.

Acknowledgments

My name might be on the cover of the book you are now holding, but there were certainly a great many folks who gave their time unselfishly to see this volume to completion.

My thanks to Gary Mitchem, the senior acquisitions editor at McFarland. It was the first time I have written a full-length biography of any person. Gary made it as seamless as possible and put many of my fears to rest.

I am indebted to my own editing team. Tom Wancho and John Wasko read through the manuscript and offered sound critique and thoughtful ideas on how to improve the text. Carl Riechers served as fact-checker. I thought I was in trouble when Carl insisted on having copies of every newspaper source I used. But that work was well worth the trouble. Carl was right on the ball with his inquiries.

Brian Meggitt from the Cleveland Public Library and John Horne from the National Baseball Hall of Fame provided photos. Thank you, gentlemen.

A big thank you to Vern Morrison and Beth Piwkowski form the Michael Schwartz Library at Cleveland State University. They were both extremely helpful in providing images of Al Rosen from their *Cleveland Press* Collection.

Cassidy Lent from the National Baseball Hall of Fame sent me Al Rosen's clip file. I have requested players' files from Cassidy on many occasions. She always comes through promptly. Her help is very much appreciated.

I am indebted to Al Rosen's oldest son, Rob, who provide insight to the Rosen family that I would not have gotten elsewhere.

All the statistics were courtesy of baseball-reference.com and retrosheet.org.

My thanks to the following, who in some way, offered a hand when I needed it: Bill Deane, Andy McCue, Bob Rosen, Jeff Miles, Morris Eckhouse, Robert Garratt, and Bob Emling.

Table of Contents

Introduction

"Rosen was the best player I ever played with. He was
a tremendous fielder and could really swing the bat.
He made himself a great player by working hard."
—Al Smith[1]

Al Rosen was the star third baseman for the Cleveland Indians in
the decade of the 1950s. From 1950 through 1956, Rosen was arguably
the greatest third baseman in the American League. The Indians won
one pennant (1954) and finished second to the New York Yankees five
times (1951–1953, 1955–1956) in that decade.

In 1953, Al Rosen was voted the Most Valuable Player in the American League. He led the league in home runs (43), RBI (145), and runs
(115). Rosen batted .336, finishing second to Washington's Mickey Vernon, who batted .337. Rosen was the first player to be voted MVP unanimously by the Baseball Writers' Association of America (BWAA). He
was also named *The Sporting News* AL and MLB MVP for 1953.

Even though Rosen proved himself between the white lines with
his skill as a baseball player, he still faced adversity. Rosen, who was
Jewish, was the recipient of taunts and jeers from fans and opposing players. Cleveland General Manager Hank Greenberg, who, like
Rosen, was Jewish, was persecuted two decades earlier for his heritage,
but to a greater degree. Instead of leaning on Greenberg for support,
Rosen met his tormentors head-on. A middleweight boxing champion
in military school, Rosen often used his fists to quiet those who chose
to make his being Jewish an issue. "On more than one occasion, you
had to assert yourself by challenging someone. You had to be better
than they were."[2]

The moniker "Hebrew Hammer" was bestowed on Greenberg
during his great career with the Detroit Tigers. The name was passed

on to Rosen, who not only could hammer a baseball, but as an amateur pugilist, often did the same to his opponents.

In a game against Chicago, the White Sox dugout was located on the third base side. A player was giving the business to Rosen, calling him a "Jew Bastard." When the inning ended, instead of moving across the diamond to the first base side, Rosen took a detour to the Sox dugout. He challenged the whole bench, but no one came out.[3]

In another instance, Rosen argued with an umpire about a call he made at third base. Rosen told the arbiter that he blew the call. The umpire told Cleveland shortstop George Strickland that he would get "that Jew Bastard" one of these days. Of course, nothing ever came of it.[4]

Rosen, who was noted for having a quick temper, played baseball with a chip on his shoulder. During his tenure as a starting third baseman, Rosen was the best player on some great Indians teams. Not only could he put up tremendous offensive numbers, Rosen showed leadership off the field as well.

On April 25, 1954, Rosen was asked to move to first base. If Cleveland had a weak link in their lineup, it was the need for a first sacker. Indians' manager Al Lopez asked Rosen to move across the diamond to man first base. Lopez assured Rosen that the move was a temporary one, maybe a couple of weeks, while the front office found a permanent solution to fill the position.

Rosen agreed to the move, putting the team ahead of himself. It was a typical case of Rosen showing his leadership on a championship-caliber team. Today, it would be unheard of to move a reigning MVP to a new position. But Rosen never thought twice about the switch.

Rookie Rudy Regalado was inserted at the hot corner, and the former University of Southern California star had a career month, batting .310 in May. Rosen's time at first base went from two weeks to seven.

On May 25 at Chicago, Rosen fractured his right index finger making a routine play at first. But true to form, he stayed in the lineup, putting the team's needs in front of his own. The finger never healed properly, and it was the major reason why Rosen's production on the diamond suffered the rest of that season and the following two years.

After his baseball career ended, Rosen stayed in Cleveland and raised his family in suburban Shaker Heights. He worked as a stockbroker, rising to president of a commodities firm in Cleveland. Through his relationship with Gabe Paul, the general manager of the Indians in the late 1960s and early 1970s, Rosen served on the board of directors of the Cleveland club.

He returned to baseball full-time in 1978, when he was offered the position of president of the New York Yankees by owner George Steinbrenner. One of the moves he made was to fire manager Billy Martin in mid-season and replace him with former Indians teammate Bob Lemon. The Yankees had a memorable division race with Boston in 1978 and eventually won the World Series.

However, the Yankees were not termed the "Bronx Zoo" for no reason, and Rosen departed the Yankees less than two years after joining them. He took general manager positions with Houston and San Francisco. He was named *The Sporting News* Executive of the Year in 1987. Two years later, the Giants won the National League pennant in 1989.

Al Rosen lived a full and rewarding life up to his death in 2015. He was never afraid to give his opinion or take an unpopular stand for what he believed was right and just. His name is revered by fans today, and his legacy has lived on for generations by Tribe fans.

The following pages are the first full-length biography written about Al Rosen, a player who not only excelled on the field, but carried himself with class, dignity, steadfastness, and a fierce competitiveness off it.

It is about time that Al Rosen was given his due.

ONE

From Spartanburg to Miami

Spartanburg, South Carolina, was founded in 1785 and is located in the northwest part of the state. The name is derived from the Spartan Regiment, a local militia unit that fought in the American Revolution.[1] The United States Census of 1920 listed Spartanburg as having a population of approximately 22,000.[2] The town grew from being a frontier trading post to a major textile center with 40 textile mills built in the 19th century.

Spartanburg is often referred to as the "Hub City" because of its wheel hub shape that was formed by the many railroad lines that came through the city. As of 2010, the population was approximately 37,000 according to the U.S. Census, making Spartanburg the ninth-largest city in South Carolina.[3] A city with eight colleges, Spartanburg is also an international city. It is the home of BMW Manufacturing Company, the automaker's only manufacturing plant in North America. Spartanburg is also home to the headquarters of Denny's Restaurants, Inc.

Albert Leonard Rosen was born on February 29, 1924, in Spartanburg to Louis and Rose Rosen (née Levine). Al Rosen suffered from asthma as a young boy. Although his breathing was labored at times, he still participated in many sports at an early age. His doctor advised Rose that it would be good for her son to spend time outdoors and to get plenty of exercise. Rose and his grandmother (Gertrude Levine) were afraid that Al might drop dead if he suffered from a severe asthma attack. But Al would never stop participating in sports. He was always active despite his illness, and eventually outgrow his asthma when he reached his teens.[4]

Rosen's grandparents, Abe and Gertrude Levine, were originally from Warsaw, Poland. Abe worked as a tailor in a department store in Spartanburg. But Gertrude did not like living in the United States and returned to Warsaw. She soon discovered she was pregnant and returned to South Carolina[5]:

> We recognized ourselves as Jews, but we weren't observant Jews. My brother and I went to Sunday school; we were neither confirmed nor bar mitzvahed. I didn't care much for Sunday school. But I always considered myself very much Jewish.
>
> As I got older, I participated more and more in Jewish affairs, became more and more identified in the Jewish communities in the states where I played and have done that ever since. I think I come from a proper Jewish heritage. I learned some hard lessons along the way in the Minor Leagues the hard way, the way Jews were thought about and the kind of hard responses that I found necessary at the time. I became very proud of the fact that I was Jewish.[6]

After Abe died, the Rosen clan relocated from Spartanburg to Miami when Al was young. The reason was twofold: Louis and Rose were having marital problems, and the couple split up. Rose described Louis, a dry goods salesman,[7] as a "handsome ne'er do well."[8] The second reason was that because of Al's asthma, a city with less humidity such as Miami would enable him to breathe with less difficulty.

"At that time, my mother and father were not seeing eye-to eye and there'd been a split," said Rosen. "Eventually a divorce ensued and we ended up living in Miami with my mother's mother, my grandmother, and her younger sister, my aunt. I had to be four or five years old because my younger brother [Jerry], who is four years younger than I, was born in Miami."[9]

Miami may have seemed like a whole different world compared to Spartanburg. Located in the southeast part of the state, Miami was founded in the 16th century by Spain, and it was called Mayaimi, meaning "sweet water." Spain ceded Florida to the United States as a result of the Adams–Onis Treaty in 1819.[10]

Florida's population soared from 29,000 in the 1920s to 100,000 in 1930 due to land expansion. Florida East Coast Railway built an extension to Miami in 1896, and the Florida Everglades were drained, which created more land to purchase. Miami was heralded as a tropical paradise that many sought as a new destination.

Rose worked as a saleslady in a dress shop to support her family. Rosen described his living situation as between poor and middle class.[11] "My mother had to work," said Rosen, "and my grandmother took care of the house."[12]

In Miami, there was a smaller Jewish population than in South Carolina. Al and Jerry often found themselves in fights, having to defend themselves against the anti–Semitism that was very prevalent in South Florida. Al Rosen never ran from a fight, and he turned to boxing to protect himself against the bigoted taunts that came his way.

> I wanted to learn how to end things. That was important. I wasn't starting trouble in those days, but when it came to me, I wanted to end it, and damn quick.[13]
>
> Like most Jewish kids who grew up in a neighborhood where you had to fight, I was very aggressive and I had this chip on my shoulder. I was looking for someone to knock it off, and look, I had my share of guys who knocked it off and whom I couldn't take. But I was ready, ready for any of them. Maybe if I'd grown up in a Jewish neighborhood, I would be a different guy. When you start out by having to fight all the time for your pride and self-respect, how are you gonna know when to stop?[14]
>
> I grew up in a neighborhood that was a real melting pot, and I was the only Jew in the neighborhood. In my neighborhood, people referred to the Greeks, and there were the shanty Irish, and the wops. I lived in what is now the middle of Miami, but in those days, it was a long way out if you lived on Tenth Avenue. I can still remember in Miami, no dogs or Jews allowed in apartment buildings. A sign right on the wall.[15]

It was a mystery to Rosen why there was so much hatred aimed at the Jews. He heard all the slurs growing up in Miami:

"Lookit the Jewboy," "Go home an' eat yuh matzos," "Sheeny," "Come on, let's get the kike."[16] It was something that he could never quite figure out. "What is it?" asked Rosen. "Is it because your nose is a little bigger, or your hair is a little curlier, or you don't go to Sunday school on Sunday morning or you're not in regular school on Yom Kippur? What is it?"[17]

When Rosen was young, he began to follow baseball more closely through the local papers. There was one ballplayer Rosen took a special interest in: Hank Greenberg. Not only was Greenberg one of the game's great sluggers, he was also Jewish.

> I was aware of Hank Greenberg from the time I was a boy. I had two favorite players, Greenberg and Gehrig. Those two I always watched. But Greenberg particularly because he was chasing Babe Ruth's [single season home run] record in 1938—I was fourteen years old then—and there was a consciousness of him being a Jew. But you're always rooting for somebody regardless of who it might be if they're after a record. I was conscious of Greenberg's try for the record and obsessed by the fact the newspapers were saying they were trying to pitch around him, to walk him, things of that nature. I can remember that he wasn't getting good balls to hit, that sort of thing.

Maybe they were afraid to pitch to him because he was doing so well, maybe because he was a Jew, maybe because they didn't want him to break Ruth's record. I can think of a combination of those things. I can remember that there was a very strong Anti-Semitic feeling in America about not letting a Jew break the revered Babe Ruth's record.[18]

In general, people are not born with the hatred of a racist or a bigot towards a certain demographic. An individual either learns this behavior in their home, or they are influenced by this hatred from somewhere outside the home. It was not just from other children that Rosen had encountered this bias. He heard anti–Semitic remarks from adults as well.

At a young age, Rosen felt that Jews were characterized as a group of pansies. He resolved to change that perception. One such experience was when he tried out for his school's football team.

In front of the other guys, the coach said to me, "What are you doing after football, Rosen?" I said, "I love football." He said, "I always thought Jews liked tennis and games like that. I didn't think they liked combat, physical stuff." What he said never left my mind. I never quite got over that. And maybe that was a defining moment for me. If a coach can feel Jews don't want to choose anything physical, I had to show him that wasn't true.[19]

While there was not a sanctioned Little League in Miami when Rosen was growing up, there were plenty of parks. There was a supervisor at each city park, and from there park leagues were developed, forming an inter-league competition throughout the city. Rosen played at the park all day, from sunrise to sundown. For the most part, he played softball. As he got older, sponsors would support the various teams so that shirts and caps could be purchased. Rosen was such an adept pitcher that he was given the name "Flipper," which was eventually shortened to "Flip." The nickname stuck with him throughout his life.

Rosen also played American Legion baseball, and as he got a little older, he went up against adults in church leagues. Rosen was able to make extra money playing in a semipro softball league.

At 14 years old, Rosen joined a traveling softball team of Miami All-Stars. He attended Miami High School for two years. But fortune smiled on him, and Rosen seized the opportunity. One day, as the tour for the softball team was nearing the end, Rosen was chatting with J. B. Lemon on a hotel porch in St. Petersburg. Lemon was the recreation director for the City of Miami, and he asked Rosen if he would like to attend military school. Rosen said that he was interested, and Lemon drove him to the Florida Military Academy, located in St. Petersburg. Rosen met with the headmaster and was offered a full scholarship.[20]

Rosen was a four-sport star (football, baseball, basketball, boxing) at the military academy. He won the middleweight boxing championship at the Florida high school tournament. He also tried to get into the welterweight tournament, but he could not get down to the requisite 140 pounds.

"One night I had to fight three bouts in one night," said Rosen. "I won the first one on a technical knockout in the second round, but the next two went the full three rounds. That was a lot of rounds in one night. I never thought seriously of turning pro, but I'm still crazy about boxing. I'd rather watch a fight show than eat. I don't care whether they're amateurs or pros, bums or champs. I love it."[21]

The Academy dropped boxing from its sports program in Rosen's senior year, but he participated in the three other sports. Rosen was more interested in sports than his education at Miami High School. As a result, he was lackadaisical about his studies.[22] Under the stringent surroundings of military school, Rosen flourished and earned a 3.8 grade point average.[23] The administrators suggested that Rosen take the entrance exam for West Point, but he decided not to.[24]

At 17 years of age, he knew that he wanted to give professional baseball a shot. Through his girlfriend's father, Lloyd Gulickson, who was a golf pro in Cleveland, he received an introduction to Cleveland's new manager, Roger Peckinpaugh, in 1941. Peckinpaugh sent Rosen to the Class C farm team, Wilkes-Barre, for a tryout. Wilkes-Barre manager Mike McNally offered Rosen a contract of $75 a month to play for Class D Thomasville.

Rosen decided that the offer made by McNally was not much more than what he could make playing semipro baseball and softball back home. Rosen declined the offer and enrolled at the University of Florida (1941–1942). After one year in Gainesville, Rosen returned home and enrolled at the University of Miami. He pledged to the fraternity Pi Lambda Phi, and he majored in business administration.

But Rosen never lost sight of his goal of the major leagues. "I knew that I wanted it," said Rosen. "I can't tell you whether I was fourteen or fifteen or when it was, but I knew I was good. I never thought I was better than anybody else, but I played semi-pro even as a kid, playing in the men's league, and holding my own."[25]

In the spring of 1942, he dialed up Gulickson again, and this time he met Boston Red Sox first baseman Jimmie Foxx. Foxx directed Rosen to meet with Boston's farm director, Herb Pennock, who sent Rosen to Class D Danville. But after a few days of workouts, Danville manager Elmer Yoter was not impressed with the young player from Miami. "Son, you're never going to be a ballplayer," said Yoter. "Go on home and get a lunch pail."[26]

There are many stories of players who were unsuccessful the first time they participated in a tryout and who were then told to forget their dream of becoming a big-league ballplayer. But miraculously, they were given a second chance. There are players who used rejection as a motivating factor to excel. Their incentive was to prove to the scout or coach who discarded them that they did have the talent and the drive to become a major league ballplayer.

The words from Yoter clanged in Rosen's ears. Flip Rosen would make Yoter eat his words. Before he could do that, he would first have to serve in the United States Navy and then prove himself at the minor league level.

Two

World War II
and Three Cups of Joe

After Yoter rejected Rosen in Danville, a friend recommended that Rosen see Frank Stein in Schoolfield, Virginia. Schoolfield was just a couple miles south of Danville. Stein, the Director of the Local YMCA, was also a bird dog scout who followed a lot of the local workouts. Stein sized Rosen up, determined that he had some talent, and advised Rosen to catch a bus to Thomasville—the same club Rosen had declined to join one year earlier.

As it was the only opportunity available to Rosen at the time, he headed to Thomasville, North Carolina. The Thomasville Tommies were a Class D club in the North Carolina State League. When Rosen arrived in Thomasville, he headed to a Nance's Café near the bus station.[1] When Rosen inquired where he would find the manager of the baseball team, a local named "Sailor" took him to the gas station around the corner. There, "getting his car filled up with petrol was the Thomasville manager, Jimmy Gruzdis."[2]

Rosen signed a contract for $90 a month and was inserted in the game that evening, getting a single in his first at-bat.[3] Gruzdis, like Stein, saw something in Rosen and worked with him daily. Rosen did not distinguish himself in his first month with the club. However, he eventually got going and was batting .300 towards the end of the season. Rosen noticed that his teammates had a nonchalant attitude about the game. They didn't react with happiness when they won a game, or with disappointment after a loss. Rosen, followed their lead, believing that these attitudes were how professional ballplayers were supposed to act.

Gruzdis pulled Rosen aside towards the end of the season to let him know that he was sending him home. When Rosen asked why, Gruzdis told him, "You're not hustling. You've stopped putting out. You're acting like these other guys. Don't you realize they're minor leaguers, and will always be minor leaguers, because that's the way they play ball?"[4]

Rosen begged Gruzdis for another chance, which the manager gave him. Rosen ended the 1942 season batting .307 in 86 games. He committed 18 errors at third base for a fielding percentage of .929.

The news that captured America's attention was the fighting in World War II over in Europe. Ballplayers were either enlisting or their draft boards were selecting them to serve in the Armed Forces. Of horror to Rosen was the Holocaust and the effect it had on Jewish people. "I think that anyone who was Jewish in those days that wasn't deeply affected by the 6 million Jews that went to the gas chambers and ovens would have to be some kind of idiot, a blathering idiot," said Rosen. "So that yes, of course, it affected me."[5]

Subsequently, Rosen returned to the University of Miami to continue working towards his degree. In the fall of 1943, Rosen played football at Miami. He was the starting left end and occasionally kicked off.

After Rosen completed a semester at Miami, he entered the V-12 program (Navy College Training Program).[6] The program enlisted young men for the Navy's officer training. Rosen stayed right at the University of Miami for his ROTC program.[7] From there, he went to Plattsburgh, New York, where he graduated as an ensign. He was assigned to Fort Pierce, Florida, for small-boat training.[8]

> I served aboard ship, made one invasion into Okinawa. We took the poor guys into the beach and we were there on D-Day. I remember on Easter Sunday when the planes were coming over. We made the one invasion and we were around Okinawa for seven days, and like everybody else who's been in combat, I was scared, but yet it's a different kind of fear because there's sort of a feeling that there's not a damn thing you can do about where you are.[9]

The fear Rosen felt on that Easter Sunday was one that, unless you were aboard that ship, might never be one that he experienced again. He was stationed on the *Procyon*, named after the brightest star in the constellation Canis Minor. The 20-millimeter naval cannon picked up a kamikaze attacking the ship from the starboard side, but it was unable to bring the plane down. A five-millimeter affixed to the stern made a direct hit just as the kamikaze pilot turned into the stern of the *Procyon*. All the crew could do was stand and watch because there was nowhere to go.[10]

Rosen was discharged from the Navy as a full lieutenant in the spring of 1946.[11] He immediately reported to Cleveland's minor league camp in Sumter, South Carolina. "There were so many of us that they put numbers on our backs," said Rosen. "I think I was 247 or something like that. We started playing games in the morning, and we played morning, afternoon, and night."[12]

Flip Rosen was initially assigned to Class B Harrisburg. But they had already made their cuts, so Cleveland assigned him to Class C Pittsfield of the Canadian-American League. Rosen was unhappy with his new assignment and thought about quitting. Laddie Placek, a Cleveland scout, talked with Rosen and implored him to stick it out. Placek preached patience and urged Rosen not to be too anxious. Placek told Rosen that he showed enough talent to eventually make it to the big leagues. Rosen took Placek's advice and reported to the Pittsfield Electrics for the 1946 season.

At five-foot-ten and 180 pounds, Rosen had grown to have an impressive physique. Often he sliced the sleeves of his uniform, which displayed his bulging biceps and his body definition even more. With his blond, curly hair and his handsome good looks, Rosen was indeed a striking figure.

Tony Rensa managed the Electrics. The 44-year-old skipper played catcher for six seasons in the major leagues, mostly as a backup. Even at his age, he still donned the "tools of ignorance" occasionally for the Electrics. Rensa used Rosen in different positions, stationing him in right field, second base, and first base, as well as third base.

Rosen was named "Player of the Day" four times in the month of May. In those four games (May 10, 12, 20, 25), Rosen batted .765 (13-for-17) with two doubles, four triples, two home runs and 11 runs batted in. Rosen was voted "Star of the League" for May by the beat writers.[13]

On June 3 against Oneonta, Rosen was hit on the right hand by a pitched ball. The result was a fractured finger that kept him out of the lineup until June 20. Rosen returned in a doubleheader against Amsterdam and hit a home run in the second game.[14]

Rosen provided the fireworks on July 4 at Wahconah Park. "Al Rosen belted a tremendous triple against the left field fence about 375 feet from home plate with Pittsfield trailing 5–4 and two men down in the ninth inning at Wahconah Park last night to give the Electrics a 6–5 win over Oneonta and an even break in the two games on the holiday," reported the *Berkshire Eagle.* The winning three-bagger by Rosen capped a 3-for-4 evening that produced three RBI.[15]

Rosen led the Electrics in many offensive categories. He topped the club in batting average (.323), home runs (15), RBI (90), and triples (19), and tied with teammate Ken Manarik in doubles with 21. Rosen's power numbers were evident in his team-leading slugging percentage (.600). Rosen was also named Player of the Year in the Canadian-American League in 1946.[16]

Pittsfield finished second in the league with a 69–47–2 record, a half-game behind the Trois Rivieres Royals. The Electrics toppled Oneonta in the playoffs but lost to the Royals in the championship round.

On September 23, Rosen's contract was sold to the Oklahoma City Indians, Cleveland's Class AA affiliate in the Texas League. Oklahoma City was piloted by Roy Schalk, a former infielder with the Chicago White Sox during the war (1944–1945). Rosen met his future roommate, Ray Boone, in 1947. Boone, a catcher by trade, was thrust into the role of shortstop due to injuries. Boone never returned to his old position, remaining at shortstop through his years (1948–1953) in Cleveland.

Rosen had a tremendous first half of the season. He batted .372 (116-for-312) and was named to the All-Star team.[17] The Texas League All-Stars went up against the first-place Houston Buffaloes on July 10, 1947, at Buff Stadium in Houston. Rosen made an immediate impact.

> Oklahoma City's Al Rosen was every inch a batting champion here Wednesday night, the 22-year-old Cleveland-bound third baseman coming through under the terrific pressure of the Texas League All-Star Game in which Houston's leaders were administered a sharply fashioned 4–2 defeat.
> While an all-time All-Star Game crowd of 11,833 paying customers overflowed into the outfield of vast Buff Stadium. Rosen smashed a homer over the left wall in the first inning as the sensational youngster provided Salty Parker's stars with what proved to be the winning run of the brilliantly waged game.[18]

Hal Middlesworth, sports editor of the *Daily Oklahoman,* gave a glowing report on Rosen to the Indians fans in Cleveland.

"Al is a line-drive hitter and he doesn't fool easily," Middlesworth told the *Cleveland Plain Dealer*. "In the field, he's still learning the ropes, but shows daily improvement. He's a good thrower. He does get his feet tangled up sometimes, though. He has become quite a favorite in our league. I don't see how he can miss hitting well against major league pitching because he's a natural at the plate."[19]

Rosen did not slow down as the season wore on and, for the second year in a row, he was named his league's Most Valuable Player, receiving six of eight first—place votes.[20] *The Sporting News* noted that Rosen was the "first Jewish star to lead [the league] in clouting."[21]

Flip Rosen led the league in batting (.349), outdistancing Jack Cassini of Tulsa (.319) by 30 points. Rosen also led the loop in hits (186), doubles (47), RBI (141), and total bases (330). Rosen was second in the league in home runs (25) and runs scored (115). His slugging percentage was a whopping .619. Rosen was the second consecutive player of the Indians to be crowned as the Texas League batting champion, as Dale Mitchell was honored in 1946.

The Jewish communities in the minor league cities welcomed Rosen. He felt at times that he was representing them out on the baseball diamond. Rosen accepted invitations to attend temple or drop by someone's house for Sunday brunch. He enjoyed meeting people in the different communities. Rosen believed there was an affinity amongst Jews to remain close and to take care of their own. As a result, he was fortunate to meet some nice people who took the time to befriend him, a stranger, but still, a person whom they could embrace.[22]

But at the ballparks and against other players, Rosen heard the same taunts he heard when he was a young boy living in Miami. America's image as a melting pot of ethnicities is very prevalent in baseball. Rosen met many different people from various parts of the country. Many people were raised with preconceived ideas and reasons for not liking a certain ethnic group. Some come by these feelings later in life. In either case, fans, umpires, and opposing players were not shy about letting their biases be known. Rosen experienced those sentiments at each stop in the minor leagues.

Rosen tried to turn a deaf ear to these taunts. However, there were times when the jeers became too loud and he felt it necessary to assert himself. If he was going to take on another player, he had to be better than they were. He felt that no matter what your race, creed or color might be, you should not be singled out. If a player was competing with tenacity and character, Rosen felt that player should earn his opponents' respect. "I heard words like sheeny and kike," said Rosen, "and that turned me off. The word kike really turned me off, and I had fights on and off the field because of this."[23]

> I can remember saying to somebody at one time that I had considered shortening my name from Rosen to Ross. It's just a passing thing that kids do to make it easier on themselves. Remember, I'm talking about very young men.

And later on, I thought, gee, I wish my name were Rosenberg so that there would be no doubt, because there were times people did not identify me as a Jew. I could never imagine why, with a name like Al Rosen. I always felt I looked Jewish, if there was such a thing as looking something.[24]

I've been judged because I am a Jew. After all, I was in the newspapers in every town I was ever in. Naturally, I'm judged as a Jew. My name is Rosen. I have a Semitic look. I certainly didn't expect anybody to think I was anything but a Jew. Sure, you hear from the stands. Sure, you hear it and you ignore it because all you do is provoke it if you take offense.

I would not play on the High Holy Days. I just merely stated my position, and that was it. Nobody ever questioned me about it.[25]

Cleveland called Rosen up to the varsity for the last couple of weeks in the 1947 season. The Tribe was in fourth place in the American League standings, 14½ games off the pace, and they were playing out the string.

Rosen made his major league debut on September 10, 1947, at Yankee Stadium. He pinch-hit for outfielder Joe Frazier in the top of the sixth inning. Yankees ace reliever Joe Page struck Rosen out in his initial at-bat. Rosen's first hit of his big-league career came in the second game of a doubleheader against Detroit at Briggs Stadium on September 22. Cleveland was trailing, 6–3, in the top of the ninth. After Jim Hegan led off with a single, Rosen batted for pitcher Ed Klieman. He rapped a single to left field off Tigers starter Frank Overmire. Rosen scored his first run in the major leagues when he trotted home courtesy of a home run by Hank Edwards. The three-run shot by Edwards turned out to be the winning blow as the Tribe won, 7–6.

Even though Rosen went 0-for-5 in a three-game series (September 11–13) at Fenway Park, there was one player who saw something special in the youngster. "He looked mighty good to me," said Ted Williams.[26]

Rosen reported to spring training in 1948 with the Indians at Tucson, Arizona. He was not welcomed with open arms. He was the hot-shot prospect who was gunning to take the third base job from Ken Keltner. The Indians' third baseman was as popular with his teammates as he was with the Cleveland fans. He broke in a year before Indians skipper Lou Boudreau. With Keltner at third base and Boudreau at shortstop, they played alongside each other for ten years. It would be a tough position for Rosen to see some playing time, despite the impressive numbers he put up thus far in the minor leagues.

"In the spring of 1948 I went to spring training with the big team," said Rosen. "When I walked into that big-league clubhouse the first time, I felt in awe. Time passes and you can't remember exactly what your feelings where, but when people ask me what my greatest thrill in baseball was, I always say it was the first time I put on a big-league suit."[27]

The Baltimore Orioles of the Class AAA International League had a working agreement with the Indians. Those players who did not make the big-league roster would be sent to the Charm City. Instead, Cleveland sent Rosen to AAA Kansas City of the American Association. The Blues were an affiliate of the New York Yankees. The Orioles had threatened to appeal the Indians' maneuver to Commissioner A. B. Chandler. Indians owner Bill Veeck explained that the only way for the Indians to obtain pitcher Charley Wensloff from the Yankees was to send Rosen to K.C. "I didn't want Baltimore to think we acted in bad faith," said Veeck. "On the other hand, the Orioles did not want to penalize us on the Wensloff deal."[28] The Indians sent catcher Hank Ruszkowski to the Orioles.

On May 14, 1948, Israel achieved statehood. Many images people had of Jews were of their being led to gas chambers and ovens by the Nazis, and not offering to fight or protect themselves. Jewish men were thought to be professional people with white collar careers such as doctors or lawyers. They were not thought of as being folks who held physical or blue collar jobs. This was the same portrayal that the football coach at Rosen's high school expressed.

Arabs and Jews had been fighting for control of Palestine since 1929. Following the collapse of the Ottoman Empire in World War I, Britain took control of Palestine. In November 1947, the United Nations voted to partition Palestine. As a result, the British withdrew. Israel held off the Arabs and gained control of their partition, becoming the first Jewish state in nearly 2,000 years.[29]

Rosen believed that the opinion of Jews changed as they banded together and fought off their enemies. He thought this also may have changed the views of Jewish ballplayers in professional baseball.[30]

Rosen wrenched his ankle sliding into second base in the second game of a double dip at Indianapolis on May 23 and missed a few games. He was batting .341 and was replaced in the lineup by Jim Dyck.[31]

Rosen had a season in one weekend against the St. Paul Saints. In consecutive doubleheaders at Lexington Field on June 19–20, Rosen strung together a perfect 8-for-8 with five home runs. His consecutive hit streak was snapped in the nightcap on June 20. A month later, the

Blues were in St. Paul again and Rosen smacked three home runs in five at-bats, driving in seven runs.

Kansas City manager Dick Bartell occasionally shifted Rosen to shortstop. Rosen now had experience playing all the infield positions as well as left field on the minor league level. He was chosen as the "Outstanding Freshman" in the American Association in 1948. He was the only unanimous choice for the League's All-Star team, receiving all eight votes.[32] Rosen finished the season with a .327 batting average in 127 games. He slugged 25 home runs, knocked in 110 runs, and had a slugging percentage of .587.

In the field, Rosen's defense was suspect. He played 102 games at third base and committed 27 errors for a .916 fielding percentage. He also played shortstop in 31 games and tacked on nine more errors.

Cleveland recalled Rosen on September 10, 1948.[33] This time the stakes were different from the previous season. In 1948 the Tribe was right in the pennant race. On September 11, Cleveland was in third place of the American League. Boston (86–49) led New York (83–52) by 3 games, and the Indians (83–53) were right behind at 3½ games out.

The Indians won 11 of 12 games between September 16–29. Cleveland vaulted into first place, leading Boston by two games. However, Cleveland lost two of three games to Detroit while the Red Sox beat Washington and New York to end the season. Rosen participated in five games after he was recalled. All five of his at-bats were as a pinch-hitter, and he singled once.

Cleveland and Boston finished the season with identical records of 96–58. The two clubs met at Fenway Park on October 4, 1948, to slug it out for the AL pennant. Gene Bearden, the rookie knuckleball pitcher, was chosen by Boudreau to start for the Tribe. Boston manager Joe McCarthy went with right-hander Denny Galehouse.

Each team put a run on the board in the first inning. Cleveland struck for four runs in the top of the fourth frame. Three of those runs came home on a home run by Keltner. Boudreau added two solo shots, and the Indians won, 8–3. Bearden (20–7) joined Lemon (20–14) as the only 20-game winners for the Tribe in 1948. Their opponent in the World Series was the Boston Braves.

On September 13, 1948, Indians pitcher Don Black collapsed at home plate as the result of a brain hemorrhage. An aneurysm caused blood to run into the spinal fluid.[34] Black was ruled out of the World

The Hebrew Hammer indeed! Although just called up to the Indians, Rosen, complete with "eye black," shows off his intensity. He would ride that passion to the American League Most Valuable Player Award in 1953 (The Cleveland Press Collection, Michael Schwartz Library, Cleveland State University).

Series (and never played again) and the Indians selected Rosen to take the fallen pitcher's place. But because Rosen had been recalled by the Indians after the September 1 deadline, the Braves had to agree to adding Rosen to the roster. The Braves granted permission to the Indians, and Rosen was added to the club.

Rosen was used one time in the Series. He pinch-hit for Satchel

Paige to lead off the seventh inning of Game Five. He popped out to second base in his only appearance, a game won by the Braves, 11–5.

Cleveland won the Series in six games. Bob Lemon won two games, including the clincher in Game Six at Braves Field. Bearden, who won Game Three, saved Game Six.

Rosen had a sideline job for the Series. He wrote articles as a correspondent for the *Miami Herald.* "The 1948 season is all over," wrote Rosen. "We won the hard way—digging, fighting for every inch. The Cleveland fans must be raising whoopee now. They have every right to do so. I'm so excited, I can't think correctly. Let's just say it's almost too good to be true. But we're the champs, and we'll be the champs for a long time to come."[35]

Rosen played in just six games and his contributions were minimal; however, he received $1,693.02 from the winner's pool, a quarter-share. A full share was worth a then-record of $6,772.07.[36]

After the Series, Rosen returned to Kanas City, where he married the former Evelyn Silverstein on October 17, 1948.[37] Evelyn was a local girl Al had met while playing for the Blues. "Flip is planning to live in Kansas City," said Rose Rosen.[38] The newlyweds traveled to Miami and then on to Cuba for their honeymoon.

Flip Rosen capped off 1948 in fine style. In what was already a memorable year, Rosen completed his work to obtain his Bachelor of Business Administration Degree at the University of Miami.[39]

When Rosen reported to spring training in 1949, he was hoping that he would stick with the Indians. Feeling that he had proved himself on the minor league level, the logical step would be to join the varsity. Of course, Keltner was a big obstacle. To replace Keltner, Rosen needed to have a good spring training. And that was the rub. In his short career, Rosen was usually a slow starter. A player who started slowly just didn't replace a seven-time All-Star like Keltner.

"The funny part of it is I know I can hit," said Rosen. "Probably the best I'll ever be is an adequate third baseman. I'll knock 'em down with my chest and throw 'em out. I don't have the natural grace of a fellow, like, say, Joe Gordon. But I can hit. All I'm afraid of is Lou Boudreau will brush me off without ever finding that out. I wouldn't blame him."[40]

When the Indians left Tucson in 1949, Rosen was in tow as the backup third baseman to Keltner. Rosen showed enough offense in the desert sun for Boudreau to keep him on the roster. He batted .358 (29-for-81) in spring training with three home runs and 14 RBI.[41]

Unfortunately for Rosen, his offense did not carry over to the regular season. He made nine starts at third base and participated in 23 games total. In 44 at-bats, Rosen batted an unimpressive .159, and he knocked in five runs through the end of June. Three of his RBI came on a bases-loaded double against Boston on June 3, an 8–1 Tribe victory.

Perhaps Rosen's mind was not completely on the task at hand. Back in Kansas City, Evelyn Rosen filed for divorce on May 11, 1949. She cited "general indignities: that Rosen argues with her, has a violent temper and said he does not love her."[42]

On July 1, 1949, Rosen was optioned to San Diego, Cleveland's AAA affiliate of the Pacific Coast League. In his fourth game for the Padres, Rosen smacked a home run at Seattle as the Padres topped the Rainiers, 5–3, in a July 4 doubleheader sweep. He also contributed a double and an RBI in the opener, a 6–1 win.[43]

In a doubleheader against Oakland on July 17, Rosen had to call on his skills as a pugilist. The Padres' Max West smacked a grand slam, his 33rd home run of the season, off the Oaks' Lou Tost. Rosen was the next batter, and Tost took out his frustration on Rosen, plunking him in the back. As Rosen walked down to first base, the two players had words, and the punches started. Rosen scored some punches to the Tost's midsection and cut the Oakland hurler under his left eye. Both players were ejected, with the Padres destroying the Oaks, 11–2 in the opener and 11–1 in the nightcap.[44]

The Indians did not recall Rosen at the end of the season like they had in 1947 and 1948. When Rosen was sent down to San Diego, Keltner was put on the shelf with a charley horse in his left leg. The injury kept Keltner out of the Indians' starting lineup until July 29. But instead of keeping Rosen on the roster to get him some experience, Boudreau, Bob Kennedy, and John Berardino shared starting assignments at the hot corner. In only 80 games, Keltner batted .232 in 1949. It was the fewest games he played and his lowest batting average since becoming a starter in 1938.

As in his other stops along the Cleveland minor league chain, Rosen performed well for the Padres. In 83 games and 273 at-bats, Rosen batted .319. He belted 14 home runs. totaled 51 RBI, and scored 49 runs. Defensively, Rosen split his time between third base (47 games) and first base (33 games). At third, he committed 11 errors for a .933 fielding percentage.

Padres manager Bucky Harris gave Rosen some of the best advice he ever received. "Bucky—one of the greatest men I've ever met in base-ball—helped me a lot mentally," said Rosen. "He kept telling me I'd hit even better in the majors."[45] As for Rosen's defense, Harris was honest. "You'll never be a George Kell, so just forget it," recalled Rosen. "Go out and hit the ball—that'll take care of your fielding."[46]

As he looked toward the following season, Rosen was optimistic that he could crack the Indians' lineup. "Personally, I'm counting on living the next few years in Cleveland," said Rosen. "I'd like to stick with the Indians."[47]

THREE

The Hebrew Hammer

Rosen approached a crossroads in his career in 1950. There was not much left to prove in the minor leagues. He had battered opposing pitchers the last three seasons, in three different leagues, batting well over .300 each year. He worked hard to improve his defense, often taking extra fielding practice. Unfortunately, his progress was negligible in the box scores. Rosen committed 27 errors in 102 games at third base with Kansas City in 1948. A year later in San Diego, he was charged with 11 boots in 47 games. There was not much improvement, and perhaps Bucky Harris knew what he was talking about.

The battle for third base would be determined in spring training. Rosen had not shown Boudreau or the Indians' front office much promise in his previous stints in Cleveland. Keltner may have been the incumbent in the battle for the hot corner, but he would need to bounce back from a subpar 1949 season. Keltner was credited for being a major factor in ending Joe DiMaggio's 56-game hitting streak on July 17, 1941. DiMaggio smashed two grounders that Keltner fielded cleanly to throw out "Joltin' Joe." Indians fans also hold Keltner close to their hearts for his three-run home run against Boston in the American League playoff in 1948. Although he slumped badly in the World Series, Keltner was a key player who helped lead the club to the pennant.

The beginning of spring training also marked the beginning of Hank Greenberg's career as the teams' new general manager. Greenberg had been the club's farm director since his retirement after the 1947 season. Greenberg was a tough negotiator on player salaries. He believed that Cleveland owner Bill Veeck, who had negotiated the players' contracts, was much too generous. There would be no bonuses for players under Greenberg's watch. "Pay for Performance" was his motto.[1]

Keltner knew he would be in for a battle to keep his starting position. Not only was Rosen knocking on the door, but there was also talk that Boudreau might shift to third base from shortstop because of his arthritic ankles. Ray Boone would step into the starting role at short. Boudreau suggested that Bob Kennedy, who usually was slotted in either of the corner outfield positions, could be used at third in a pinch. "Kenny apparently has come down here with the idea of winning that third base job," said Boudreau. "I look for him to put up a terrific battle."[2]

As the weeks went by, it became apparent to Greenberg that Keltner had lost a step in the field, and his bat was missing its usual pop. "Ken Keltner, our regular third baseman, was getting old; he couldn't play anymore in my opinion," Greenberg wrote later. "All Keltner could do was drink and smoke with the rest of the boys, like Joe Gordon and Lou Boudreau. He had no discipline whatsoever."[3]

But Boudreau insisted that the competition for the third base job was too close to call. In the April 9 edition of the *Cleveland Plain Dealer*, beat writer Harry Jones shared a capsule view of each player's performance thus far. Jones wrote his comments about each player as if he were handicapping a thoroughbred race:

- *Ken Keltner*—He'll probably spend much time in the barn, for that old zip is gone.
- *Al Rosen*—A frisky young colt who has not yet shown the ability to which he has been credited. He has improved greatly in the field, but there has been no power in his punch, and time is running out.
- *Lou Boudreau*—He won't collapse in the stretch. Moreover, he has seen the light, and if need be, he will move from shortstop to third base in the best interest of the club. Early trials indicate he will hit.
- *Bob Kennedy*—A competitor. They won't keep this one in the barn very long. He'll be on the track, spurring the others on. He may be in the outfield one day and the infield the next, but he'll be in there.[4]

A few days later, the time came for Boudreau to make roster cuts. It may have been a surprise to some that it was Keltner who was shown the door. "I kept hoping Keltner would hit like he did two years ago," said Boudreau. "Then maybe he could get by on his fielding. It got pretty obvious that he wasn't going to hit with his old power. It's a sad thing, but we've all got to face it. It's going to happen to me some day."[5]

Boudreau was not pleased about releasing his friend and teammate.

It was also apparent that he was not too keen about Rosen taking over the hot corner. With Boudreau, it was not a question of if Rosen will fail, but when he would fail. It was certainly not the type of encouragement a young player could expect from his manager. "I kept Keltner around this long because Rosen has looked as bad or worse," said Boudreau. "Maybe Rosen will perk up now that he knows the job is his until he plays himself off it. I don't know how long I can go with Rosen. If he hits, then maybe I can overlook his poor fielding. If he doesn't hit, he will be out of there in a hurry and Bob Kennedy will be my third baseman."[6]

"This is a young man's game," said Greenberg, who also released greybeards Mike Tresh and Satchel Paige before showing Keltner the exit sign. "We have too many players who are hoping for one more good year. We plan to dispose of them before the season opens, because if they're on the club we'll be tempted to use them, and the younger fellows will be handicapped by having to sit on the bench."[7]

When it was suggested to Rosen that he would have mighty big shoes to fill at third base after Keltner's departure, Rosen simply replied, "I've got pretty big feet."[8]

It did not take Keltner long to latch on to another club. Boston Red Sox manager Joe Cronin contacted Keltner to join the Red Sox. Keltner only played in 13 games for Boston before getting his release on June 6, 1950.

The Indians opened the season on April 18 against Detroit. Before a crowd of 65,744 at Cleveland Stadium, the Indians lost, 7–6, in ten innings. The crowd chanted "We want Keltner" right from the first pitch. But Rosen showed his mettle, cranking his first big league home run in the bottom of the eighth inning off Tigers starter Fred Hutchinson. The two-run blow that reached the left field seats tied the game up at 6–6. "It felt great at the time," said Rosen, "but they don't mean a thing when you don't win."[9] He added that he felt right at home and that he was not the least bit nervous as the Tribe's Opening Day third baseman.

Rosen went deep again against the Tigers two days later, but then his bat cooled. As the weather started to heat up on the lakeshore, so did the Indians' young third baseman. He batted .281 in May, but in June, he was scorching, batting .308 with 11 home runs and 32 RBI. He showed a good eye at the plate, walking 19 times and whiffing only seven. By the end of the month, Rosen had smacked 21 home runs and trailed league-leader Ted Williams by three.

Under the careful tutelage of assistant coach Oscar Melillo, Rosen was becoming quite a fielder as well. "He almost worked me to death, but he taught me how to play third," said Rosen. "My two chief faults were holding the glove between my legs in fielding the ball and throwing crossfire to first. We often stayed on the diamond so long after infield practice that Manager Lou Boudreau had to throw us off."[10]

Melillo, who was a good-fielding second baseman for the St. Louis Browns in the 1920s and 1930s, worked with Rosen to keep his hands in front of him when fielding the baseball, as well as reminding him to stay low and keep on his toes. If Rosen forgot these instructions, Joe Gordon would yell across the diamond to Rosen to "get down low."

His efforts did not go unnoticed by his peers. "The change in Rosen's fielding is amazing," said the Yankees' Hank Bauer. "I roomed with him in Kansas City and even Flip will admit he was a poor fielder in those days. If you had seen him before, you wouldn't believe it was the same person."[11]

Rosen's hot bat also was a main factor that kept Cleveland in contention for the American League flag. The Tribe was in third place, five games behind front-running Detroit and one game behind second-place New York, as the curtain came down on the month of June.

One of Rosen's biggest games of the year came on July 1 against Detroit. He slammed two home runs and drove in five runs in the Indians' 7–4 victory. Rosen homered off Hal White in the first and third innings. The night before, Rosen touched 'em all in his last at-bat in the seventh inning, giving him three consecutive home runs. Rosen commented about how he held a baseball bat, with his fingers about two inches from the bat handle. "Choking the bat gives me balance,"[12] he said.

Of course, Rosen was not doing all the heavy lifting. Another new addition to the Cleveland starting lineup was first baseman Luke Easter. The tall, (6'4") left-handed-hitting power hitter was signed by Cleveland after he played two years with the Homestead Grays of the Negro National League. In his first year in the minors, Easter clubbed 25 home runs and drove in 92 runs at San Diego in 1949. Easter was 34 years of age when he made his major league debut on August 11, 1949.

Like Rosen, Easter had a veteran blocking his path to the majors. In his case, it was Mickey Vernon. In 1949, Vernon, also a lefty, batted .291 for the Tribe. He was the incumbent to retain his starting position at first, and Easter started the season in right field. In the early stages of the 1950 season, Vernon's lumber took a slumber, and he batted .189

The Rookie and the Pitcher: Al Rosen and Bob Lemon celebrate another Indians win. Rosen often called Lemon his closest friend on the Tribe. Their friendship carried past their playing days as they reunited in New York in 1978 to drive the Yankees to a World Championship (courtesy Cleveland Public Library).

in 90 at-bats. On June 14, Vernon was traded to Washington for pitcher Dick Weik. Easter moved to the infield, and the Indians now had two new power hitters at their corner infield positions. Kennedy, Boudreau's "ace in the hole" if Rosen did not work out at third, replaced Easter in right.

Easter carved his name into Indians and Cleveland Stadium history on June 23, 1950. In a 13–4 shellacking of Washington, Easter clubbed his 10th and 11th homers of the season. It was his second one in the sixth inning that made the 26,627 in attendance "ooh" and "aah" with delight. Easter sent a 3–0 offering from Washington reliever Joe Haynes high and far to right field. The baseball landed over the auxiliary scoreboard that adjoined the facing of the right field stands in section four. The tremendous clout has been measured at 477 feet, the longest ball hit at Cleveland Stadium.

While Easter was a bigger-than-life personality, Larry Doby was more serious and thought that a player should handle himself in a business-like manner.

"Luke was a great big, easy going, devil-may-care, jolly, kind of guy who took a ribbing and dished it out," said Rosen. "Larry, maybe inside, I think he may have looked at Luke like an Uncle Tom type. It was often said in our clubhouse that if you could have put Larry Doby's talent with Luke Easter's outlook, you'd have the greatest player on two legs." [13]

There were more changes coming to the infield. Ray Boone became more of a fixture in the starting lineup, as Boudreau's career as a player was winding down. Like Keltner, Boudreau had lost a step in the field, and his bat speed had slowed. Boudreau was also battling an injured right shoulder that limited his usual high productivity. Boudreau was once dubbed the "Boy Manager" when he took the helm of the Indians in 1942 at the age of 24, and his best days were clearly visible only in the rearview mirror.

Boone's partner at the keystone position was Joe Gordon. But "Flash" also was winding down a spectacular career. Although he started the most games at second base, his replacement was waiting in the wings. Bobby Avila, like Boone, showed a propensity to hit the baseball around the ballpark and added a dimension of much-needed speed on the basepaths. The kid from Veracruz, Mexico, made 52 starts for the Indians in 1950.

The Tribe's infield was in transition as the season played out. That they could stay in the race with so many personnel changes was a credit to Boudreau.

Cleveland's real strength was in its pitching staff. They boasted one of the best in baseball. Starters Bob Feller, Bob Lemon, Early Wynn, Mike Garcia, and Steve Gromek could stack up against any other staff in the major leagues.

The Indians checked into the All-Star break in third place with a

46–32 record. Detroit (49–26) was still leading the pack, three games over New York (47–30) and 4½ over Cleveland.

Rosen pulled even with Williams for the league lead in home runs with 25, which was also the high-water mark for the major leagues. It caught some by surprise when Rosen was left off the American League roster for the All-Star Game. Yankees manager Casey Stengel selected eight of his own players to make the trip to Comiskey Park for the mid-summer classic.

"That Rosen was left off the All-Star team is an injustice to his performance, especially when Gerry [*sic*] Coleman and Tommy Henrich are on the squad," said Greenberg. "It reveals a flaw in the selection system. The inclusion of eight players in the Yankee lineup smacks of favoritism. Rosen's play this year has been most outstanding and his fine hitting record would make him valuable to the American League squad if only as a pinch-hitter."[14]

In addition to his hitting, Rosen's glovework was near the top of the third baseman in the league. At the time of the break, Rosen and Kell had each committed six errors, while Kell was the only third baseman selected to the AL roster by Stengel. Coleman, who normally played second base, could serve as his backup, if needed. As unfair to Rosen as it may have seemed, he would just have to wait his turn to receive All-Star recognition. The Indians were well-represented on the AL squad with Hegan, Doby, Feller, and Lemon receiving invites from Stengel.

The Tribe came out of the chute in the second half on a winning note. They posted a 9–4 record on the Eastern swing part of their schedule. By the end of July, Cleveland pulled within two games of the Tigers, who were now in a virtual tie with New York for first place. Rosen had a tremendous month as he batted .315 with eight home runs and 24 RBI. He was now batting .296 with 29 home runs and 88 RBI. Easter was also proving his resolve, showing a stat line of 21/60/.288 through July.

Off the field, Rosen was corresponding with Terry Blumberg. Terry was from Dothan, Alabama, but she was a student at the University of Miami, while Rosen made his off-season home in Miami Beach. Terry's Aunt Miriam and Al's Aunt Sari were old friends.[15] They pushed for him and Terry to meet. Eventually he did ask Terry out. They hit it off, but he had to report to Tucson for spring training. They wrote to each other during the season. Terry made a trip to Chicago to visit a friend and watch her first major league game.

After the game, Rosen took Terry to Soldier Field for the College

All-Star Football Game. They sat next to Boudreau, along with some of their teammates. "Flip introduced me to his teammates," said Terry. "We left before the game was over to beat the crowd and all the players yelled to us as we departed, 'Don't forget the curfew.'"[16]

On August 20, in the second game of a doubleheader against Chicago, Rosen smacked his 33rd home run of the year off Billy Pierce. The blast set a Cleveland record for home runs in a season by a right-handed batter. The previous mark was set by Gordon, who clouted 32 homers in 1948.

New York took control of the AL, posting a 38–20 record over August and September. The Tigers stayed in the race, and Boston took over third place. The Indians finished in fourth place with a 91–62–1 record, seven games out of first place. The Indians, who played each AL rival 22 games a season, held a winning mark against every club, with one exception. The Tribe posted an 8–14 record against New York.

Rosen led the AL in home runs with 37. He also drove in 116 runs, a team high, batted .287, and walked 100 times. The 37 home runs remains the most by a rookie for a season in Indians history.[17] It was the high-water mark for American League rookies until 1987, when Oakland's Mark McGwire crushed 49 home runs.[18]

Rosen led all AL third baseman in assists with 322. Offensively, Easter performed just as well. He left the yard 28 times, drove in 107 runs (second on the team), and batted .280.

Although there was no argument about the great years Rosen and Easter had, neither player was named AL Rookie of the Year. That honor went to Walt Dropo of the Red Sox. The big first baseman belted 34 home runs and drove in a league-best 144 runs while batting .322.

The bigger news came on November 10, when Indians owner/president Ellis Ryan and Greenberg made a managerial change, dumping Boudreau and appointing Al Lopez the new skipper. Lopez caught for 19 seasons in the majors. He was most recently the manager of Indianapolis of the American Association. Over a three-year span (1948–1950), Lopez led the Indianapolis Indians to a 278–182 record.

Boudreau was not asked back as a manager or player. "I was hurt because they didn't ask me if I would stay on as a player. It would have been an uncomfortable situation, but I was disappointed they didn't give me the opportunity."[19]

As for Lopez, he liked the makeup of his new team and saw no reason to change what was already working well. "I never saw Al Rosen

Al Rosen is greeted by his mother, Mrs. Rose Gould, before an Indians game at Cleveland Stadium. Mrs. Rosen and Flip's grandmother, Gertrude, were the positive influences in his life. Both women were strong supporters of his early athletic career and offered a strong shoulder in his dealing with anti–Semitism as a young boy (The Cleveland Press Collection, Michael Schwartz Library, Cleveland State University).

play in a Cleveland uniform," said Lopez. "but I saw him play plenty, and often to my sorrow, when he was with Kansas City. Easter had a terrific year, and everyone tells me this kid Avila has a chance to become one of the real good ones."[20]

Rosen's stardom on the baseball diamond provided him with perks he may not have otherwise been offered. From October 11 to November 5, a team of AL stars went up against a team of NL stars in a 33-game schedule. The barnstorming tour began in Montreal and ended in San Francisco, reaching 29 cities in all. While in Miami on October 21, Rosen was the guest at a testimonial dinner given in his honor at Hickory House in Miami Beach. He received an assortment of gifts at the dinner and was the honored guest at halftime of the University of Miami-Boston University football game. "It was the greatest day of my life,"[21] said Rosen.

While the barnstorming brigade moved across the country, one of the other players Rosen sought batting advice from was Ralph Kiner. The young slugger from the Pittsburgh Pirates broke into the big leagues in 1946. Kiner led the NL in home runs from 1946–1950, topping 50 homers twice.

Kiner suggested to Rosen that he consult Greenberg instead. "Hank Greenberg was my instructor," said Kiner. "When we were roommates in Pittsburgh, he helped me plenty in becoming a more consistent long-ball hitter. You're lucky he's the general manager of the Indians. If I were you, I'd go to him for help."[22]

Rosen heeded Kiner's instruction and went to see Greenberg. The former and current AL home run champions worked together as Greenberg was glad to see that Rosen was not resting on his laurels and wanted to improve himself. Greenberg advised Rosen to stand a bit closer to the plate to give himself a better shot at connecting on the outside pitches.

"I'm not as big as Walt Dropo or Kiner," said Rosen. "I must compensate for size in other ways. By moving up, I can get more distance on those outside pitches. Perhaps some persons who saw Hank work with me had the idea, because I was being pitched outside, that I was learning to hit to right field. That's not so. My power is to left and I'll gladly take all my hits there."[23]

The 1951 edition of the Cleveland Indians was not much different from the one that finished the 1950 season. Joe Gordon retired and was now a player/manager for the Sacramento Solons of the Pacific Coast League. Lou Boudreau, like Keltner, signed on with the Boston Red Sox a week after his release from the Tribe. The pitching staff remained largely intact from the previous season, as was the rest of the team. Four veterans were signed to add experience to the bench: outfielders Barney McCosky and Sam Chapman, infielder Snuffy Stirnweiss, and catcher Birdie Tebbetts.

The newcomer that everyone had their eye on was rookie Harry Simpson. An outfielder, Simpson, or "Suitcase Simpson," as he came to be known, would push left fielder Dale Mitchell for playing time. The left-handed-batting Simpson was signed by Cleveland in 1949 after playing with the Philadelphia Stars of the Negro National League from 1946--1948. Simpson tied teammate Jack Graham for the team lead in home runs (33) in 1950. "Suitcase" led the club in doubles (41), hits (225), and slugging percentage (.578).

As the players reported to Tucson for spring training, three members of the Indians' infield were more at ease and were anticipating a little less stress. "It certainly is different this spring," said Rosen. "Most of us feel relaxed and confident because we are pretty sure of holding our jobs."[24]

"It'll be easier," said Ray Boone, "without so many big wheels around. We won't have to worry about making mistakes for fear of being benched."[25]

"We feel confident," said Luke Easter, "but we're also dog-gone anxious to do our best. Look how many fellows came down here before they had to."[26]

Rosen and Boone especially felt a bit of relief, since they replaced two icons that Tribe fans embraced wholeheartedly. "Sometimes, Joe Gordon would signal me to move over a step or two toward second base and then I'd look into the dugout and see Lou frantically waving me back toward third," said Boone. "I decided finally that the only way out for me was not to look. Then if everything worked out all right nothing was said. If it didn't, I just took my bawling out and let it go at that."[27]

Rosen knew all too well what Boone was facing as a young player trying to make a go of it. "I was the same way while Kenny Keltner was around," said Rosen. "I guess I had an inferiority complex. It wasn't until Ken left the ball club and I knew I was the third baseman that I settled down to play ball the way I knew I could."[28]

The 1951 season started in Detroit on April 17. The pitching matchup featured two future members of the Hall of Fame: The Tribe's Bob Lemon and the Tigers' Hal Newhouser. Although "Prince Hal" was on the downside of a great career, he pitched a dandy of a game. He scattered eight hits and surrendered two runs, both unearned. Unfortunately for Newhouser, the Tiger's offense was helpless against Lemon. The right-handed hurler claimed the 2–1 win, giving up two hits, striking out four, and walking one. Avila, Easter, and Rosen combined for five of the eight hits off Newhouser.

Because Cleveland promoted Simpson to the varsity, they deemed their other prospect, Minnie Miñoso, expendable. On April 30, Cleveland traded Miñoso to the White Sox as part of a three-team trade including the Philadelphia Athletics. Cleveland also dealt pitcher Sam Zoldak and catcher Ray Murray to Philadelphia, and Chicago sent left-handed reliever Lou Brissie to Cleveland.

It turned out to be a bad deal for Greenberg and the Indians. Brissie was a mediocre pitcher for the Tribe. Miñoso blossomed into a star with Chicago, leading the AL in triples (14) and stolen bases (31) in 1951. Although Miñoso returned to the Indians several years later, his best years were with the White Sox.

Rosen got off to a fine start in 1951, but he slumped in May, batting .239. It was the second month since he became a regular player that Rosen whiffed (15) more times than he walked (11).

If there were any doubts about Rosen's toughness as a player, or his desire, they were put to rest on June 1. During warm-up before a game against the Senators at Cleveland Stadium, a throw from Bob Kennedy slipped through Rosen's glove and smacked him right in the nose. The force of the baseball broke Rosen's nose, for the tenth time in his life. But Rosen played the game and went 2-for-3 against Senators' starter Julio Moreno. Cleveland won the game, 2–1 behind Early Wynn's three-hitter.

On June 10 against Boston, fracture number 11 occurred in the top of the sixth inning of Game One of a double dip. Rosen took a ground ball off the bat of Walt Dropo to the face. Rosen was laid out flat because of the impact. He was removed from the game and Stirnweiss took his place at third base. Rosen was kept out of the nightcap, causing him to miss his first game since becoming the Indians' starting third baseman the year before.

"I saw it all the way, but it came too fast for me to duck or get my glove up,"[29] said Rosen, whose nose was bulging and eyes were badly swollen, resembling a panda. When it was suggested to Rosen that the recent incidents might impair his vision, he cracked, "Is there anything in the rules that says you can't take a seeing-eye dog out to third base with you?"[30]

"Al could be out for several days," said trainer Wally Bock. "A nose hemorrhage could cause plenty of swelling and he may have trouble getting his eyes open in the morning."[31]

Perhaps Bock was being overly cautious. The Indians hit the road to begin a trip out east, beginning in Philadelphia. Rosen accompanied the team and arrived at Shibe Park early so that Bock could treat his swollen face. Despite his maladies, Rosen insisted that he play. Lopez acquiesced, and Rosen banged out three hits including a double and a three-run homer. It was Rosen's seventh dinger of the season, and he collected four RBI in the Indians' 8–6 win over the Athletics. His effort helped Bob Feller improve his record to 9–1. "We stayed with it," Rosen said of his treatment. "Just knocked off for a while to get something to eat. I can't give too much credit to Wally. I just wouldn't have made it without him. At noon, my eyes were like slits and I had a couple of bulbs under them."[32]

"It was pretty simple," said Bock. "There was an awful lot of congestion and we just spread it. Flattened it out. Al's going to have those raccoon eyes for a while, but the swelling is way down."[33]

Feller hurled the third and final no-hitter of his career on July 1 against Detroit at Cleveland Stadium. "Rapid Robert" struck out five and walked three in the 2–1 victory to raise his record to 11–2. An error by Boone in the top of the fourth inning, his 20th of the season, opened the door for the Tigers to score their only run. Easter knocked in both runs for the Tribe.

At the All-Star Game break, the leaders in the AL looked like this:

Team	Won	Loss	Percentage	Games Back
Chicago	49	29	.628	---
Boston	47	29	.595	1.0
New York	45	29	.581	2.0
Cleveland	44	32	.535	4.0

Rosen slumped again in July, as he batted .209 for the month with three home runs and 15 RBI. At the break, Rosen had 12 home runs to his credit as opposed to the 25 he cracked a year earlier by the same time. Despite this, Cleveland posted its best monthly record at 22–8. In a matter of three weeks, the AL race was turned upside-down. The Yankees claimed first place, two games up on Cleveland and three on Boston. The White Sox fell to fourth place, 7½ games back.

Cleveland's rise in the standings could be attributed to two of their starting pitchers. Both Early Wynn (4–1, 2.81 ERA) and Mike Garcia (6–1, 1.78 ERA) pitched marvelously in July, providing the Tribe ample opportunities to put wins on the board.

On August 15, Rosen smashed a first-inning grand slam into the left field seats at Sportsman's Park. The blast highlighted a seven-run outburst off St. Louis Browns starter Ned Garver. The home run was Rosen's fourth in the last six games. It was also his fourth grand slam of the season, tying him with eight other players. The last to accomplish the feat was Sid Gordon of the Boston Braves in 1950.[34]

The Indians defeated the Browns as Wynn upped his record to 13–11. More importantly, it was the Tribe's 13th win in a row, and they were holding on tight to first place over New York by 2½ games. The winning streak ended the following day as St. Louis shut out Cleveland, 4–0.

After their win streak was halted, the Indians' bats went cold. From August 23 to September 1, Cleveland's record was 4–6. In those ten games, all played at Cleveland Stadium, they never scored more than three runs. And that only happened twice: on August 25, they lost to the Yankees, 7–3, and on August 31, they were defeated by St. Louis, 6–3.

The Indians victimized Garver again on September 2, when they became the 27th team to hit three consecutive home runs in one inning. Simpson got the parade going with an inside-the-park job in the bottom of the fourth inning. He was followed by Rosen, who smashed his 23rd, and then Easter, who hit his 21st. Asked if the park job by Simpson helped relieve some tension, Rosen said "Yep, I think that did it. We hit a good pitcher and he had good stuff. He slowed up in the late innings after we'd been belting his fast pitches."[35]

The win nudged the Tribe to a half-game behind New York, which was idle. On September 9, New York (86–49) and Cleveland (88–51–1) were in a virtual tie for first place.

Two days later, the Tribe was in Philadelphia for a doubleheader. The baseball found Rosen once again. With the score tied, 2–2, the Athletics loaded the bases against Cleveland starter Mike Garcia in the bottom of the fifth inning. Steve Gromek entered the game and retired Gus Zernial on a pop to Rosen at third. However, Billy Hitchcock lined a single to center field to plate two runs. Doby charged the ball and threw to third to try for the baserunner advancing to third base. But his throw took a bad hop, smacked Rosen in the face, and rolled over to the stands. The runner scored and Philadelphia took a 5–2 lead.

Blood gushed from a cut over Rosen's right eye, onto the front of his jersey. Bock attended to Rosen with ice packs to try and stop the bleeding. Bock wanted Rosen to leave the game, but he would have none of it. "Tape 'er up and let's get on with the game,"[36] said Rosen.

The Indians came back to win the game, 6–5. But they dropped the second game by a score of 9–5. New York lost both ends of a doubleheader to St Louis. As a result, Cleveland moved ahead of the Yankees by a full game.

An item about Rosen appeared in the *New York Daily News* on September 22, 1951. "Al Rosen, Cleveland third baseman, is a native of Miami, Fla," wrote Ed Sullivan. "Of Jewish parentage, he is a Catholic. At the plate, you'll notice he makes the sign of the cross with his bat."[37]

Like many players who are superstitious at the plate, Rosen made an "X" with the end of his bat on home plate before he stepped into the batter's box. However, the "X" was thought to be a cross, signifying that Rosen must be Catholic. "I went back to my apartment from a road trip and found several bags of mail," said Rosen. "Half the letters were from irate rabbis, the other half contained St. Christopher medals [St. Christopher is the patron saint of safe travels]. I stopped making 'Xs' after that."[38]

The Indians closed the season with a 4–9 collapse. Conversely, the Yankees posted a 12–5 record to end the campaign. New York captured its third straight pennant, and eventually, their third straight world championship.

Cleveland, which finished five games out of first place, could look to its head-to-head matchup with the Bronx Bombers as a reason why they finished in second place. New York and Cleveland met 22 times during the season, with the Yankees winning 15. The Tribe had also taken 16 of the first 17 games from Detroit. But in the last ten days of the season, Detroit took four of their final five games.

Cleveland had three 20-game winners in 1951: Wynn (20–13), Garcia (20–13) and Feller (22–8). Feller led the junior circuit in wins, while Bob Lemon led the league in losses (17–14).

"Bobby Avila and Ray Boone developed as a second base combination faster than we had any right to think they would," said Lopez. "Al Rosen and Luke Easter did not have the kind of seasons we expected of them, but you must remember that both of them not only were handicapped by injuries [Easter had a sore right knee], both of them played many a time when they should have been resting. No, I certainly won't feel depressed at the prospect of opening the 1952 season with that infield."[39]

Larry Doby and Feller were more direct in their post-season comments.

"That's the story of the Cleveland failure to win the pennant," said Doby. "The three of us [Rosen, Easter and Doby] were supposed to be the big guys of the Cleveland attack but nothing happened. [Cleveland] just couldn't win the 'big one,' while the pennant-winning Yankees made it a repeated habit of grabbing off every 'money' decision that cropped up."[40]

"As everyone knows, we had a poor season offensively," said Feller. "Al Rosen and Larry Doby both had ordinary seasons at bat. Luke Easter had a bad knee. The pressure, as a result, fell on the fellows who aren't supposed to hit much."[41]

Rosen finished the season with 24 home runs 102 RBI, and he batted .265. He finished second to Easter (27 HR, 103 RBI) in both power categories. The only Cleveland player to bat over .300 in 1951 was Avila (.304). If Rosen was feeling down that he had an off-year, he had a fan in Boston. "Rosen is a good, sound ballplayer, with a lot of ability and guts," said Ted Williams, "I saw him get his nose broken in a game against us. I thought the fellow would bleed to death before they could do something for him."[42]

Prior to the start of spring training in 1952, the Indians held a pre-camp batting school for a select number of players. The five pupils who were extended an invitation were Rosen, Boone, Simpson, Doby, and Easter. The instruction began February 19 and lasted 10 days, right up the start of spring training. Supervising, as well as instructing the players were Greenberg, Lopez, and Indians great Tris Speaker. "All these fellows, remember, have proven they can hit better than they hit last season," said Greenberg. "We're not trying to add any points to their best average. We're just trying to help them back to it."[43] The early batting practice was a welcomed exercise by the Tribe players. Rosen, who had been very diligent in his preparation, used a five-point plan to improve his batting.

1. Rosen gave up golf, which he loved to play, but he suspected it was causing him to swing with an uppercut. Professional golfer Sam Snead told Rosen, "You don't see me swinging a bat."
2. He practiced his swing under the watchful eye of ex-big leaguer Max Carey, who noticed that Rosen was uppercutting the ball.
3. He studied films of Ted Williams hitting so that he could close his eyes and see the Splendid Splinter's level swing.
4. He worked on leveling off his swing in front of a mirror for an hour a day.
5. On the advice of his doctor, he began to eat several carrots a day in an effort to improve his vision for night games.[44]

Perhaps Rosen was on the way back from his position inside the batter's box, but it appeared as if his defense was still an issue. At least to one observer this was the case. New St. Louis Browns manager Rogers Hornsby was asked for his assessment of Rosen. "He can hurt you with a bat, but in the field he is liable to get himself killed,"[45] said Hornsby.

Rosen was not one to take guff from anyone, not even a great player like Hornsby.

"I don't know where Hornsby ever saw me play," said Rosen. "I remember meeting him once, several years back. If he did see me play, it was probably five years ago in the Texas League. How can he come into this league and pop off without ever seeing me in a major league game? They should give credit to a person who tries to improve."[46]

Perhaps the Rajah should have been more worried about his own team, as he was fired after just 51 games and a 22–29 record.

The Editors of *Sport* magazine came out with their predictions for the 1952 Major League season. Their pick to win the American League was Cleveland.

> We are of the opinion that the Tribe's pitching staff is the very best in the league—good enough, in fact, to carry the club to its first pennant since 1948. The league's best pitching staff has the benefit of the league's best catching from Jim Hegan. The Indians' quiescent batting attack will be more menacing if Larry Doby and Al Rosen can hit their potentials. A pennant for Cleveland will be made possible according to our charts, by the descent of the Yankees and the Red Sox.[47]

Perhaps *Sport* was on to something as the Indians broke out of the gate by winning their first seven games. On April 29, the Indians

Indians Opening Day lineup in 1952 at Comiskey Park (courtesy Cleveland Public Library).

trounced the Athletics by a score of 21–9. Rosen had his best day as a big leaguer, posting career highs in home runs (3), hits (4), runs (4), and RBI (7). Rookie outfielder Jim Fridley led the hit parade, going 6-for-6, tying a modern league record for the most hits in a nine-inning game. The Tribe collected 25 hits and 40 total bases in the romp.

The Indians made a bit of history on May 3 in Washington. With Hegan injured, Birdie Tebbetts became the starting catcher. His backup was Quincy Trouppe. The 39-year-old Trouppe played most of his career with the St. Louis Stars of the Negro National League. Trouppe was playing winter ball in Venezuela when Greenberg reached out to him about joining the Tribe. Trouppe replaced Tebbetts in the bottom of the seventh inning. Sam Jones, who pitched for the Cleveland Buckeyes in 1947, entered the game in relief of Lou Brissie. Thus, Trouppe and Jones became the first African American battery in American League history.

Rosen smacked six home runs, drove in 12 runs, and batted .348 in April, and he was just getting started. He started off May with a nine-game hitting streak, and his slash line for the month read 4/18/.333. It looked as if the due diligence he had put into his off-season workouts was paying off. As the month of May came to a close, Rosen's 10 home runs and 30 RBI led the circuit, and he trailed teammate Bobby Avila in runs, 28 to 26.

One adjustment Rosen made was to drop his arms so that the bat was at shoulder length. "I used to hold my bat high," said Rosen. "I was successful with this stance in both the Texas League and the American Association. I was always a .300 hitter with it. And in the majors I hit for distance but not frequently enough. I began to experiment and found I was upper-cutting too much."[48]

The result was a much more level swing. One of Rosen's hitting heroes, Ted Williams, had such a swing, level and compact. "I admire the levelness of Williams' swing," said Rosen. "I'm positive all batters do. I certainly hope I can emulate it."[49]

As a team, the Indians lost three starters early in the year to minor injuries: Doby (thigh muscle), Hegan (sore arm), and Avila (sore leg). But the injured trio did not miss much time due to the seemingly magical trainer's skill employed by Bock.

As May ended, the Indians were on top of the AL standings, sporting a 25–17 record. Included in that record was a two-game sweep of the Red Sox at Fenway Park and a three-game sweep at Yankees Stadium in early May. The Yankees were in fifth place but were 3½ games off the pace. Except for Detroit, the rest of the league was only separated by six games. The Indians posted a 12–15 record in June. The Yankees got a measure of revenge when they took three of four from the Tribe at Cleveland Stadium. After that series, the Senators came to Cleveland Stadium and swept a three-game series.

A crowd of 69,468 crammed their way into the lakefront stadium for a doubleheader against New York on June 15. Lopez juggled his lineup. Dale Mitchell, a terrific batter, was out with a leg injury suffered when he stepped off a high curb in Boston. Reserve Pete Reiser took over in left field. Easter had been ineffective at the plate. He was batting .213 with nine home runs as of June 14. Rosen was moved to first base to replace him. Hank Majeski, who was purchased from the Athletics on June 10, took over at the hot corner. "Maybe I'd get used to it after a while," said Rosen about playing first base, "but you get an entirely different perspective over there."[50]

New York won the first game, 8–2, behind a complete game by Eddie Lopat. The Bronx Bombers also won the nightcap, 4–2, behind Bob Kuzava.

The Yankees now had a 2½-game lead over the Tribe, who dropped to third place behind Boston. "Yeah, it helps to win two but it's going to be tough all the way," said Casey Stengel. "Look at us. Couple of weeks ago we're way back and now we're on top again."[51]

At the All-Star break, the top of the AL looked like this:

Team	*Won*	*Loss*	*Percentage*	*Games Back*
New York	45	29	.608	---
Chicago	44	34	.564	3.0
Cleveland	42	33	.560	3.5
Washington	39	34	.534	5.5

Rosen had a marvelous first half, and his name was listed numerous times on the leaderboard for offensive categories in the AL. He ranked first in RBI (53), first in slugging percentage (.577), tied with Yogi Berra (15) for second in home runs, second in hits (92), second in runs (50), and third in batting average (.330).

Unlike his rookie season when he was left off the AL All-Star squad, Rosen outpolled George Kell, who was now with Boston. Rosen finished first in the voting for the AL starting third baseman by 50,000 votes for the July 8 exhibition at Shibe Park. "I thought it would be impossible to beat out Kell," said Rosen. "George is an established star. I was surprised when I polled one million votes. I thought that was quite an achievement. But to beat out Kell ... how about that?"[52]

Mitchell and Avila joined Rosen in the starting lineup. Rosen, who was slotted in the cleanup spot, went 0-for-1 with a walk and a run scored as the NL won, 3–2, in the rain-shortened game that went five innings. Bob Lemon, who gave up a two-run home run to the Cubs' Hank Sauer, was charged with the loss.

On July 26, 1952, Mr. and Mrs. Myer Blumberg of Dothan, Alabama, announced the engagement of their daughter Terry to Al Rosen.[53] Two weeks later, Terry made her first trip to Cleveland. She was accompanied by her father on the journey north. There were lavish engagement parties thrown for the couple in sprawling estates in Shaker Heights.[54]

Terry also went to a game for the first time at Cleveland Stadium. Unfortunately, it was not a pleasant experience. "During my first visit to Cleveland one particularly vitriolic fan made all sorts of remarks about Flip," said Terry. "They were simply horrible. I was nearly in tears. Unable to stand it any longer without answering him back, I left in the sixth inning."[55]

For Rosen, the month of August in 1952 was a tale of two halves. He entered August batting .311, but as the month wore on, his batting average began to drop. From August 1–17, Rosen hit .210 (13-for-62) to drop his average to .297. His production numbers were on the wispy side with two homers and seven RBI. Included was a 1-for-7 effort against Chicago in a doubleheader at Cleveland Stadium on August 17.

Greenberg looked to strengthen the club as the season headed into the home stretch. The Indians made two deals that would be beneficial now and in future years. On August 7, they acquired outfielder Wally Westlake from Cincinnati for two players to be named later and an undisclosed amount of cash. "I'll guarantee you one thing. If Westlake gets in one of those hot streaks, Al [Lopez] will find a place in the lineup for him. I don't know where it will be, but when he's hitting you couldn't ask for a better ball player," said Indians coach Tony Cuccinello, who coached with the Reds in 1951.[56]

The second deal occurred on August 18, 1952. Cleveland sent infielder John Berardino, $50,000, and a player to be named later (minor league pitcher Charles Sipple) to Pittsburgh for pitcher Ted Wilks and shortstop George Strickland. At the time of the deal, Ray Boone had committed 20 errors at shortstop, and the Tribe brass looked for a player with a better glove, which was Strickland. "Strickland won't hit much—an occasional long ball maybe—but he's a good fellow to have around in case of an emergency. He covers a lot of ground, got a good pair of legs, and he throws very well," said Cuccinello.[57]

The Indians started an East Coast swing on August 19 in Boston. Cleveland led the Red Sox, 5–2, going into the home half of the seventh inning. Wynn was on the hill for the Tribe, and all looked well as he retired the first two Sox batters he faced. But a walk to Dom DiMaggio was followed by a bunt by Billy Goodman. Wynn fielded the baseball by the third base line but was knocked off-balance when Rosen ran into him. Wynn ate the ball, and Boston now had two runners on. Clyde Vollmer singled to center field to plate DiMaggio. The ball got past Doby, and the runners moved up to second and third base. Dick Gernert stepped into the batter's box and lifted a soft fly ball to right field. Simpson moved in but lost the ball in the summer sun at Fenway Park. It fell at his feet. Two runs crossed the plate, and the game was now tied, 5–5. "I saw it when it first came toward me," said Simpson. "Then I never saw it again until it hit the ground."[58]

The game remained tied until the bottom of the ninth inning, when Goodman opened with a two-base blast to center. Al Benton bunted down the third base line, and Wynn tried to nail the quick-starting Goodman at third. He missed by a shade. Gernert was handed an intentional pass to load the bases.

> Al Lopez brought in Mike Garcia to pitch out of the jam. He didn't fail by much. He retired Hoot Evers on a foul to Al Rosen. [Sammy] White bounced one towards shortstop. Rosen raced over, made a diving attempt to grab the ball in between bounces but it went through him to Ray Boone. Boone fired the ball to Jim Hegan at the plate but it arrived as Goodman was brushing off the seat of his pants after a winning slide."[59]

The scenario described above was taken from the game story in the *Boston Globe* on August 20. It is interesting to note that the *Cleveland Plain Dealer* and the *Cleveland News* took dimmer looks at the play, chastising Rosen for not being able to field the ball on what was termed a "roller" or an easy grounder. The Cleveland scribes also wrote that Rosen was in the way of Boone's throw home, causing him to double-clutch, which allowed Goodman to score.

But the fielding issues were only part of the problem. Rosen went 0-for-5 in the game and grounded into two double plays. After the game,

Lopez announced that he was going to sit Rosen down for the next two games at Fenway. "He can't seem to do anything right," Lopez said of Rosen. "I hope a rest will do the job." Lopez continued, "We need Rosen, but the way he's playing now he's hurting both the team and himself."[60]

Lopez looked like a genius when Rosen got back into the lineup on August 22 and went on a 12-game hitting streak. From August 24–31, Rosen knocked in at least one RBI a game, and totaled 19 in that span. He also smacked five home runs. He had his highest production numbers for the season in August, slugging seven home runs and driving in 26 runs. Zernial and Rosen were tied at the top of the RBI leaderboard with 92.

Cleveland closed to within two games of New York at the end of August, as they went a combined 37–24 through July and August. Between the two months, the Tribe played 11 doubleheaders, putting a strain on their pitching staff. Lemon and Garcia led the league with 36 starts, Wynn had 33, and Feller had 30.

On September 1, Cleveland wrapped up a road trip in St. Louis with a doubleheader against the Browns. The Indians won the first game, 9–3, with Rosen going 3-for-5 at the dish and scoring two runs.

In the nightcap, St. Louis led 2–1 when the skies opened up in the fifth inning. Play was halted for just over an hour. When it resumed, the Indians scored three runs off Satchel Paige in the top of the sixth inning, but rain intervened once again. Although it rained for only eight minutes, the field was deemed unplayable, and it resembled a small lake. The Indians were unable to retire the Browns in time, and the final score reverted back to a 2–1 verdict in favor of St. Louis. The Indians' brass protested the game, charging that:

1. The Browns had improper equipment to cover the field.
2. A deliberate attempt was made to avoid putting the field in playing condition by verbal orders from the team president (Bill Veeck).
3. American League rules call for every effort to be made to complete the regular schedule during the last visit of a club.[61]

Because the game was made official with the Indians batting in the top of the fifth inning, it ended a 12-game hitting streak by Rosen.

The scene got uglier with both front offices hurling charges and counter-charges at one another. Rosen, who was no doubt frustrated at the outcome of the second game, challenged a heckler outside the

Indians' clubhouse to a fight, but it was quickly broken up by St. Louis' finest.

American League President Will Harridge threw out the protest three days later. "While this type of incident is regrettable, it has happened many times and can only be charged to the elements over which the game has no control,"[62] said Harridge.

Al Rosen and Terry Blumenthal on their wedding day, October 13, 1952, in Dothan, Alabama. Their nuptials capped a big year on the field for Rosen in 1952. Cleveland's star third baseman led the league in RBI with 105 and he was voted to start in his first All-Star Game (The Cleveland Press Collection, Michael Schwartz Library, Cleveland State University).

Hebrew Hammer

On September 14, the Yankees (86–57) led the Indians (84–60–1) by 2½ games. Cleveland ended the season winning nine of their last 10 games. But they could not catch the Yanks, who closed out the season with an impressive run of their own, winning 13 of 15 games. Cleveland ended the season in second place, two games out of first. Ironically, Cleveland was 10–12 against the Yankees during the season.

The Indians again had three starters win 20 games or more: Wynn (23–12, 2.90 ERA), Lemon (22–11, 2.50 ERA), and Garcia (22–11, 2.37 ERA). Rosen led the AL in RBI (105), smacked 28 homers, and for the first time since he made the majors, batted over .300 (.302). Doby led the league in home runs (32) and slugging percentage (.541). Doby finished second to Rosen in RBI (104). Easter, who was demoted to Indianapolis for part of the season, still finished second in homers (31).

The October 8 issue of *The Sporting News* ripped off a portion of *Casey at the Bat* and slanted the verbiage to the Indians' season.

Oh, somewhere in this favored land
The sun is shining bright;
The Band is playing somewhere
And somewhere hearts are light;
And somewhere men are laughing,
And somewhere children shout;
But there is no joy in Cleveland
The mighty Indians have struck out! [63]

There was some chatter that Cleveland, most everyone's favorite to win the flag, lost the pennant or "choked." But Lopez took the high road, using the team's fast finish as his logic for the team not giving up or folding. He saw no reason that his club needed to be broken up, but perhaps instead it needed some minor tweaks.

Al Rosen's life changed immeasurably on October 12 when he exchanged "I dos" with Terry. The ceremony took place at Emmanuel Temple in Dothan. Jerry Rosen served as best man.

The couple spent their honeymoon in Acapulco, Mexico.

FOUR

It's Unanimous!

Finishing two games behind to New York for the American League pennant in 1952 was a hard pill to swallow for the Indians. They had a great season, but the Yankees were a better club. For two years in a row, Cleveland served in the role as the proverbial bridesmaid instead of the bride. They were left to wonder how to close the gap between the Bronx Bombers and themselves.

Hank Greenberg, perhaps deciding that the roster needed only a slight tinkering instead of a major overhaul, made few moves in the off-season. The biggest deal was acquiring pitcher Bob Hooper from the Philadelphia Athletics for pitcher Dick Rozek and minor leaguer Bobby Wilson. The other addition was Jim Lemon. The big, right-handed outfielder broke in with the Indians in 1950 but was called up to active duty for the Korean War. He was scheduled to be discharged from the Army on January 18, 1953, in time for spring training.[1] The former Texas League home run champion in 1950 (39 home runs at AA Oklahoma City) would be a welcome addition.

Also returning to the club was outfielder Bob Kennedy. He had played in only 22 games in 1952 before being called to active duty. Like Lemon, Kennedy would be present for the start of spring training.

There was one critic of Greenberg's lack of activity. Joe Trimble, the Yankees beat writer for the *New York Daily News*, predicted an easy season for the Bombers. "The [Indians'] management has seen fit to stand pat with a group of CHRONIC QUITTERS, and second place, which they seem to like, should be their lot. New York, replete with youthful talent in its regular lineup, and a seasoned, deep pitching staff is the class of the league. This could be the easiest flag of them all."[2]

It may have been a harsh characterization by Trimble, but the Yankees were the AL kings four years running. Until another team dethroned them, New York was the king of the American League.

The Indians held their "batting school" once again at their minor league training camp in Daytona Beach. Eighteen players were slated to attend the early drills that began on February 14. The mandatory reporting date for the whole club was 10 days later in Tucson. On the contract front, Rosen received a substantial increase in his salary to $22,000. Rosen was quick to accept terms of his deal, which nullified the cut he took in 1952 and added a bit more.

As spring training opened, there was no shortage of story lines. Although Rosen agreed to terms, Larry Doby and Early Wynn held out. Both stars seemed ready to remain at home until they received acceptable terms.

Another late arrival was second baseman Bobby Avila. Checking in two weeks late, Avila showed up limping, favoring his right ankle. Avila claimed that he was injured in an automobile accident in his native Mexico. However, the Indians learned that Avila had hurt his ankle sliding into a base while playing winter ball in Mexico. Players who were born in North America were forbidden from moonlighting in winter ball. But a player born in Mexico, Puerto Rico, Cuba, or Venezuela could participate and, in many cases, the player was treated as a national hero in his homeland. Avila's narrative changed from "he didn't play any baseball" to "he hadn't played all that much." Greenberg was rather sour about the topic of Avila playing winter league ball. Cleveland brought a case against Avila to Commissioner Happy Chandler. But nothing came of it. Even if Avila did play winter ball, he did not break any regulations. He only incurred Greenberg's wrath.

There were position battles that gave the beat writers stories to fill the daily sports pages. At shortstop, Ray Boone and George Strickland went head-to-head. Would Lopez go with Boone's bat or Strickland's glove? Lemon was also given the opportunity to unseat Dale Mitchell in left field. Mitchell had been the starting leftfielder since 1947. A solid batsman, Mitchell hit below .300 only once (.290 in 1951). The battle for right field was between Kennedy, Wally Westlake, and Harry Simpson.

As the spring forged ahead, Lopez's lineup began to take shape. Wynn and Doby came to terms on their contracts. Because of his ability to hit, Boone was getting the nod over Strickland at short. Mitchell was holding down the left field job. "Suitcase" Simpson was having a good camp. It looked as if veterans Kennedy and Westlake would be riding the pine. One player who offered an unbiased view on the Tribe's offense was pitcher Sal Maglie of the New York Giants. New York made their spring training home in Phoenix and opposed the Indians on a regular basis. "I'd rather pitch against Brooklyn than against Cleveland," said Maglie. "The Indians have more left-handers and very tough ones. You have to pitch your heart out to stay even with the Indians pitchers."[3]

Players were shocked to learn that former Indians owner Alva C. Bradley, who owned the Indians from 1927–1946, died of a heart attack on March 29 in Florida. Bradley was instrumental in moving Sunday doubleheaders to Cleveland Stadium as well as installing lights at the ballpark on the shores of Lake Erie.

Outside his ownership of the Indians, Bradley was a major factor in hiring U.S. Senator A. B. "Happy" Chandler as the commissioner of baseball following the death of Kenesaw Landis in 1944. Bradley chaired a committee to search for Landis' replacement. Although many owners favored National League President Ford Frick, Bradley favored a replacement who came from outside the game.[4]

Bradley was a philanthropist and served as president of many boards. At age 36, he became president of the Cleveland Chamber of Commerce. When asked what his biggest hurdle would be in spotlighting the city, Bradley answered, "The assimilation of our vast and growing foreign population. Getting these people to come here and live is one thing. Making Clevelanders of them is another. There must be aroused in them some spirit of civic pride before they are really citizens."[5]

The Indians' beat writers differed on their predictions regarding the American League flag. Harry Jones of the *Cleveland Plain Dealer* wrote that it was foolish to make predictions in April of what might happen in October. "Let's simply say now that New York is the team to beat, that Cleveland has an excellent chance, that Chicago is the dark horse and that Philadelphia and Washington have fourth-place potential."[6]

Ed McAuley of the *Cleveland News* wrote, "They've called out the man with the net for less than this--but I pick the Cleveland Indians to win the pennant. I've become convinced that the world champions won't be as tough as they were last season, when they finished only two games ahead of the Tribesmen."[7]

A season of baseball was set to get under way, and the Yankees were strong in every facet of the game. However, all it takes is an injury to a front-line player, and the season can come undone. And an injury to a key player is exactly what happened to Cleveland in only the fourth game of the year. On April 18 at Comiskey Park, the Indians lost to the White Sox, 7–6. The game itself mirrored any Little League game played across America.

Both pitching staffs combined for 26 walks, which was just four free passes short of the MLB record set on May 9, 1916, in a game between Philadelphia and Detroit.[8] The Indians also committed four errors and left 14 runners on base. Of the seven runs the Indians gave up, only two were earned.

But the real misfortune of the day occurred in the fourth inning. Easter was hit on the left foot by a pitch from Chicago's Lou Kretlow. "Man, that Kretlow sure throws a big curve—but not that big," said Easter. "I saw it coming tight. I stepped back. Thought I was back far enough. But it kept curving. It dropped right on my foot. Plop!"[9]

"The X-rays show a serious fracture of the large metatarsal bone," said Cleveland trainer Wally Bock. "He'll be in the hospital three days and will be laid up for five, six weeks—maybe longer."[10] Unfortunately for the Indians, Bock's assessment turned out to be a tad conservative.

The loss of Easter was surely felt. Other than Doby, Easter was the only viable power hitter from the left side of the plate. Bill Glynn took over at first base for Easter, and although he was also a left-handed hitter, that was the only similarity he shared with Easter. Glynn was a good glove man who was used many times as a defensive replacement late in games. But as a hitter, he didn't measure up to Easter for average or power.

The pressure to provide some punch for the Tribe's offense fell to Rosen and Doby. Rosen was hot at the onset of the season. He got a base hit in the first 11 games of the season, and 18 in the first 19 games, which resulted in a .362 batting average.

Rosen's early-season success was what the Indians' flailing offensive attack needed. As the curtain came down on the month of May, Rosen was batting .338 and led the league in both home runs (10) and slugging percentage (.619). Doby had slumped to a .230 average in the same period, leaving Rosen to carry the offense.

But one player could carry an offense only so far. Behind Rosen and the Tribe's vaunted pitching staff, they were in second place at the end of May.

Team	Won	Loss	Percentage	Games Back
New York	27	11	.711	---
Cleveland	22	15	.595	4.5
Chicago	25	18	.581	4.5
Washington	23	20	.535	6.5

Beginning on June 2, the eastern clubs of the AL made their way west. Cleveland had a 14-game homestand against Boston, Philadelphia,

Washington, and New York. The Indians went 8–2 in the first 10 games and awaited the Yankees to close out the homestand with a four-game set.

Indians fans may have steered their attention away from baseball on Monday, June 8, 1953. One of the greatest natural disasters rolled through Cleveland. A tornado that claimed 112 lives in Flint, Michigan, made its way through Bowling Green and then to Cleveland's west side. After the tornado ripped through the city, it was estimated by Cuyahoga County Auditor John J. Carney that there was over $50,000,000 in damages. Over 400 city workers, with the assistance of volunteer workers, attempted to clear debris and fallen trees. An additional 2,000 utility workers labored through the evening to restore gas, electric and phone service. Transit repairmen, numbering close to 600, worked around the clock to restore overhead wires.

An additional $500,000 worth of damage was estimated to have hit 13 school buildings. One grade school had its roof crash through the building and took the second floor with it. "If this storm would have happened when the children at these schools were in classes, I am sure we would have had hundreds of casualties," said Superintendent Mark C. Shinnerer. "At least one class of children would have died there."[11] Nine deaths and 221 injuries were attributed to the tornado.

On the baseball front, the Indians were a hot club to be sure. But the Yankees posted a 10–0 record while the Indians went 8–2, increasing their lead over the Tribe by two full games. They had won 14 straight games as the boys in pinstripes invaded Cleveland Stadium.

The Yankees swept Cleveland with little difficulty. The final two games, a Sunday double-dip on June 14, drew 74,708 fans to the park. It was the largest crowd in the big leagues since August 28, 1951, when the Red Sox and Indians played a doubleheader in front of 75,997 spectators at Cleveland Stadium. It may have been appropriate that on this day, Americans celebrated "Flag Day," as Old Glory flew unfurled throughout the country. It could be argued that the Yankees, who ran their winning streak to 18 games, wrapped up the AL flag on this day.

Rosen went 12-for-52 (.231) during the homestand. His batting average dropped from .338 to .309. "They beat some very good pitching in this series and with a break here or there, we would have won two or three of them." said Lopez. "Over 100 games are left and we're certainly not finished."[12]

Indians fans may have had a different take on the weekend's results.

"The Indians made a number of mistakes throughout, but the greatest was showing up for the second game," wrote Harry Jones. "They made a fight for it for eight innings in the opener [a 6–2 loss] but offered no opposition at all for Vic Raschi in the nightcap [a 3–0 loss]. The fans even tired of booing them."[13]

The trading deadline was the next day. Boone's name was at the center of trade talk rumors. He was batting .241 and in 31 games had committed eight errors. He had not started a game since May 27 as Lopez made the switch to Strickland. The rumors turned to fact when Cleveland and Detroit made an eight-player deal ahead of the deadline. Boone, pitchers Steve Gromek, Dick Weik, and Al Aber were headed to Tiger Town in exchange for pitchers Art Houtteman and Bill Wight, infielder Owen Friend, and catcher Joe Ginsberg. "When I found out that he [Boone] was traded, my wife and I both cried, we were so upset," said Rosen of his close friend and road roommate. "That was the first time that anyone close to me was traded."[14]

Houtteman was a right-handed starting pitcher. Although he won 19 games for the Tigers in 1950, he led the league in losses in 1952 with 20. He did not pitch well early in the 1953 season (2–6, 5.90 ERA). Yet he was still considered the key player coming to Cleveland. Boone was often criticized for his defense and his lack of range at shortstop. Detroit manager Fred Hutchinson inserted Boone as his everyday third baseman. The move worked brilliantly as Boone excelled in a Tigers uniform for six seasons.

The Indians left Cleveland for an extended trip east. After taking two of three games from the Athletics and thee of five from the Senators, they split a four-game series with the Red Sox. Easter rejoined the club in Washington on June 22, hoping to give the offense a shot in the arm. They headed to Yankee Stadium for three games against New York. This time the Indians turned the tables, sweeping the Bombers.

Before the final game, when Casey Stengel was holding court with the Gotham reporters, he pointed to Rosen and said, "That guy hasn't hurt us with the bat all year."[15]

The pitching matchup for the finale looked to be a dandy with Wynn facing Whitey Ford. The Indians got their bats going in the first frame, when Dale Mitchell and Bobby Avila led off with singles. Rosen came to the plate. Ford was deliberate as he checked on the baserunners and took a little too much time for Rosen's liking. He called time and stepped out of the box, but Ford fired a pitch. Home plate umpire

Ed Rommel ruled the pitch a strike. "I said it loud enough for him to hear and before Ford delivered the ball," said Rosen. "I stepped back and Rommel called it a strike."[16]

Lopez was ejected for arguing the call with Rommel. "I told him I'd run him out of the game if he didn't stop and he said, 'Go ahead and run me out.' So I did."[17] Just as Lopez reached the visitors' clubhouse, Rosen smacked his 16th home run into the left field seats to give the Indians a 3–0 lead.

Wynn (7–5) threw a complete-game three-hitter in the 4–1 Tribe win. He backed his outstanding pitching performance with a home run of his own in the fourth inning. Rosen fared much better on the team's swing through the East, batting 20-for-58 (.345) with four home runs and 16 RBI.

Rosen connected for his 17th homer of the season off Detroit hurler Ned Garver on June 30 at Briggs Stadium. Rosen had the distinction of being the first player in the junior circuit to hit a round-tripper in every ballpark in the league that season. It was Rosen's second HR in two days. Three days later, he connected against Billy Hoeft of the Tigers. Rosen had homered in five consecutive games,driving in 10 runs. He missed tying the AL record of six, shared by Lou Gehrig (August 28–September 1, 1931) and Kenny Williams (July 28–August 2, 1922).

Rosen was voted as the starting third baseman for the American League for the 20th All-Star game at Crosley Field in Cincinnati. Rosen easily outdistanced George Kell of Boston, 1,058,244 votes to 731,559.[18] Stengel, who was piloting the AL, selected Larry Doby, Bob Lemon, and Mike Garcia as reserves.

The Indians closed out the first half of the season with a five-game series (July 10–12) at Comiskey Park. The White Sox had lost two of three to the Indians in Cleveland the previous week. But despite that series, the Chisox were on an impressive 21–5 record run since June 13. Chicago took over second place, nudging ahead of Cleveland by a half-game. The series in Chicago was an important one for the Indians, giving them a chance to recapture second place and stay in the AL race.

In the opener, Feller shut out the White Sox, 3–0, in a ten-inning affair. Rosen knocked in one of the runs and Easter the other two, all in the top of the tenth frame. But that was the extent of the good news from the Windy City. The White Sox won four straight contests, including bashing Cleveland in the second game (16–5) and the fourth game of the series (14–2). It was less than an ideal way to end the first half of the season. Chicago tightened their grasp on second place. Now the Tribe was chasing two teams instead of just the one. As the All-Stars made their way to Cincinnati, the American League standings looked like this:

Team	Won	Loss	Percentage	Games Back
New York	56	26	.683	----
Chicago	52	32	.619	5.0
Cleveland	48	35	.578	8.5
Boston	47	39	.547	11.0

At the break, Rosen led the league in several offensive categories: home runs (22), RBI (72), and slugging percentage (.587). Part of his success was taking what the pitchers were giving him. He was facing a steady diet of outside pictches, and he was feasting on them by going the other way.

Rosen credited his new hitting approach to spring training instructor Tris Speaker. If a player was going to follow the advice of someone, one couldn't do better than "The Grey Eagle." Over a 22-year career, mostly with the Red Sox and Indians, Speaker batted .345. Rosen took the advice of Speaker, and instead of trying to pull every pitch, he "would take the outside pitch to right field."[19]

At the owners' meeting in Cincinnati, Cleveland was selected as host of the 1954 Mid–Summer Classic. It was the second time Cleveland would play host to the MLB's best, as the 1935 contest at Cleveland Stadium was the first. Ted Williams, who had just returned to the States after serving in the Korean War, threw out the first pitch at the All-Star Game. The National League toppled the AL for the fourth straight year, 5–1. Rosen, who played the entire game, went 0-for-4 at the plate.

Besides the adjustments he made in his approach to hitting, Rosen offered another key to the success he was having in 1953. There was another change he had made away from the ballpark that also helped him. His reasoning may have come to a surprise to some. "Married life is the only life for a ballplayer," said Rosen. "I feel wonderful. Mentally, I've never felt better in my life. A ballplayer who is single, is on the road continually. Even when the team is at home, he's looking at four walls of a hotel room. For me it's such a delight now to come home, see my wife's lovely smile, eat a home-cooked meal and not have to talk baseball."[20]

Cleveland opened the second half of their season at home. The teams from the East were the opponents in a 12-game homestand. The Tribe posted a 2–3 record against both the Athletics and Red Sox before the Yankees visited. Behind complete-game wins by Lemon, Garcia, and Wynn, the Indians swept the New Yorkers. In the finale on July 23, Rosen went 3-for-5, scoring two runs and unloaded his 25th home run on the year. The Indians never looked back in their 10–2 win.

Despite Cleveland kicking sand in the faces of the world champions the last six games, they couldn't make their way up the standings. The Indians' "big three" of starting pitchers were posting decent seasons as the season headed to August. Bob Lemon (14–9, 2.86 ERA), Mike Garcia (12–6, 3.31 ERA), and Early Wynn (11–8, 3.72 ERA) each won more than 20 games in 1952. It did not look promising that the trio would duplicate the feat in 1953. But the lack of depth on their pitching staff was the real issue. Bob Feller's dominant years were behind him. Rookie Dave Hoskins was pulling double duty as a spot starter and a reliever. The acquisition of Houtteman from Detroit was supposed to shore up the rotation. But through July, he was pitching poorly. In nine starts, Houtteman was 2–6 with a 7.02 ERA.

Rosen was having the greatest year of his career. In July, he batted .309, slugged nine homers and drove in 30 runs. As a result, he led the circuit in home runs (26), RBI (85), and slugging percentage (.589). Boone was second in slugging percentage (.530) and apparently found Briggs Stadium much to his liking.

"As far as I'm concerned, I have yet to see a better clutch hitter," said St. Louis Browns pitcher Harry Brecheen of Rosen. Brecheen hurled in the NL for a number of years. "He's the best hitter in the American League. And there's none better in the other league. Rosen has no real weakness. Even when you get him out, he usually hits the ball hard. I'd rather face any other player than Rosen in a clutch spot."[21]

Rosen was tied with Boston's Billy Goodman for fourth in batting with a .315 average at the end of July. Washington's Mickey Vernon led the league at .328. It may not have occurred to anyone at the time, but the batting race would become the focus of the fans and the press as the season wore on.

The Tribe made their final stop in St Louis for a three-game set with the Browns on August 14. St. Louis owner Bill Veeck had failed to find a local buyer for the perpetual losers of the American League. Overtures were made to ownership groups in various other cities, but nothing seemed imminent as far as a sale was concerned. The Browns won their only pennant in 1944 (and lost in the World Series to the Cardinals), a war year when many of the game's stars were pressed into military service. The Cardinals developed into a perennially competitive club in the

NL. The Cards had won nine pennants and six world championships since 1926. Naturally, they became the more attractive and popular team to the St. Louis baseball fans. The Cardinals may have been the Browns' tenants at Sportsman's Park, but it was the landlord who continued to suffer at the gate. August Bush, Jr., bought the Cardinals in 1953 and purchased Sportsman's Park from Veeck, renaming it Busch Stadium. Now the Cards owned the ballpark and the Browns were paying rent.

Flip Rosen had a terrific series. In the three games, he went 6-for-13 with three runs and five RBI. Rosen also cracked his 29th home run of the season and increased his RBI total to 101. It was the fourth straight season Rosen eclipsed the century mark in RBI. But the Indians dropped two of three games. They had been battling the Browns since 1902. and Cleveland held the advantage in wins (680–446). The Indians also had a winning record (327–231) at Sportsman's Park/Busch Stadium. It was the last time Cleveland would play a game in the Gateway City for 44 years. In 1997, major league baseball began interleague play, and the Indians returned to St. Louis. But for now, the Browns were headed to Baltimore for the 1954 season.

Cleveland closed August on a 12–2 run. Unfortunately, the Indians were too far back to catch the Yankees as the standings looked this way when August ended:

Team	Won	Loss	Percentage	Games Back
New York	86	43	.667	----
Chicago	78	52	.600	8.5
Cleveland	76	54	.585	10.5
Boston	72	60	.545	15.5

Perhaps the Indians were out of the pennant race. But a different race ensued that gave the fans reason to check the daily box scores. It seemed unlikely that Rosen could get hotter at the plate in August than he was in July. But he did. Rosen hit nine home runs again and drove in 37 runs. He batted .354 (45-for-127) and was making a run at Mickey Vernon for the batting title. Vernon was leading the league with a .329 average. But Rosen was right on his heels, hitting .325. With a month to go in the season, there was plenty of time for Rosen to overtake the Washington first baseman.

Another statistical race to keep an eye on was the chase for home run supremacy. Heading into September, Rosen was tied with Gus Zernial of Philadelphia with 35 round-trippers. Rosen had 122 RBI, enjoying a big lead over Yogi Berra, who had driven in 95 runs.

No player in Cleveland history had won the Triple Crown (league leader in home runs, RBI, and batting average). But Rosen was making a run at being the first. If Rosen was hot in August, he was boiling in September. From September 5--27, Rosen put together a 20-game hitting streak. It proved to be the longest of his career. Rosen batted .392 (31-for-79) with seven home runs, 20 RBI, and 25 runs scored.

On September 25 against Detroit, Rosen had a spectacular day, going 4-for-6 with two home runs, four RBI, and four runs. The homers gave Rosen 43 on the season, which toppled the team record of 42 home runs by Hal Trosky in 1936. Rosen raised his average from .329 to .332.

Al Rosen demonstrates the batting stance that struck fear in American League pitchers. The determination shows on Rosen's face, a characteristic that his teammates admired and one that caused anxiety for his opponents (National Baseball Hall of Fame and Museum, Cooperstown, NY).

On the same day, Vernon went 0–for--4 against the Athletics, and his batting average dropped to .333.

The next day, Rosen went 2-for-4 and raised his average to .333. The Senators played a night game at Griffith Stadium and knew full well about Rosen's day. Vernon responded with a 3-for-4 game and raised his average to .336. "I was leading most of the season," said Vernon. "But Al got hot and started getting two or three hits in nearly every game for the last two weeks [of the season]."[22]

The last game took place on September 27, 1953. Indeed, it would take a Herculean effort by Rosen to catch Vernon on the final day of the season. The Indians front office arranged for the play-by-play of the Athletics-Senators game to be wired to the press box at Cleveland Stadium. The result of each Vernon at-bat was announced to the crowd. Rosen did his best impression of the Roman god by going 3-for-4 against the Tigers and former Indians teammate Al Aber. Vernon was holding his own, going 2-for-3 over at Griffith Stadium.

Rosen came to the plate in the ninth inning, presumably his last at-bat of the season. But Aber could not get the ball over the plate. and the count went to 3-and-0. Rosen refused to walk and swung at the ensuing pitches from Aber. Rosen finally put a ball in play with a grounder to Tigers third baseman Jerry Priddy. The throw from Priddy across the diamond to first baseman Fred Hutchinson nipped Rosen at the bag. Although it appeared to the fans that he was safe, umpire Hank Soar gave him the thumb. Of course, the umpires in the grandstand booed lustily. "Don't blame him," said Rosen. "Soar knew I was out. Hutchinson knew I was out. I knew I was out. I wouldn't want to win the title from Mickey on that play. I would know in my heart always that I really didn't make it."[23]

"Everybody on the bench thought I was safe," said Rosen. "I tried to leap to first base. But I did a quick step and missed the bag."[24] Lopez emerged from the first base dugout to argue the call, but Rosen waved him off.

Vernon lined out in the seventh inning to Elmer Valo in right field and was 2-for-4. The statisticians got to work in the press box at Griffith Stadium. Even if Vernon had one more at-bat and made an out, he would still nip Rosen by a margin of .0011. An announcement was made over the speaker system that no matter what occurred if Vernon got another at-bat, he would win the batting title. Cheers erupted from the 3,704 fans who had turned out to cheer Vernon on.

However, Vernon's teammates made sure that he would not come to bat again The Senators trailed the Athletics, 9–2, in the bottom of the eighth inning. Neither club was playing for anything as the Senators came up to bat. With two down, Mickey Grasso doubled to left but was picked off second base by A's pitcher Joe Coleman. In the bottom of the ninth inning, pinch-hitter Kite Thomas rapped a single to left field but was thrown out trying to stretch the hit into a double. Eddie Yost popped out on a pitch that was said to be a foot over his head. Pete Runnels grounded out to end the game. "I had nothing to do with any conspiracy theory," said Washington manager Bucky Harris. "If the players ran the bases poorly or swung at bad pitches, it was their own doing. Anyway, they won't be fined."[25]

The Indians went 16–8 in September and surpassed Chicago for second place in the American League standings. For the third straight season, the Indians finished in second place to New York. The only positive was that the Indians would get a bigger pot ($51,850.62) to share from the World Series money than Chicago, which finished in third place ($34,567.08).[26] Perhaps Joe Trimble of the *New York Daily News* did have it correct when he wrote prior to the season that 1953 might be the easiest flag to raise for the Yankees.

The final American League standings for the first division looked this way:

Team	Won	Loss	Percentage	Games Back
New York	99	52	.656	---
Cleveland	92	62	.597	8.5
Chicago	89	65	.578	11.5
Boston	84	69	.549	16.0

In 1953, Rosen had one of the greatest seasons of any Indian in franchise history. He led the league in home runs (43), RBI (145), runs (115), and slugging percentage (.613). He collected 201 hits and batted .336. Rosen came within a percentage point of winning the Triple Crown. No player in an Indians uniform has come closer. The 43 home runs were the most by an AL third baseman for 47 years. In 2000, Anaheim's Troy Glaus clouted 47 round-trippers (46 as a third baseman and one as a designated hitter).

The rest of the Indians club fared well. Doby batted .263, which was the lowest in his career to that point. But he smacked 29 home runs and drove in 102 runs. However, he led the league in strikeouts with 121 whiffs. Mitchell (.300), Avila (.286), Westlake (.330), and Strickland

(.284) all proved to be offensive assets for the Tribe. Surely the loss of Easter hurt, and when he returned to the lineup, all he could muster was seven home runs and 31 RBI.

Lemon (21–15, 3.36 ERA) was the only Cleveland pitcher to win 20 games in 1953. Wynn posted a 17–12 record, but his ERA ballooned to 3.93. His record is indicative of the offensive support he received, almost five (4.97) runs a game.

Rosen was voted the American League's Most Valuable Player in 1953. He was the first player to win unanimously since the electorate was expanded to three writers from each league city in 1938. When he was told of the news, Rosen could not believe it. "Terry and I sat down and both of us cried," said Rosen. "We're so happy. This is the most tremendous thing that has ever happened to me. I'm still weak and getting cold shivers. To think that I'm the first whoever did it. It might never happen again. Winning this award is the greatest Thanksgiving gift possible."[27]

Rosen became the third player in franchise history to win the MVP Award, following George Burns (1926) and Lou Boudreau (1948). As of 2021, Rosen is the last Indian to win the award.

That was not the only good news coming from the Rosen household, Al and Terry were expecting their first child. The new addition to the Rosen home was due to arrive before Al left for spring training in Tucson.

FIVE

111–43 and
a Fractured Finger

Rosen was honored on January 18, 1954, as the "Man of the Year" by the Cleveland chapter of the Baseball Writers' Association of America. The Ribs and Roast dinner was held at the Hollenden Hotel. But before Rosen received all the trappings that came with the honor, he and Terry were blessed with their first child, Robert Terrell, at noon. Rosen paced the hospital floor in eager anticipation. "I really got nervous after it was all over," said Rosen. "This is much, much tougher than playing the Yankees."[1]

Rosen looked forward to spring training after the birth of his son. He had been taking bets that his first-born would be a boy. "When we report to spring training in Tucson, I expect to collect about $750 in wearing apparel and cash," said Rosen. "My wife told me from the beginning that it would be a boy and I knew she wouldn't be wrong."[2]

As if a new son wouldn't keep him busy, Rosen was hosting a television sports show on WXEL, Channel 8. WXEL was the television home of the Indians, and in 1954, the station planned to televise all the Indians' road games. However, the home dates would be blacked out.

The Indians felt that solidifying the first base position would be their biggest need. Easter never fully recovered from the broken bone in his left foot, and at times he was seen hobbling. He may have been rushed back into service before he was ready, as Bill Glynn was not giving the club much production in his absence. On October 1, 1953, Greenberg sent minor league pitcher Bill Abernathie to Brooklyn for first baseman Rocky Nelson. The Indians were expecting a big season from Nelson. In 1953 with AAA Montreal, the left-handed-swinging first baseman belted 34 home runs and drove in 136 runs. He was named the International League MVP. But the road to first base in Flatbush was blocked by Gil Hodges.

Al Rosen shows off his Man of the Year Award from the 1953 season at the Cleveland Chapter of the Baseball Writers' Association of America "Ribs and Roast" dinner in January 1954. Rosen had good reason to be excited, as his oldest son, Robert, was born earlier that day (courtesy Cleveland Public Library).

They made a deal with Washington on January 20, 1954, exchanging backup catchers. Joe Tipton was sent to the Senators for Mickey Grasso. On February 19, they extended an offer to Easter to come to spring training. The big move of the off-season happened on the same day. The Indians sent minor league pitchers Bill Upton and Lee Wheat to the Philadelphia Athletics. In return, the A's sent outfielder Dave Philley to Cleveland. Both clubs denied that there was cash involved in the deal.[3] Philley, a veteran player of several seasons, played primarily with the White Sox and the A's. He batted .303 in 1953 and led all right fielders in assists with 16. Philley became embroiled in a contract dispute with the A's, and the Indians jumped in with their offer to acquire the switch-hitter. "He [Greenberg] wanted Philley all right ... he needed him," said A's general manager Earle Mack. "But he didn't want to let Wheat go. Finally, he gave in this afternoon. Chicago [White Sox] and Detroit dropped out when he continued to demand $25,000 to sign a contract."[4]

Philley took his profession seriously and competed intensely in any activity he attempted. Up to this point, the outfielder from Paris, Texas, played mostly on second-division clubs with the White Sox and Athletics. Even though he had not been in a pennant race thus far in his career, it did not stop him from giving an opinion as to why the Indians were coming up short to New York year after year. In Philley's opinion, the Indians were too complacent, and they lacked the desire and determination to get past the Yankees. Philley did not think the Yankees were that much better talent-wise, but their desire to win was stronger. One Indians player who Philley singled out as having the desire was Rosen.

"Now don't get me wrong. Not all the boys have it [complacency]," said Philley. "Take Rosen. There's not a better fighter or hustler in the game. But you know yourself, there are some of the men on this team who think about individual performance, rather than team play. This is a TEAM game."[5]

Perhaps there was some validity in Philley's comments. However, his remarks may have been considered rather harsh, considering he was a newcomer to the Indians.

Although the addition of Philley was made to strengthen the club, it may have been hard to find the club's reasoning on how their next move made the team stronger. On April 12, the Indians signed pitcher Hal Newhouser. Referred to by many as "Prince Hal," Newhouser was a star pitcher for the Detroit Tigers and a former teammate of Greenberg's. In 15 years with the Tigers, Newhouser amassed a record of 200–148 with a 3.07 ERA. He was given his unconditional release on July 22, 1953. The southpaw hurler had been experiencing a sore shoulder and compiled just 21⅔ innings in 1953. His last appearance was on July 5 that season. "Unconditional release ... that's a couple of words I've always heard about. But they never really meant much until right now," said Newhouser.[6]

Newhouser, 33, reported to Tucson to see how his arm responded to pitching in the exhibition schedule. Until his pitching showed him and the Indians he belonged on the club, Newhouser refused to sign a contract. He wanted to be sure that he could contribute to the club and not be a detriment. "He's a great competitor and if his arm is all right, he'll be a tremendous help to us," said Greenberg. "It certainly is worth the trial."[7]

Rosen's league-leading 43 homers in 1953 gave him 132 round-trippers over the last four seasons. There were some in spring training who wondered if Rosen might be the slugger who would eclipse Babe Ruth's record of 60 home runs in 1927. Rosen didn't buy into the speculation. He noted that if a player were to break the Babe's record, there were other attributes to be considered. "If Ruth's record is ever broken, a bigger, stronger man than I will do the job. Furthermore, he'll probably be an outfielder, who doesn't play nine innings under the pressure that's on the infielders, and he'll play in a home park which has at least one short field."[8]

Despite Rosen winning the MVP Award the previous season, not all Tribe fans believed that Rosen could maintain his high level of performance. In the *Cleveland News*, one fan took pen to paper to push for a new third baseman.

> *Have you ever thought of polishing up a good man to play third base for the Indians? Unless Al Rosen is an exception to the rule, he may not have a very good year in 1954 as it will be his post "Pomp and Ceremony" year and you know how that always works out. Unless he is a strong-minded man, the jinx will have its usual effect.*[9]

The Indians did have another third baseman on their roster who grabbed the attention of the front office. Rudy Regalado was signed off the University of Southern California campus in 1953. That season, Regalado batted .320 between Class A Reading and Class AAA Indianapolis. He continued to swing the lumber in spring training in 1954. In 76 at-bats, Regalado smacked nine home runs, drove in 19 runs, and batted .447.[10] His natural position at USC was first base. However, Regalado worked out at second and third base since there were already three experienced players at first base with Easter, Nelson, and Glynn. "This Regalado looks like the real thing," said Giants pitcher Larry Jansen.[11]

Rosen also worked out at first base on occasion so that he could get comfortable with the new glove (borrowed from Detroit's Walt Dropo), not to mention learning the new defensive alignments that would be required of him. It may have seemed more logical for Lopez to leave everyone at their natural positions instead of forcing two players to learn new defensive posts. But the Indians insisted that they were satisfied with their allotment of first baseman. Any move of Rosen to first base would be a last resort.

The Indians did lose two bench players in a game against the Cubs on March 24 in Mesa, Arizona. First, backup catcher Mickey Grasso fractured his left ankle sliding into second base. Harry Simpson fractured his left arm in a play at the plate when he collided with Chicago pitcher Omar Lown. Simpson's left arm struck Lown's right knee on the play.[12]

Both players reported to AAA Indianapolis at the completion of their rehabilitation. Only Grasso made it back to Cleveland in 1954.

One change that was made off the diamond would be just as noticeable to the Cleveland fan base. Jack Graney, who was paired with Jimmy Dudley as the radio team on station WERE, was retiring after 21 seasons behind the mic. He was replaced by WERE sportscaster Ed Edwards. Graney, a former outfielder with the Cleveland Naps/Indians (1908–1922) was a member of the Indians' first world championship team in 1920. After his playing career, Graney worked primarily as a car salesman before becoming the Indians' lead radio announcer in 1932. He had the distinction of being the first player of a professional or collegiate sport to make the transition to the broadcast booth.

Gordon Cobbledick, sports editor of the *Cleveland Plain Dealer*, and Harry Jones, Indians beat writer for the *Plain Dealer*, both picked the Yankees to finish in first place. Both scribes saw some chinks in the armor of New York. The veteran writers predicted the Tribe to finish behind the Bronx Bombers. "Both teams are capable of finishing anywhere from first to fourth," wrote Cobbledick. "In view of the quality of competition in the second division, neither could land lower than fourth without the intervention of a railroad wreck or an H-bomb attack."[13]

"You could pick the Indians to win the American League pennant this season and get away with it, I suppose," wrote Jones. "You could pick them for no other reason than the fact they are long overdue. But frankly, I can't. While it seems highly improbable that they will finish [second] for the fourth year in a row—no team has ever been consistently second-best—I still must pick them to come in behind the Yankees. Maybe close behind."[14]

Beat writers who covered teams for *Scripps-Howard Newspapers* were not as charitable. The poll of 24 writers picked the Tribe to finish third behind New York and Chicago.[15]

Cleveland broke out of the gate with a 3–6 record. The team's slow start was not the fault of Glynn, the primary starter at first base. He was batting .419 (13-for-31) through the first nine games. However, Lopez wanted to make a switch, and Rosen moved from third base to first while Regalado took over at third on April 25. "Maybe Regalado can give us the lift we need," said Lopez. "The way we've been going we need a lift from somebody. I hope he can do it."[16] When the reporters asked Lopez about moving Rosen to first instead of Regalado, he replied, "Rosen has had some experience at first base, and I know he can do the job. Maybe Rudy can do it, too. I know he played some first base in college, but Rosen has had actual pro experience at that position."[17]

The move across the diamond may have not been welcomed by Rosen, but he was a team-first player. Although Lopez made it known to him that Cleveland was in pursuit of a permanent first sacker, Rosen was happy to help in any way he could. But there was another reason why Rosen switched positions: "I moved because Al Lopez asked me," said Rosen. "If he had asked me to walk across Lake Erie, I would have tried."[18]

The club responded by winning six straight games. Rosen's new digs seemed to agree with him. He went 9-for-21 in those six games and raised his batting average from .294 to .345.

Regalado did not carry the burden of playing third base alone. Al Smith, who broke in with the Indians in 1953, proved to be a valuable commodity for Lopez. Smith could play all three outfield positions as well as third base. Smith was more than an adequate batsman who had some power. He was a competent player who went about his job in a quiet, efficient manner.

The Indians broke camp with 33 players, and they had to pare their active roster down to 26 by the cut-down date on May 12. Easter and Nelson were used primarily in pinch-hitting roles, and it appeared they would be sliced from the roster. Nelson, who batted .163 in spring training, could not get it going with the Tribe. Deemed expendable, Nelson was sold to Montreal of the International League on May 7, 1954. "No member of the Indians was ever given so much opportunity and no man ever took so little advantage of it. Both because the Indians sorely needed a first baseman and because his minor league career warranted a fair trial, the job was forced upon him," wrote Jones.[19]

Cleveland optioned Easter to AAA Ottawa of the International League. Although the Indians did have a working agreement with the Ottawa club, Big Luke's days in Cleveland had apparently come to an end.

Rosen had one of his biggest days of the season on May 18 at home against Boston. The Red Sox jumped to a 3–0 lead heading into the bottom of the second inning, knocking Indians starter Art Houtteman out of the game. Rosen led off the bottom of the second with a homer, his seventh of the year.

Cleveland sliced Boston's lead to 3–2 going to the fifth inning. The Red Sox had runners on first and second with one out when Billy Goodman smoked a grounder to second. Avila fielded the ball and threw to Strickland for the force, but the runner came barreling into the Indians' shortstop and his relay to first was short of the mark. Rosen fielded the ball and saw that the runner on second base was attempting to score. He threw a perfect strike to catcher Jim Hegan to get the runner at the plate to end the inning.

Rosen hit another home run over the left field wall in the sixth inning to knot the game up at 3–3. But something was amiss, or so thought Boston skipper Lou Boudreau. The Bosox manager noticed that Rosen's bat was discolored in one area and signaled the Red Sox backstop, Sammy White, to take a closer look. White saw six small nails driven into the grain of the fat part of the bat. White protested to home plate umpire Charley Berry. The arbiter threw the bat out of play, ruling it illegal. However, Rosen's home run still counted.

"Look it isn't the bat, it's the batter," said Rosen. "I put these tacks in because the bat was beginning to check. The wood was beginning to separate at the grain. I liked the bat and wanted to keep it from splitting. The nails don't add anything. They're not in the part where the bat meets the ball. If anything, they would tend to throw the bat off-balance. The Red Sox were simply trying to upset me, psychologically."[20]

Rosen added a double, making it a 3-for-4 day, with three RBI and two runs.

"Rosen's awesome demonstration at the Stadium last night in itself may have proven nothing more than that the Red Sox haven't much high-grade pitching," wrote Ed McAuley of the *Cleveland News*. "But taken in conjunction with Al's earlier work, those two home runs and one double must be regarded as significant. Many times this season, he has been retired in efforts to hit behind the runners, when his selfish interests clearly called for him to try for the full distance."[21]

Rosen had an incredible month at the plate in May. He smacked six home runs in five consecutive games (May 15–19). On May 21, he went 1-for-4 against Baltimore (a single) and missed tying the all-time mark of seven home runs in six games set by George "High Pockets" Kelly of the Giants in 1924 and Walker Cooper, also of the Giants, in 1947.

The Indians—White Sox game on May 25 at Chicago was a game that Rosen would not forget, for a whole different reason. The Indians

Al Rosen and one of his favorite pieces of lumber take time to pose for pictures with fans before a home game at Cleveland Stadium (National Baseball Hall of Fame and Museum, Cooperstown, NY).

were leading the White Sox, 2–1, heading into the bottom of the fifth inning at Comiskey Park. Nellie Fox led off with a double to right field. After Minnie Miñoso grounded out, three consecutive singles by Ferris Fain, Cass Michaels, and Sherman Lollar plated two runs and gave the Chisox a 3–2 lead. Jim Rivera came to bat and smashed a hard grounder toward first base. Lollar, the baserunner at first base, blocked Rosen's view as the ball smacked Rosen's right index finger, fracturing the digit. The White Sox won, 4–2.

The finger swelled up but Rosen, being the tough player that he was, did not leave the game. "Today they would have sent me to the hospital, x-rayed me and put me on the disabled list," said Rosen. "I was equally at fault. I wanted to play."[22]

Rosen knocked in at least one run in 25 of 29 games from April 25 through May 29. In the streak, Rosen totaled 45 RBI.

Despite the injury to Rosen, the Indians were playing sizzling baseball. They were winning at a torrid place and held a slim lead over Chicago as the calendar turned to June. The Indians turned in a solid performance, going 22–7 for the month, which included a 11-game winning streak from May 13–23.

Team	Won	Loss	Percentage	Games Back
Cleveland	28	13	.683	---
Chicago	28	15	.651	1.0
New York	25	17	.595	3.5
Detroit	20	17	.541	6.0

The Indians were getting solid offensive contributions from both Bobby Avila and Rosen. At the end of May, Avila led the league with a .388 average. Rosen was second with a .361 mark. Rosen topped the league in homers (13), RBI (49), and slugging percentage (.660). "Rosie will be glad to be one-two with me," said Avila. "I be glad to be two-one with Rosie on top. If we both are high, I think maybe it mean the pennant."[23]

On the pitching side, Lemon, Steve Gromek of Detroit, and Bob Keegan of Chicago were tied for the league lead in wins with seven. Early Wynn had six victories.

On June 1, Cleveland acquired outfielder Vic Wertz from the Orioles in exchange for relief pitcher Bob Chakales. That possibly marked the best trade made by Greenberg in his tenure as general manager in Cleveland. Wertz, a left-handed stick, could hit the long ball and for average. Chakales had appeared in three games for the Tribe. "I think Vic can do us a lot of good," said Lopez. "He's going to be good insurance in case anything happens to our other outfielders. He hits a long ball and may give us some added scoring punch."[24]

The following day, the Indians headed to New York for a three-game series with the Yankees. Although Rosen was still penciled in the lineup, he received little relief from his injured finger. "I soak it regularly and all it does is keep it clean," said Rosen. "Does it hurt much? Well, you saw me swing."[25]

The opener had all the makings of a great pitching matchup with Early Wynn (6–2) facing Allie Reynolds (5–1). Late-arriving fans may have missed the early fireworks, as the Yankees scored seven runs in the first inning. Four of those runs were charged to Wynn, who did not record an out.

But the Indians battled back, scoring three runs in the third and fourth innings. A home run by Avila in the top of the ninth tied the score, 7–7, while Smith's solo shot in the top of the tenth inning delivered the win. Indians relievers (Don Mossi, Ray Narleski, Bob Hooper, Mike Garcia, and Hal Newhouser) held the Yankees without a hit from the second inning on. "This is a game where you got to bleed and believe," said Philley, who made a defensive gem when he reached over the fence in right field to rob Eddie Robinson of a two-run homer in the fifth inning.[26] "I think it was the most important game we ever won at Yankee Stadium," said Lopez.[27]

However, the Yankees took the next two games and the series. Cleveland led Chicago by mere percentage points, while New York was right behind them, two games off the pace. The Indians continued their road trip, heading to Philadelphia. But more importantly, they would face the A's without Rosen. X-rays revealed that he had a chip fracture on the tip of his right index finger, and he returned to Cleveland to meet with the team physician, Dr. Dan Kelly.

"I suppose I should have had the thing x-rayed the day after it happened," said Rosen, "but I thought the swelling would go down and it would be all right. Later on, I was convinced something was broken. We had important games with the White Sox, Tigers and Yankees coming up so I asked Lopez to let me stick it out. I know I wasn't helping the team much, but I don't think I was hurting it either."[28]

Dr. Kelly put Rosen on a rehabilitation schedule and prescribed some time off so that the finger could mend. He sat out for ten days, and when he returned, he was limited to pinch-hitting duties.

As if losing Rosen didn't hinder the offense enough, Avila was also put on the shelf as the result of a chipped fracture of his right thumb. The injury occurred in the first game against the Yankees when Hank Bauer made a hard slide into second base in the first inning. "I would say Bob Avila's thumb is not hurt as badly as Al Rosen's finger was, and that Rosen's may be much better in a day or two," said trainer Wally Bock. "In fact, both should be much better by then."[29]

The Tribe went 6–2 while their two hitting stars, Rosen and Avila, were nursing their injuries. Five of those wins were a sweep over Boston at Fenway Park (June 11–14). Sam Dente and Hank Majeski filled in for Avila at second base. Glynn started the first three games in Rosen's absence, but he went 1-for-11 at the plate. Lopez made the move to bring in the newly acquired Vic Wertz to play first base. Wertz had played the outfield his entire career in the big leagues, and at 29 years old, he would be learning a new position on the fly. Despite Wertz batting .202 at Baltimore when Cleveland acquired him, Lopez knew that Wertz would be an offensive upgrade over Glynn. And the club needed that hitting potential. Any inadequacies Wertz might have had while learning to play a new position could be tolerated because of his skill as a batsman.

Rosen started at first base in both games of a doubleheader against Boston on June 20 at the Stadium. By the end of the month, Rosen moved back to third base, replacing Regalado. "Red Hot" Rudy played a competent third base. But four errors from June 13–June 23 coupled with a batting average that dipped to .268 in late June sent Regalado to the bench.

Rosen struggled with his hitting stroke in June. Of course, he missed part of the month because of his injured finger. But even when he returned, his finger was never fully healed. In 17 games and 53 at-bats in June, Rosen batted .264. He hit only one home run and totaled seven RBI. "It was mangled," said Rosen, referring to his injured finger. "All of a sudden, I was just another out."[30]

Cleveland's record in June was 20–9. They won their first five games of July and eight of the first nine. The Tribe swept Chicago in a four-game holiday weekend set at the Stadium, with each game decided by one run. Doby was the offensive player of the series. The Tribe's center fielder was 8-for-15 with eight RBI and five runs. He cracked a home run in each game, culminating on the Fourth of July with his 15th dinger of the season.

The Indians closed out the first half of the docket with a four-game series at Comiskey Park. The White Sox gained some revenge, sweeping the Indians and shutting them out twice by identical 3–0 scores. Those four losses in Chicago enabled the Yankees to gain precious ground. The Bombers finished June with a 20–10 record and won 11 of 12 games in July before the All-Star break.

As the season headed to the All-Star Game break on July 11, the AL looked this way:

Team	Won	Loss	Percentage	Games Back
Cleveland	56	27	.675	---
New York	56	28	.667	0.5
Chicago	54	31	.635	3.0
Detroit	35	44	.443	19.0

The AL race looked to be a white knuckler for Tribe fans in the second half of the season. But for all the excitement the Indians were generating, the talk around Cleveland centered on the murder of Marilyn Sheppard in suburban Bay Village. The 30-year-old woman, who was four months pregnant, was the wife of prominent Dr. Sam Sheppard. Her body was found on the morning of July 4, 1954, in a pool of blood. Her death was caused by repeated blows, maybe as many as 25, to her head with "an instrument having a sharp edge." The blows to her head and face made her unrecognizable.

Dr. Sheppard was napping downstairs when he heard his wife's pleas for help. He raced to the upstairs bedroom of their lakeside home. "I was clobbered from behind," said Dr. Sheppard, who blacked out after he was attacked.[31]

Over the ensuing weeks, the murder case of Marilyn Sheppard gripped the nation. Readers read with fascination the accounts of the investigation. People could not get enough information about the case. Eventually, Dr. Sheppard was tried for the murder and found guilty. On appeal, Sheppard won a "not guilty" verdict on November 16, 1966. To this day, the murder of Marilyn Sheppard remains unsolved.

Although Rosen missed some time on the field and began the season playing third base, he nonetheless received the most votes as the starting first baseman for the AL in the All-Star Game. Rosen (1,452,736 votes) easily outdistanced Ferris Fain of Chicago (991,507). Rosen accounted for more votes than any player at any position in the AL. Only Stan Musial of St. Louis (1,468,377 votes) surpassed his total. The other Tribesman to get a starting nod was Avila (1,386,144 votes) who won a tighter race with another South Sider, Nellie Fox (1,051,392).[32]

Two other players formerly of Cleveland were also listed on AL manager Casey Stengel's lineup card: Ray Boone at third base and Minnie Miñoso in left field. Lemon, Garcia, and Doby joined Rosen and Avila in representing Cleveland and the American League.

Avila led the circuit with a .341 batting average while Smith topped the league in on-base percentage with a .414 mark. Doby had picked up his production in the power department. At the break, Doby had swatted 15 home runs (second in the league) and driven in 61 runs (fourth). Rosen followed close behind with 14 home runs and 59 RBI.

The baseball world turned its eyes to Cleveland Stadium for the mid-summer classic, and Rosen shifted his attention to a different icon for some batting advice. He was batting .350 when he returned to the club after sitting out with his injured finger. At the break, his average had plummeted to .313. Rosen sought advice from perhaps the greatest hitter in baseball, Ted Williams.

> Ted told me, "Choke up on the bat at least two more inches. Any time you're hurt and not getting around there's only one thing to do, slide your hands up higher on the bat. It makes you bring your bat around quicker. It's that easy!"
>
> To me, Williams is the final word when it comes to batting ... like wisdom from heaven. I slid my hands up on the bat two inches.[33]

The suggestions from "Teddy Ballgame" proved worthwhile. Of all the stars who descended on Cleveland, Rosen shined the brightest. He belted two home runs. The first was a three-run shot off Robin Roberts in the third inning. His former roommate, Ray Boone, followed that blast with a round-tripper of his own. Rosen smacked his second home run, a two-run shot, off John Antonelli in the fifth frame.

The 69,751 fans hollered with approval as Rosen's dash around the bags was only part of the story. Avila went 3-for-3 with two RBI and a run. With the NL leading, 9–8, in the bottom of the eighth, it was time for a third member of the Tribe to contribute. With one down, Doby pinch-hit for pitcher Dean Stone and smacked a solo homer off Gene Conley into the left field stands. The AL loaded the bases that same inning, and Nellie Fox singled home the final two runs in the AL's 11–9 win in a true slugfest.

"Those homers are the best tonic possible for Rosen's state of mind and the whole team,"[34] said Lopez. Not only did Rosen stay in the entire game, he played the last inning at third base. On the day, Rosen went 3-for-4 with five RBI and two runs.

"I felt obligated to play because the fans had given me more votes than any other member of the American League team," said Rosen. "On the other hand, I felt that because of my sore finger and the fact that I had been in a bad slump I wouldn't do the team any good."[35]

Rosen conferred with Casey Stengel before the game to discuss whether Rosen should play. At the time, there was a rule stating that the players who were voted to the starting lineup must play at least three innings. Stengel said he would not break the rule without consulting

Commissioner Ford Frick. In the end, it was decided that Rosen would start the game, take one at bat, and then a decision would be made as to the rest of the game.[36]

Lopez may have been on to something when he indicated that the All-Star performance by Rosen might jump start him in the second half. Rosen tallied one or more RBI in the next eight games. By the end of July, Rosen's batting average inched up to .324, second to Minoso's .332. He had smacked 19 home runs, trailing Doby by three. Doby hit 11 homers in July and led the AL with 22. Rosen drove in 22 runs, tying him with Miñoso for the league lead with 78 RBI.

The Indians were leading the Yankees by 2½ games as the schedule turned to August. The triumvirate of starting pitchers, Lemon (13–5), Wynn (14–7), and Garcia (12–5), were leading the way. Houtteman (10–5) pitched well, while Feller (8–2) proved he could still be a key contributor at age 35. Many clubs would be envious of the surplus of starting pitching Lopez had at his disposal. Chicago White Sox manager Paul Richards did not share that view. "They'll win if they get the pitching," said Richards, "but I doubt whether their pitching will hold up."[37]

Rosen started out in a slump in August, and unfortunately it continued through the whole month. From August 1–12, Rosen went 3-for-42 at the plate, and his batting average plunged to .294. On August 8, the Tribe faced Philadelphia in a doubleheader at Cleveland Stadium. In the third inning of the opener, Rosen was hit on the left elbow by a pitch from the A's Arnie Portocarrero. The result was a lump the size of a baseball near his elbow. "I really hurt," said Rosen. "In fact, I felt as if I was going to be sick—that's why I had to stop and put my head down."[38] Rosen stayed in the game and played in the nightcap as well, although he went 0-for-7 for the day.

Rosen hit a homer on August 13 at Detroit, his 20th of the year in a 10–1 Indians win. The clout inspired *Plain Dealer* sportswriter James Doyle to submit the following:

> *Flip Rosen slammed one on the nose*
> *At long, long last, to end his woes.*
> *Had Flip's flop lasted one more day,*
> *He might have gone completely gray.*[39]

In the opener of a doubleheader sweep against Baltimore on August 15, Rosen dove and caught a line drive off the bat of Jim Fridley. Rosen landed on his left shoulder but didn't think much of it. "I woke up at 6 this morning and was in terrific pain," said Rosen. "I had an idea it might be bursitis because I had it in the same shoulder a couple of years ago."[40]

Indeed, it was bursitis and Rosen sat out for a few days. "I don't feel right sitting on the bench at a time like this," said Rosen, referring to the pennant race. "But as Dr. Kelly explained, there is no use taking chances. In a day or two, it'll be all right."[41]

On August 25, the Indians played their last game in Philadelphia, and they did not return there until 2010 with interleague baseball. Like the Browns the year before, the Athletics were relocating. In 1955, the A's called Kansas City home, leaving Philadelphia as a one-team baseball city. Like the Cardinals of St. Louis, the Phillies were in the National League. The A's had not been competitive in the AL for two decades, winning their last pennant in 1931. Their attendance at Connie Mack Stadium had been in a downturn for a few years, and in 1954, they drew 304,666 fans for the season.

Rosen especially enjoyed playing at Shibe Park/Connie Mack Stadium. He had more success hitting there than in the other road AL parks. He hit for the highest average (.327) in his career there. He also smacked the most home runs (17) there and drove in the most runs (61).

However. as a team, the Indians flourished in August, posting a 26–6 record. A 16–2 mark from August 6–22 bolstered their impressive record. Going into September, the top of the AL standings looked this way:

Team	Won	Loss	Percentage	Games Back
Cleveland	95	36	.725	---
New York	89	41	.685	5.5
Chicago	85	47	.644	10.5
Detroit	57	73	.438	37.5

The race for the AL pennant became a two-team dash for the flag. But the Tribe quelled any hopes the Yankees had of catching them. Cleveland ripped off their second 11-game win streak from September 8–20. Included in that streak was a doubleheader sweep of the Yankees on September 12. The Indians won behind their two 20-game winners: Lemon (22–6) won the opener, 4–1, and Wynn (21–11) cleaned up matters in the second game, leading Cleveland to a 3–2 win. Rosen played in the first game and went 2-for-3 and two RBI. "So, down we go after five straight world's championships, and up comes Cleveland, and that is life," said Casey Stengel.[42]

"This was the way we wanted it," said Lopez. "We wanted to beat the Yanks ourselves. This was the way we wanted to win the pennant."[43]

A crowd of 85,563 jammed into Cleveland Stadium for the twin-bill. As of 2021, this mark is still the all-time high for a regular-season game in the major leagues. The throng was a major league attendance record that stood until the Dodgers moved to Los Angeles in 1958 and played their home games at the Los Angeles Coliseum, which had a seating capacity of over 93,000 for baseball games. The Dodgers hosted three games in the 1959 World Series against Chicago. Each game drew over 92,000 fans.

Rosen nursed a sore thigh muscle and a strained back as the regular season neared its conclusion. He sat out a handful of games to get healthy for the World Series. Doby was also nursing a sore thigh muscle. Lopez thought it was imperative that his two stars rest, but also that the Tribe still needed to secure the pennant. "We want to keep winning," said Lopez. "First, we've got to clinch the pennant. Secondly, we'll be playing clubs with a chance for World Series money. It wouldn't be fair to their competitors if we took it easy from now on."[44]

The Indians coasted to their first pennant since 1948. They set an American League record for the most wins (111) in a season and the highest winning percentage (.721). The 111 wins eclipsed the previous record of 110 set by the 1927 Yankees, the Murderers' Row club. The Indians went 11–11 against both New York and Chicago. But their record against the remaining five teams was 89–21.

The final AL standings went like this for the first division:

Team	Won	Loss	Percentage	Games Back
Cleveland	111	43	.721	---
New York	103	51	.669	8.0
Chicago	94	60	.610	17.0
Boston	69	85	.448	42.0

Avila won the AL batting championship with a .341 average. Although Ted Williams batted .345, he had 386 at-bats and a player had to have 400 or more to be considered for the league leader.[45] One reason for Williams missing the 400 at-bat requirement was that he led the league in walks with 136.

Doby led the AL in home runs (32) and RBI (126). Lemon and Wynn were tied atop the AL in wins (23), while Garcia had the lowest ERA (2.64). Lemon tied Bob Porterfield of Washington for the most complete games (21), and Wynn paced the circuit in starts (36).

On May 25, the date Rosen injured his finger at Comiskey Park, he was batting .372. He finished the 1954 season batting an even .300, losing 72 points on his batting average. He belted 24 home run and totaled 102 RBI. He knocked in 100 or more runs for the fifth straight season. In 304 at-bats when Rosen played third base, he batted .276 with 11 home runs and 51 RBI. At first base, he had 155 at-bats and batted .348 with 13 home runs and 48 RBI.

The Indians were matched against the NL champion New York Giants in the World Series. Game One was scheduled for September 29 at the Polo Grounds. The Giants were not picked by many to win the NL flag. The same *Scripps-Howard* writers who viewed Cleveland as a third-place club also predicted that the Giants would finish in fourth place behind Brooklyn, Milwaukee, and St. Louis.[46] New York led Brooklyn by 5½ games at the All-Star break. They were never seriously threatened following a strong August and September, when they posted a combined 32–20 record.

The final NL standings for the first division looked this way:

Team	Won	Loss	Percentage	Games Back
New York	97	57	.630	---
Brooklyn	92	62	.597	5.0
Milwaukee	89	65	.578	8.0
Philadelphia	75	79	.487	22.0

The Giants may not have had as many league leaders as Cleveland, yet they were a formidable club. Willie Mays swatted 41 homers and led the league in triples (13). Don Mueller led the senior circuit in hits (212), while Johnny Antonelli was second in wins (21) and led in ERA (2.30).

Neither the Polo Grounds nor Cleveland Stadium was constructed as a baseball-only facility. The Polo Grounds especially was shaped like a horseshoe. The measurement down the left field line was 279 feet, and it was 257 feet down the right field. It would take a tremendous clout to hit a home run to center field. A distance of 455 feet lay between home plate and the center field wall.[47]

Cleveland Stadium was a bit more symmetrical for baseball. The distance down both lines measured 320 feet, while the center field fence measured 404 feet from home plate.[48]

The Indians were 9–5 betting favorites as they departed for New York to play Games One and Two.[49] If you were the superstitious sort, you may have bet against the Indians after they departed by train from the downtown train terminal on track number 13.

Game One featured Bob Lemon for Cleveland and Sal Maglie for New York. With the score tied, 2–2, the Indians mounted a rally in the top of the eighth inning. Doby led off with a walk and Rosen followed with a single to put runners on first and second base. Don Liddle came in from the pen to face Wertz. The Indians' first baseman, who had three hits and drove in the first two runs, smashed a ball to center field. Mays got on his horse and made a terrific back-to-home plate catch in deep center field. The runners advanced, but the Indians could not score. The catch is one of the most iconic plays in major league history.

The Giants won the game in the bottom of the tenth inning when Dusty Rhodes, a left-handed batter, lifted a three-run homer off Lemon just over the fence in right field. The misfortune of the events of the first game were that Wertz's smash would have been a home run in Cleveland Stadium, while Rhodes' home run would have been a harmless fly out. But the truth was that the Indians left 13 men on base, and it is hard to win with that much population stranded on the bags.

After the Indians dropped a hard-fought Game One, it would be interesting to see how they would they respond in Game Two. Lopez sent Wynn to the mound to face Antonelli. Al Smith's first inning lead-off home run represented the only run the Indians could muster. Once again, they left 13 men on base. Again, it was Rhodes who came to the rescue for New York. He delivered a pinch-hit single in the fifth and a solo home run in the seventh frame to lead the Giants' offense. Antonelli struck out nine and notched the complete-game win in New York's 3–1 victory.

After the game, the Giants flew to Cleveland. They checked into their hotel, ate a good dinner, and got a full night's sleep. The Indians took the train back home and did not arrive until the wee hours of the next day. It's important to note that there were no travel days. The Giants made good use of their limited travel time, while the Indians did not.

Ruben Gomez faced Mike Garcia in Game Three at Cleveland Stadium. Although the home fans were ready for the Indians to mount a comeback, it didn't happen. The Giants took a 6–0 lead and cruised to a 6–2 win. Mays had two RBI, while Rhodes once again served as a pinch-hitter and knocked in two more runs. Rosen sat out the game, nursing his sore leg. "We're still a good ball club but we can't win without hitting and we're not getting it," said Lopez. "Maybe we'll snap out of it. We have to. Rosen's injury has made a big difference in the series. If he can go, he'll be back in there."[50]

Lopez brought back Lemon to start Game Four in an act of desperation. The Giants raced out to a seven-run lead, scoring six runs off Lemon (five earned), and cruised to a 7–4 win. It was a devastating letdown for Cleveland. Of the Indians regulars, only Wertz had a good Series, batting .500 (8-for-16) with a homer and three RBI. Smith (.214) and Rosen (.250) were the only players in the starting lineup to bat over .200 for the series.

"I was so emotionally drained [after the 1954 World Series loss] that my wife and I checked into the Statler Hotel in downtown Cleveland after the fourth game, left our children with my in-laws, and I took two sleeping pills and I slept for 36 hours, just tried to sleep it off," said Rosen. "Oh, it was a horrible experience. I mean really ... it's an unbelievable thing. It's tough to lose. Defeat is a very difficult thing."[51]

There were many viewpoints as to why New York swept Cleveland in the 1954 World Series.

"Either the Yankees or the White Sox would have shown more life," wrote John P. Carmichael of the *Chicago Daily News*. "You can't imagine the Yanks leaving 26 men on base in two games ... or the Sox under Paul Richards standing around as if counting the house. The shame of the Indians is so pronounced because they made a record run of 111 victories to get in the Series."[52]

Local scribes pointed to the injuries of Rosen and Doby, combined with the poor hitting (.133 average) of batting champion Avila as the reasons for the Tribe's downfall. Franklin Lewis of the *Cleveland Press* believed that the Indians were through after losing the two close contests in New York. Futility and hopelessness took over the Cleveland club.[53]

One critic had this to say about the Indians setting a record for wins in a season while winning the AL pennant. "There are five Pittsburghs in that league, they didn't beat much."[54] The Pirates finished last in the NL in 1954 with a record of 53–101.

Years after his career had ended, Rosen talked about how the damaged index finger affected his career.

After that injury, I was never the same player. I didn't let my hand heal properly. I think the Cleveland club missed out in handling that situation, but we were all equally guilty. Should I have done what the players do today? You get hit by a pitched ball today, you're out, you're on the disabled list, you get yourself perfectly back in shape--but we didn't do it that way when I played.[55]

Six

Decline and Retirement

Sports fans in Cleveland had plenty to keep themselves occupied after the 1954 season ended. Maybe the success of the other teams that the city followed could wash the bad taste of the World Series from their mouths.

The Cleveland Browns of the National Football League began the 1954 season with a 1–2 record. They were on a four-game win streak as they prepared to face the Philadelphia Eagles at home on November 21. A win was imperative if the Browns were going to continue their march to a fifth straight Eastern Division Championship.

Ohio State University was tuning up for its annual slugfest with the University of Michigan on November 20 in Columbus. On the line for Woody Hayes' squad was the culmination of an undefeated season, a trip to the Rose Bowl, and a possible National Championship.

As the Thanksgiving holiday drew near, sports fans discovered another reason to give thanks in addition the success of the gridiron teams. On November 16, Cleveland acquired slugger Ralph Kiner from the Chicago Cubs for an undisclosed amount of money, although guesses on Kiner's purchase price ranged from $60,000 to $75,000.[1]

"Wherever he is used, he will strengthen the position," said manager Al Lopez. "He gives us that extra-long ball hitter and you can't have too many of those."[2] Indeed Kiner could take a pitcher deep with the best of them. At the time of the trade, he had smacked 351 home runs in nine seasons for an average of 39 home runs per year. In the first seven years of his career, Kiner either led or tied for the league lead in home runs.

Every National League team passed on acquiring Kiner, or more likely, Kiner and his $65,000 contract. The Cubs were then free to deal with teams from the junior circuit. "We felt we had to do something about our outfield, and it looked like Kiner didn't fit," said Wid Matthews, Cubs Director of Player Personnel. "The move was made with

100% endorsement of our manager, Stan Hack. He thrives on speed, and so do I. Kiner didn't fit into that pattern."[3]

"I'm surprised they waived him out of the National League," said Yogi Berra. "I don't think he will help Cleveland much fielding, but he sure ought to hit over there. Maybe he'll wind up in the front office helping Hank Greenberg run the joint."[4]

The Cleveland–Chicago deal had three different transactions: Cleveland sent pitcher Sam "Toothpick" Jones to the Cubs on October 13, 1954. The Indians acquired Kiner on November 16. On November 30, Cleveland sent outfielder Gale Wade to Chicago.

It was a shock to many when Kiner requested a 40 percent cut in his salary, to bring his salary to $40,000. However, Commissioner Ford Frick intervened and ruled that the contract Kiner had signed with the Indians would be invalid because it was not in accordance with the rules of a player salaries. The maximum a club could cut a player's salary was 25 percent. Kiner, after meeting with Frick, settled for a contract of $49,000. "Basically, I wanted a fresh start in the American League," said Kiner. "I want my performance to determine the basis for my future salary. I did it because I want to prove my value and I have confidence in myself."[5]

Unlike his new teammate, Rosen did not take a pay cut in his 1955 salary. Rosen worked locally for a securities firm, Bache & Company. He took time off from his off-season job to sign his 1955 contract. Greenberg and Rosen came to terms on a $40,000 deal that matched his 1954 salary. Despite a drop in his statistics, Greenberg considered that Rosen battled through most of the season with a fractured index finger. "I'm very well satisfied," said Rosen. "We weren't far apart to begin with."[6] With regards to the injured finger, he still could not bend the digit around the handle of a baseball bat. "It doesn't hurt much," he said. "I just can't bend it very far."[7]

Rosen reminded Greenberg that in 1940, Detroit gave him a $10,000 bonus for moving to left field to make room for Rudy York at first base. Rosen figured he had a little more coming his way since he made the transition from third to first base. "Yes, but that was me, and this is you," said Greenberg.[8]

Dave Philley, the Tribe's right fielder, found his contract negotiations with Greenberg more combative. Philley batted .226 with 12 home runs and 60 RBI in 1954. He threatened to retire from baseball and enter the lumber business in Texas if Greenberg did not offer him a square deal. "And here's the hope that if Hank refuses to relent, Dave will do a lot better with the Texas lumber than he did with the lumber he was swinging at baseballs last season," wrote James E. Doyle in the *Plain Dealer*.[9] The Indians and Philley eventually came to terms.

On the day Rosen inked the dotted line at Cleveland Stadium, one of the Indians' prized prospects was getting his first look at the big league park. Rocky Colavito came to town for his off-season job of selling season tickets. Colavito socked 38 home runs and drove in 116 runs at AAA Indianapolis. Despite the gaudy numbers, the addition of Kiner assured that Colavito would return for another season in the Circle City.

One prospect who did join the varsity in 1955 was pitcher Herb Score. The hard-throwing southpaw had been named Minor League Player of the Year by *The Sporting News* in 1954.[10] Score, who was Colavito's roommate since their days at AA Reading, went 22–5 with a 2.62 ERA. He completed 21 games and shattered the league strikeout record by whiffing 330 opposing batters in 251 innings.[11]

In a pre-season poll in *American Weekly* magazine, 28 sportswriters were asked to make their predictions for the pennant winners in each league. A two-team race in the AL was forecast, with New York (14 first-place votes) and Cleveland (13 first-place votes) the favorites to take the flag. In the NL, the scribes selected New York the top club with 13 first-place votes. Milwaukee came next with eight votes and then Brooklyn with seven.[12]

Plain Dealer beat writer Harry Jones predicted that the Indians would finish first and that New York would be "10 to 15 lengths behind, might have trouble finishing second."[13] PD Sports Editor Gordon Cobbledick was a little more conservative with his selection. While predicting that the Tribe would finish at the top of the heap, Cobbledick did not predict a double-digit winning margin. "The Yankees and White Sox will fight it out for second place, with the Yankees having an edge, but not a wide one."[14]

Sports Illustrated also picked the Tribe to reign again over the AL. In its baseball issue, with Rosen on the cover, Red Smith gave his view of the pennant race in the AL. "This is the same team that won 111 games in 1954, plus Score, plus Kiner. In the World Series, these slow-footed, brawny aborigines didn't look like the Indians who fought at Little Big Horn, but there isn't a real tough Custer in the whole American League."[15]

A sore leg kept Rosen sidelined near the end of spring training.

But he was in the starting lineup Opening Day on April 12 as Cleveland beat the White Sox, 5–1, at Cleveland Stadium. Rosen went 0-for-3 with a walk. Kiner smacked a solo home run in his Indians debut, while Al Smith added a two-run shot to pace the offense.

Perhaps the most compelling day of the young season occurred on May 1, 1955. The Indians hosted Boston in a Sunday doubleheader. Feller started the opener and hurled the 12th one-hitter of his career. The Indians blanked the Red Sox, 2–0. In the nightcap, Score took the mound and struck out 16 batters. The Tribe won, 2–1, to complete the sweep. Feller held the modern-day record when he whiffed 18 Tigers on October 2, 1938. "No kidding, I think a one-hitter is better than a flock of strikeouts," said Score. "One is great pitching and the other is throwing. I made a lot of mistakes. I always sleep good before a game and then stay awake after one. Especially when I make mistakes."[16]

During the second game against Boston, Rosen pulled a muscle in his left leg. He was replaced at third base by Hank Majewski. Doby suffered a groin injury, and he was also sidelined for a few days.

On May 6, the Athletics made their first visit to Cleveland since changing their postal code to Kansas City, and the Indians won four straight games. Wertz played in the first two games of the series but had to be taken out of each game because he was battling a wounded left hand. Rosen volunteered to move to first base and replace Wertz in the series-ending doubleheader. Rosen smacked his fifth home run of the season in the nightcap.

"My leg was better, but still a little tender," said Rosen. "I wanted to get a couple of games under my belt before going into New York and figured first base was a good spot as long as Vic couldn't play. You don't get as much running or as many balls that require that quick start there. I came through without a twinge and everything is fine."[17]

Smith was the leader on offense, going 5-for-9 with three home runs, five RBI, and four runs in the twin-bill. Smith's versatility proved to be an asset for the Indians in 1955. Smith started 40 games at third base and 104 games in right field. He batted .306, tops on the team at season's end. "At the plate, Al Rosen gave me some suggestions on hitting. He showed me how to choke up and use a lighter bat, making me a better hitter," said Smith.[18] He was dubbed the "Lookee Here Kid" by his teammates for his happy-go-lucky personality.[19]

Following the series, the Indians needed to make several roster moves in order to get down to the requisite number of 25 players. One of those players on the chopping block was pitcher Hal Newhouser. The veteran lefty appeared in two games with 2⅓ innings pitched. He was given his outright release, effectively ending his career. "Whether I go someplace depends on what kind of deal I can make," said Prince Hal. "It came as a surprise when Al Lopez gave me the news."[20] Cleveland sold Harry Simpson to Kansas City, while infielder Joe Altobelli was optioned to AAA Indianapolis. Simpson broke in with the Indians in 1951. Cleveland thought so much of Simpson then that they dealt Minnie Miñoso to Chicago. The front office considered Simpson a top prospect, and the team gave him every opportunity to secure a regular job. But Simpson never panned out. Meanwhile, Miñoso achieved stardom on the South Side.

On May 13, the Tribe began a three-game set in Baltimore. After two rainouts, the two clubs split a Sunday doubleheader. The O's took the opener, 4–1. In the second game, Rosen aggravated his left leg muscle running the bases in the first inning.[21] Mike Garcia tossed a complete-game shutout in the 5–0 win.

The re-injury to his left leg kept Rosen out of the lineup for 11 days. "The leg hurts as though somebody's sticking a hot poker in it," said Rosen, "but the agony of not being able to play is much worse."[22] The Indians went 2–5 in his absence, as Smith filled in at third base. After the Indians dropped a 4–1 decision to Chicago on May 24, Lopez admitted that not having Rosen in the lineup left a big void. "We just have to get more base hits," said Lopez. "Sure, we miss Al Rosen. He's a big man in the lineup. Al worked out tonight and seemed better but I don't think he'll be ready to play for two or three days."[23] Rosen returned to the lineup on May 26 against Chicago. The Tribe closed the month with a 5–1 record. As the month of May closed, the American League leaders are below:

Team	Won	Lost	Percentage	Games Behind
New York	30	13	.698	---
Cleveland	27	15	.643	2½
Chicago	25	16	.610	4
Detroit	22	20	.524	7½

The first two months of the season were a cause of concern for Rosen. Through May, he was batting .219 (23-for-105) with six home runs and 21 RBI. Nagging injuries and the injured finger contributed to his downturn. To Rosen's credit, he didn't use his injuries as an excuse. Some of the fickle fans at Cleveland Stadium showed their unhappiness with Rosen, and the "booing" became louder as the season wore on.

With Wertz out because of a jammed thumb, Rosen moved back to first base. The Indians looked for some offensive help and a third baseman in case Rosen's move to first base was a longer one than expected. On June 15, 1955, the Indians sent outfielders Dave Pope and Wally Westlake and $20,000 to Baltimore for third baseman Billy Cox and outfielder Gene Woodling. Westlake, a key contributor on the pennant-winning team in 1954, saw his time get cut with the acquisition of Kiner. Pope, also a reserve outfielder, was having a solid year. Through 35 games, he smacked six home runs, collected 22 RBI, and was batting .298.

Woodling returned to Cleveland for his second tour of duty (1943–1946). He reported to the Indians, happy to be with a team in the pennant race. But the deal hit a snag when Cox returned to his home in Newport, Pennsylvania, saying he did not want to report to the Indians. Cox had been one of the better third basemen in the National League when he was with Brooklyn from 1948–1954. A capable hitter, Cox could also play shortstop and second base.

Cox broke in with the Pittsburgh Pirates in 1941, and he roomed with Lopez. But despite his connection to the Indians' skipper, Cox retired. He last played in a game for Baltimore on June 11, 1955. Cox left the game when he pulled the hamstring in his left leg while running to first base in the third inning.[24] The Indians made the following statement: "After repeated attempts to persuade Billy Cox to join the Cleveland Indians, [we] have today received final word from him that his leg is in such condition that he is unable to play and will not change his mind about joining our club."[25]

The Orioles sent an undisclosed amount of cash back to Cleveland as compensation for Cox retiring. Although the exact amount was not known, it was believed that the O's returned the $20,000 with an additional $10,000 the Tribe's way.[26]

On June 28, 1955, the Indians hosted the Athletics. The Tribe scored six runs in the second inning to jump-start them to a 7–5 victory. Even the official scorer took pity on Rosen and his hitting slump, A pop fly towards the third base line, about 20 feet from home plate, was not caught by A's third baseman Hector Lopez. Official scorer Frank Gibbons of the *Cleveland Press* announced that Lopez would be charged with an error. However, Gibbons changed his ruling to a hit when he learned that Lopez did not touch the baseball when he went to catch it. The result was a two-hit game for Rosen and an RBI. Still, Rosen was looking for answers. "If I didn't think I'd come out of it, I'd quit baseball right now," said Rosen.[27]

As the season made its way to the halfway point, the Yankees distanced themselves a bit more from the pack in the American League:

Team	Won	Lost	Percentage	Games Behind
New York	55	29	.655	---
Cleveland	50	34	.595	5
Chicago	47	33	.588	6
Boston	48	36	.571	7

County Stadium in Milwaukee hosted the All-Star Game on July 12, 1955. No Indians player was voted to the AL starting lineup. Rosen was batting .233 at the break, with 11 home runs and 50 RBI. Rosen finished third in the All-Star team voting (1,004,553 votes), trailing Jim Finigan of Kansas City (1,659,278) and George Kell of Chicago (1,528,166).[28]

But Lopez was the AL skipper based on Cleveland winning the pennant in 1954. Lopez had the responsibility of naming the pitching staff and the reserves to the AL squad. Like many managers in that position, Lopez stockpiled the rosters with his own players, including Rosen, Avila, Smith, Doby, Score, and Wynn. Rosen replaced Finigan in the sixth inning and went 0-for-2 at the plate as the NL squeaked out a 6–5 win.

"Rosen's batting average for the three seasons preceding the present one was .313," wrote Gordon Cobbledick of the *Plain Dealer*. "He is currently batting .233. He has averaged 35 home runs in the last three seasons. He has hit 11 to date this year. That alone is enough to account for the Indians' offensive failures. Couple it with Avila's .272 batting average and you wonder, not that the Tribe isn't on top, but that it is so close to the top."[29]

Rosen came out of the break swinging. He smacked a solo home run in back-to-back games on July 14–15 against New York. Rosen smacked seven home runs in July, the most he hit in any month in 1955.

As a team, the Tribe posted a 20–11 record in July, while the Yankees struggled to a 12–17 mark. Chicago was also very much in the mix, going 20–12. The Indians' pitching staff was doing its part to keep the club in the race. Wynn (13–5) and Lemon (12–7) were leading the way through July.

On July 31, 1955, the Indians claimed pitcher Sal Maglie on waivers from the New York Giants. In seven seasons with New York, Maglie had a record of 95–42 with a 3.13 ERA. "The Barber," as Maglie was known for his close, inside pitches, was a familiar face to the Tribe. Cleveland made their spring training home in Tucson, Arizona, while the Giants trained in nearby Phoenix. The two teams faced each other numerous times each spring.

Rosen experienced stiffness in his neck and shoulders that was caused by muscle spasms.[30] He missed a handful of games, but the season continued its downward spiral for the Tribe third baseman. But his maladies were nothing compared to Vic Wertz's. He played his last game that season on August 24, when he became ill. Originally, it was thought that a virus had infected Wertz, but his sickness proved to be more serious. The diagnosis was poliomyelitis, more commonly known by the shortened name of polio. Wertz, a veteran left-handed power stick, would be hard to replace in the Indians' lineup. However, with the seriousness of his disease, the Tribe's misfortune took a back seat to pulling for Wertz to recover.

Cleveland, New York, and Chicago battled for first place in the American League over the last two months of the season. The Indians won 11 of 13 games from September 3–13. Cleveland had sole possession of first place with a record of 90–55. The Tribe had a two-game lead over New York (87–56) and 4½ games over Chicago (85–59) on September 13.

But the Indians could not hold the lead. They lost six of nine games while the Yankees stepped it up and won 9 of 11 games. It was certainly a disappointing end to the season. For the fourth time in five seasons, Cleveland finished second to New York. Ironically, the Indians had winning records against the Yankees (13–9) and the White Sox (12–10), but they had difficulty with fourth-place Boston (11–11) and cellar-dweller Washington (9–13).

Team	Won	Lost	Percentage	Games Behind
New York	96	58	.623	---
Cleveland	93	61	.604	3
Chicago	91	63	.591	5
Boston	84	70	.545	12

"It's no disgrace to lose to that team," Lopez said of the Yankees. "What've they won now? Nine out of 10? Well, that's going some. I guess they deserve to win."[31]

"A lot of people criticize Al Rosen and Bobby Avila because they didn't have a good season," said Lopez. "Maybe they didn't, but they hustled all the way and I can't ask for anything more."[32]

Because of injuries, Rosen could not seem to get going offensively. As a result, the fans booed him with gusto. Although he tried to block out the boo-birds, he heard their cries of displeasure. Not living up to the high standards that he set for himself was killing Rosen. He knew he had been a disappointment to the fans. But Rosen was his own worst critic. He was a bigger disappointment to himself.

Gene Woodling and Ray Boone also weighed in on the fans booing of Rosen. "I've played in both leagues," said Woodling. "The Cleveland fans are the worst. And you can print it."[33]

"I certainly feel sorry for old Rosey," said Boone. "Cleveland is a poor town. I thought I used to get it pretty good in Cleveland and I probably deserved it because I couldn't do the job. But I'll say one thing—it was never as bad as Rosen got."[34]

Cleveland did not have a 20-game winner on its pitching staff for the first time since 1938 (not including the war years). Bob Lemon started out with a 5–0 record in April, but he did not pitch as strong the rest of the season (18–10, 3.88 ERA). Herb Score (16–10, 2.85 ERA) was named American League Rookie of the Year. He set a major league record for the most strikeouts by a rookie with 245. He broke the record set by Grover Cleveland Alexander of the Philadelphia Phillies, who totaled 227 punchouts in 1911. Dwight Gooden of the New York Mets eclipsed Score's strikeout total when he whiffed 276 batters in 1984.

For Al Rosen, the 1955 season could be filed away and forgotten. He played in the fewest games (139) since he became a starter. In 492 at-bats, Rosen totaled 120 hits for a batting average of .244. He hit 21 home runs and drove in 81 runs. He trailed Doby (26) and Smith (22) in the home run department, but his 81 RBI led the team. Rosen still had tremendous control at the plate, as his walks (92) more than doubled his strikeouts (44).

Cleveland released Kiner (18 home runs, 54 RBI, .243 batting average) on October 24, 1955. Perhaps it would have been more prudent to promote Colavito instead of signing the aging Kiner. "The Rock" had another superb year at Indianapolis. He knocked 30 home runs, drove in 105 runs, and batted .268 at Indianapolis.

The next day, the Indians shipped Larry Doby (26 home runs, 75 RBI, .291 average) to the White Sox. In return, the Indians received shortstop Chico Carrasquel and outfielder Jim Busby. The *Plain Dealer* described the trade in a nutshell, writing that the Indians "sacrificed power for defense and speed."[35]

The key to the deal was Carrasquel. A four-time All-Star, Carrasquel's defensive play inspired the trade. The Indians were counting on him to shore up the infield. "As much as we hated to let Doby go," said Greenberg, "we feel we improved the team. It was necessary to trade someone with his ability to fill the weakness we had at shortstop. Carrasquel was the man we wanted, of course, but Busby was no throw-in. We had to have an outfielder to take Doby's place and Busby has the ability. He is a very good defensive outfielder."[36]

Rosen took a $10,000 cut in his salary, lowering it to $30,000 for the 1956 season. "I had it coming," said Rosen. "I had an awful season. If I'd just had an ordinary year, we would have won the pennant. There were a few others who went into a tailspin, too, but my slump hurt the club more than anyone's."[37]

Rosen also deemed that his injured finger from the 1954 season had finally healed. "Now I can bend the fingers completely around a bat without any pain," said Rosen. "Why the finger bothered my hitting, I don't know, but it did. It's perfectly healed now, though. The doctor has checked it completely. At first it was thought an operation would be necessary, but the rest this winter cured it without surgery."[38]

Although his finger may have been healed, Rosen soon had another injury to be concerned about. While vacationing in Miami, he was involved in an automobile accident that resulted in a neck injury. Although x-rays revealed no broken bones, damage to the vertebrae on the left side of his neck caused a pinched nerve. An orthopedic collar was affixed to his neck.

"I was going in the curb lane about 20 miles an hour," said Rosen. "In front of me a lady was driving her car about the same speed. She stopped short and I had to do the same. But the man driving the car behind me crashed into our car and knocked us into the one in front. We were pancaked. I'm really fortunate that I didn't hurt my right hand at all."[39]

Rosen endured a sore toe, a sore shoulder, and a sore thigh because of the auto accident. However, he reported to spring training early and worked out daily with Cleveland coaches Tony Cuccinello and Red Kress. Some of the local scribes pronounced Rosen "washed up" and said he had become apathetic about playing baseball.

Hebrew Hammer

"No one is going to write my obituary," said Rosen, "whoever does will be sorry. I have no intentions of quitting baseball. I've put a lot of effort into this game—it's my profession, and I intend to stay in it as long as I can, three or four more years, I hope. It's true that when I find I no longer can help a major league club, I'll quit."[40]

Rosen, who worked for a brokerage firm in the off-season, was criticized for his choice of occupations. Many suggested that Rosen had moved on already from his baseball career and was spending more time studying the ticker tapes and stock charts. Rosen took exception to these charges. Rosen wondered why it was okay for some players to go hunting or run a gas station in the off-season, while he was chastised for working in the investment business. He knew that baseball, while providing a comfortable living for his family, was not forever. He "had the foresight and the ambition to learn a business for when he hung up his spikes."[41]

Rosen's renewed outlook worked in the Arizona sun, as he batted a healthy .464 in spring training.[42] The Tribe received a surprising boost as Wertz made a full recovery from the dreaded polio that afflicted him a year earlier. Wertz, a rejuvenated Rosen, and rookie Rocky Colavito were expected to replace the power shortage caused by the release of Kiner and the trade of Doby to Chicago.

Plain Dealer sports editor Gordon Cobbledick predicted a third-place finish for the Indians, finishing behind New York and Boston. Cobbledick's opinion was a simple premise: The Yankees were good enough to win in 1955, why shouldn't they be the pick for 1956? Indians beat writer for the *Plain Dealer* Harry Jones picked Cleveland to finish in second place in the AL. "I seriously doubt that they improved enough to overhaul the Yankees even though they finished only three games behind the Yankees in 1955,"[43] wrote Jones.

Rosen started out slowly, batting .216 in April. He straightened out in May, raising his average to .301 on May 16. Rosen's power numbers were abysmal, just four home runs and 17 RBI. On May 18, the Washington Senators came to Cleveland Stadium for a two-game set.

The first game of the series was a tough one offensively for Rosen. In the bottom of the first inning, with a man on second base and no outs, he struck out. In the third, with runners on first and second and no outs, he lined into a double play. In the sixth, with runners on first and second and two outs, Rosen flied out. On the evening he left four men on base. The boo-birds were in fine form this Friday evening.

90

Six—Decline and Retirement

In the top of the ninth inning, with the Tribe leading, 4–3, the Senators' Pete Runnels tripled to left field. As Runnels made his slide into the bag, he crashed into Rosen.[44] The Tribe's third baseman lay in a heap, as he tore ligaments in his right knee and wrenched his right ankle. A small portion of the 7,747 in attendance cheered loudly during and after the collision.[45]

"It was the nastiest, most bush, meanest thing I ever heard," said Lopez. "These fans don't deserve a winner. They don't even deserve a major league club. He tries to cut down the tying run by blocking third base and he gets badly hurt—and I mean bad. So, what do the miserable fans do? They cheer his pain. It was shameful, absolutely shameful. They're bush, that's what they are—bush."[46]

Rudy Regalado took over at third base as Rosen did not get back into the starting lineup until June 5. The Yankees, sparked by a 21–10 record in May, jumping out to a big lead over their American League rivals:

Team	Won	Lost	Percentage	Games Behind
New York	29	13	.690	---
Chicago	18	15	.545	6½
Cleveland	20	17	.541	6½
Boston	20	19	.513	7½

Lopez shined the spotlight on the Indians' main problem in the early going of the 1956 season. In his verbal undressing of Tribe fans, Lopez mentioned that to date, Rosen led the club in RBI with 17. Vic Wertz had 16 RBI. When you consider that Yogi Berra and Mickey Mantle were leading the AL with 33 and 32 RBI, respectively, Rosen's total paled in comparison. The Indians were not hitting, proven by their team batting average in April (.239) and in May (.235).

While Rosen sat out, it gave him an opportunity to put himself in the shoes of Joe Fan. He caught several Indians games via television. "Now I know why fans get burned up at me whenever I leave men on base," said Rosen. "It's the natural thing to do. I got burned up myself watching our guys leave 'em on. I found myself second-guessing, too. Whenever I'd see someone strike out or pop up, I had the feeling he could have done better. I suppose the average fan thinks the same thing about me."[47]

On June 24, the Indians toppled the Senators at home in a rain-shortened game that was called in the bottom of the sixth inning.

91

Rosen socked his eighth home run of the season in the fifth inning. The two-run shot sailed over the fence in left-center field. The round-tripper marked the 1,000[th] career hit for Rosen. He joined Vic Wertz and Dale Mitchell as the only current Tribesmen who topped the 1,000-hit mark.

At the All-Star break, Rosen owned a batting average of .313, with 12 home runs and 45 RBI. But injuries, specifically a right leg injury in July that was re-aggravated in August, cost him approximately two weeks of playing time in the second half of the season. The injuries coincided with a reduction in his offensive production. Rosen totaled three home runs and 16 RBI for the rest of the season. His batting average plummeted to .267.

Another critic of Rosen's play on the diamond came to the forefront in September. Greenberg gave a speech to the Sigma Delta Chi, a national journalism fraternity, at the Manger Hotel on September 17, 1956. Greenberg alluded to Rosen's head not being in the game and suggested that perhaps he was better off elsewhere.[48]

When Greenberg was asked if that meant Rosen was going to be traded, he responded: "I haven't talked to Rosen recently, but some of his close friends, whose views I respect, have told me he thinks he can't play here. Confidence is an important factor in anyone's makeup, and I'm afraid Rosen has reached the point where he can't play here anymore. In justice to him, maybe we should trade him, and if we do I hope he does well wherever he goes."[49]

Rosen responded quickly to Greenberg's criticism. He cited the automobile accident as the reason for his injuries to his shoulder and neck that impeded his play all season. "I always give 100 per cent on the field. It may not be evident to the fans or those in the press box, but in my heart I know I'm giving my very best every instant. I couldn't live with myself otherwise. A standard is always set by any player who has had success, and naturally when I don't reach the standard, a number of people take offense to it."[50]

Feller made the final start of his career on September 30, 1956, against Detroit at Cleveland Stadium. A paltry crowd of 5,910 showed up to bid "Rapid Robert" adieu. The Tigers won the game, 8–4. Feller started four games in 1956 and lost three of them.

Cleveland lost the season series to New York (10–12), Chicago (7–15) and Boston (9–13). However, the Indians finished in second place because they beat up the second division teams (62–26) of the American League.

Team	Won	Lost	Percentage	Games Behind
New York	97	57	.630	---
Cleveland	88	66	.571	9
Chicago	85	69	.552	12
Boston	84	70	.545	13

The Indians' second-place finish enabled them to receive a bigger slice of the World Series shares pie. Full shares for the Indians ($1,649.05) were more than $500 than the full shares for the third-place White Sox ($1,112.75).[51]

In 1956, Rosen played in 121 games with 15 home runs and 61 RBI, and he batted .267. Wertz rebounded from his polio-shortened 1955 season to club 32 home runs, and he knocked in 106 runs, both team highs. Colavito had a solid rookie season (21 home runs, 65 RBI, .276 average). Smith batted .274, belted 16 home runs, and drove in 71 runs.

However, the rest of the regulars had low averages, including Avila (.224), Busby (.235), Carrasquel (.243), and Jim Hegan (.222).

The Tribe touted three 20-game winners: Lemon (20–14, 3.03 ERA), Score (20–9, 2.53 ERA), and Wynn (20–9, 2.72 ERA). Lemon won his 200th career game on September 11 in a 3–1 victory over Baltimore. Score led the league in strikeouts for the second consecutive season with 263 punchouts.

Not only did Feller retire, but Lopez resigned as manager of the Indians. In six years with the Indians, Lopez's won-lost record was 570–354. As of 2021, he holds the highest winning percentage (.617) of all managers in Indians history. The man known as "Senor" took over the White Sox, and just like when he piloted the Tribe, Chicago finished in second place to the Yankees in 1957 and 1958. Lopez led the Sox to the AL pennant in 1959, the first flag to fly on the South Side since 1919.

Except for 1954 and 1959, Casey Stengel's Yankees won a pennant every season from 1949 to 1960. The two years they lost out were to teams managed by Lopez.

Kerby Farrell replaced Lopez. Farrell managed AAA Indianapolis of the American Association to a 92–62 record in 1956. The 1957 season was Farrell's only one as the Tribe's skipper.

Rosen, at the age of 32, retired from the Indians on January 30, 1957. He retired with a lifetime batting average of .285, 192 home runs, 717 runs batted in, and a slugging percentage of .495. Rosen's fielding percentage at third base was .961. At the time of his retirement, Rosen trailed only Earl Averill (226), Hal Trosky (216), and Larry Doby (202) in career home runs.[52] As of 2021, Rosen ranks tenth all-time in Cleveland Indians history in home runs.[53]

Flip Rosen was employed full-time now at Bache. Rosen said that he was retiring "because I can't do the job anymore."[54] But Greenberg wasn't buying it. "We'll know whether Rosen's with us when we go to spring training," said Greenberg. "It's no secret that he's been talking about retiring all winter, but he hasn't given us any official notice."[55]

From the ballfield to Bache: Al Rosen trades in his Indians uniform for businessman attire. Rosen attacked both careers with the same intensity. His success transferred to his stockholder trade (The Cleveland Press Collection, Michael Schwartz Library, Cleveland State University).

Rosen told the Associated Press why he retired from baseball, and it had nothing to do with the booing of the fans.

> For what the Indians were paying me every year, they could have booed me all day and night. I'm lucky. I retired from baseball before it retired me. But you can't say the same thing about some other players. They are just hanging on and they won't have a thing going for them when they are forced to leave the game. They'd be better off learning something else then reading comic books or going to the movies.[56]

Rosen was asked what he thought of the Indians' prospects for the 1957 season. "Don't count them out. They have a terrific player in Roger Maris [an outfielder from Indianapolis]," said Rosen. "This kid may do for the Indians what Mickey Mantle did for the Yankees."[57]

Maris started in center field for Cleveland in 1957. On June 15, 1958, the Indians traded him to Kansas City. From there, Maris was dealt to the Yankees on December 11, 1959. It took a former MVP to recognize a future MVP. Maris won back-to-back MVP Awards with the Yankees in 1960–1961, two years removed from when he wore an Indians uniform.

In February 1957, Al and Terry Rosen welcomed their second son, Andrew. As the Indians reported to Tucson for spring training, stories swirled that perhaps Rosen would return to third base for the Tribe. The stories in the daily newspapers were rampant with speculation about whether Rosen was talking to Farrell or if he missed baseball enough to end his retirement. It is always troublesome when the media writes stories about the personnel who are not with the team instead of focusing on those who are in camp.

Rosen met with Greenberg in March 1957. Greenberg told the media that he thought Rosen might be thinking over his decision and that he missed baseball.[58] Maybe Rosen missed the game more than he thought or that he cared to admit. Rosen called Farrell to let him know that he was ready to end his retirement. That decision was reversed when Greenberg gave the thumbs-down to Rosen's contract requests. "Rosen wanted approximately a 50 per cent increase," said Greenberg. "He wanted to be rewarded to leave his job. I told him we couldn't reward him except for performance on the field. I said it was impossible to give him the increase merely because he had a good job out of baseball."[59]

When asked about the negotiations, Rosen said:

> When I announced I was going to retire I didn't realize how much I'd miss baseball. I never thought I'd come to the point of wanting to return. I instigated it and I'm sorry now that it all happened.

Al Rosen at home with his family. Terry and Al administer a baby bottle to baby Andrew while older brother Robert looks on. Al and Terry's third son, James, would arrive three years later (courtesy Cleveland Public Library).

If I had gone through with it [returning to baseball], it certainly wouldn't have been any bed of roses. Some of the press seemed hostile. And I don't know what the public reaction might have been.[60]

According to Cobbledick, Rosen's former teammates did not want him to return to the club.

Rosen convinced them months ago that he had lost all desire to play. Many of them were convinced earlier that he had lost the ability to play. It is no exaggeration to say that to have brought him back now, at his own terms, would have had a demoralizing effect on the Cleveland Indians.

It's a fact brought to light in many conversations with many players in Tucson. They don't want him back.[61]

On April 3, 1957, the *Plain Dealer* took a poetic shot at Rosen in the editorial pages. The piece was entitled "Anticlimax—or Al Rosen's Fall from Grace":

On February First, my lad Al Rosen said "I'm through";
"I've got a brand new broker's job, and quite a lot to do,

Six—Decline and Retirement

Though baseball has been good to me, I feel it's time to quit,
So now I'm hanging up my spikes—and there's an end to it!"
The papers all applauded Al. "You're smart," they said, "to stop,
While you are still a brawny lad, and very near the top,
And when we need a broker, Al, we'll promptly go
To see the up-and-coming lad who sells for Bache & Co."

Now anticlimax is something all men should strictly shun,
And when you say: "I've quit," stay quit; don't go as Al has done.
For when a thing is final there is nothing more to say,
You cannot make revisions on decisions every day!

So Al is still a broker, and a broker he will stay
(At least until Hank Greenberg greatly elevates his pay.)
But, since this isn't likely, our Al will stay retired.
We wish it hadn't happened to a guy we have admired! [62]

Rosen may have retired from playing baseball, but he was not far from the game. In 1958 he hosted a show on WEWS Channel 5 titled "Direct Line," which was sponsored by the Ohio Bell Telephone Company. The 15-minute program preceded selected Indians games with Rosen interviewing a variety of guests, including Tris Speaker and new Indians general manager Frank Lane.

Perhaps Rosen's pregame show served as a springboard to bigger and better opportunities. From 1959—1960, Rosen teamed with veteran broadcaster Chuck Thompson to call the Saturday Game of the Week on NBC. "Baseball has been part of me for so long that I missed it," said Rosen. "It's been good to get back and see the players and even to revisit the ballparks I played in. There are still some players left who were around when I quit. They are getting fewer, though."[63] Rosen added that he didn't bring up his day job as a stockbroker during a telecast unless his broadcast partner brought it up.

In July 1960, Al and Terry announced the birth of their third son, James.

For the past decade, the City of Cleveland had become a football town. The Browns participated in 10 straight championship games between the All-America Football Conference and the National Football League. Their success was unmatched in the professional ranks. Cleveland had a strong high school football tradition. As mentioned earlier in the chapter, Ohio State University was a powerhouse on the collegiate level.

As the Browns took off in popularity, the Indians struggled.

Rosen charts pitches at spring training in Tucson during spring training in 1965. He served as a batting instructor for several seasons during spring training (The Cleveland Press Collection, Michael Schwartz Library, Cleveland State University).

Naturally, fans gravitated to a winner. The Browns' success relegated the Tribe to second-class citizens.

Considering the Indians' loss of recognition to the sports fans in Cleveland, dwindling attendance followed. The Indians had cracked the one million mark in attendance once (1959) in the last six seasons, with 1,497,976 fans pushing their way through the turnstiles at Cleveland Stadium. That was also the last time the Indians fielded a team that was in contention for the World Series. Even in their pennant-winning season in 1954, Cleveland only drew 1,335,472 patrons.[64]

There was speculation that the Indians would relocate to another city because of the low attendance figures.[65] Another reason for the low attendance was Cleveland Stadium. The old lady on the shores of Lake Erie was only 30 years old, but it was not a great facility for viewing a baseball game. The ballpark had a capacity of over 72,000 for baseball. Most days, fewer than a quarter of that figure attended an Indians game. The stands were far from the field, and poles that supported the upper deck led to an impeded view for some fans. Cold weather blew into the stadium from Lake Erie. Sometimes it was not until mid–May that the climate was comfortable enough for fans to watch baseball.

The Wahoo Club, an adult booster club for the Indians, was the result of a grassroots effort. The Wahoo Club is the Official Booster Club of the Cleveland Indians. The organization took its name from Chief Wahoo, the cartoonish caricature that the club sewed on some versions of the Indians' caps and jerseys.

A group of former players, including Bob Feller, Mike Garcia and Rosen, were part of the organizing body. Also part of the group were Gabe Paul, Indians president and general manager; Nate Wallack, Tribe public relations director; John Nagy, Cleveland Recreation Director; and Gordon Cobbledick.[66] Rosen was selected as president.

"The Wahoo Club will actively support the Indians of course, but they are not our only interest," said Rosen. "We'll be backing the kids on high school and college teams and the many sand lotters in our area. We're interested in baseball and the young men who play it. We'll do anything we can to promote interest in the game."[67]

The Wahoo Club resembled the Touchdown Club, a booster support group for the Browns. Luncheons and speaking engagements featuring major league players would be on the docket. The Wahoo Club is still a viable and prosperous organization. Currently, there are over 1,500 members who attend luncheons and take road trips to see the Tribe play ball in different major league venues.[68]

On April 5, 1966, a group of Cleveland's young business leaders was formed and for no better reason was called "Group 66." The group's purpose centered around assisting Cleveland Mayor Ralph S. Locher in getting projects under way that otherwise might have to wait until funds were available for planning or for the projects themselves. George

Steinbrenner, president of Kinsman Marine Transit Company, organized the group that included 29 members.[69] Among the other members were Kenny King, Jr., vice president of the Kenny King restaurant chain; Jess A. Bell, president of Bonne Bell Inc.; Marc A. Wyse, president of Wyse Advertising Agency; and Rosen.

One of the projects of the group included refurbishing Cleveland Stadium. Rosen headed the project to put a fresh look on the venue. "This will be no broom-sweeping job," said Rosen. "We're talking about making the Stadium a showplace—a place where people can really enjoy themselves."[70]

Improvements called for steam-cleaning the interior of the stadium, repaint the inside using different colors and color schemes, revamping the concession operation, new lighting, landscaping, improved restrooms, and a new sewer project. "This has long-range implications," said Rosen. "When we are done, we will have a real showplace, something to be proud of."[71]

But restoring the Stadium was not the only improvement project Rosen took on. He also aspired to improve Little League baseball. Or at least to better the experience for the fathers and their sons. Rosen's sons, Rob and Andy, began to play Little League baseball, and Rosen was right there with them, acting as their team's manager. The work inspired Rosen to author a book: *Baseball and Your Boy*, published by The World Publishing Company in Cleveland.

Rosen covered all aspects of playing, weaving personal accounts of his own career into the book. He also covered the roles of the player's father, mother, and manager. Rosen also wrote about sportsmanship and the length of practices. Los Angeles Dodgers manager Walter Alston and St. Louis Cardinals great Stan Musial both contributed blurbs praising the book.

"My aim is to help the boy get started," Rosen wrote in the preface. "Not to make him a future major leaguer but a youngster who can get fun and satisfaction out of his years in a boys' league. And the best break he can have is parents—and especially a father—who take an interest in his playing and encourage his progress."[72]

Rosen ascended in his career as a stockbroker, becoming vice president at Bache.

In an interview with the *Cleveland Plain Dealer*, Rosen discussed his strategy when advising customers on the stock market. He educated himself on different stocks by reading and researching many different sources. Rosen was on the lookout for clues to see if a company just had a bad day or a bad week, or if it was in a downward spiral. For Rosen, it was important to identify these trends, but also to determine the direction in which the various stocks were moving. In his opinion, a person who chooses a broker has every right to have high expectations of him. And although the experience of a broker is important, the chemistry between the broker and the customer must be present. Rosen said that "chemistry grows when the broker knowing [sic] his customer and their needs."[73]

In 1967, tensions between Israel and neighboring Arab states Egypt, Syria and Jordan heightened due to diplomatic friction.[74] Back in Cleveland, a different kind of skirmish was taking place. Dorothy Fuldheim, the 74-year-old journalist from WEWS TV5, wanted to go to Israel to cover what would become known as the Six Day War.

But Fuldheim was stonewalled by her bosses, and they refused to give her permission to travel to Israel. Management's primary reasons were sound: her age and the numerous danger risks while entering a potential war zone would not be worth the story. Fuldheim, who was Jewish, agreed to a bodyguard—someone who was "strong, good-looking, [and] bright" and had "a good name," said Fuldheim. "I don't want to run around Israel with just anyone."[75]

Someone suggested Al Rosen. He agreed and requested that armed guards travel with them throughout the trip. They visited the wounded and dying, officers and political leaders, and the women and children who were left behind.[76] Fuldheim and Rosen cried tears of joy as the Israelis became the victor: "for those whose memory marched with Tenth Battalion on that boulevard in Tel Aviv that June day," said Fuldheim.[77]

Rosen called the effort of the Israelis "one of the greatest exhibits of unity—of singleness of purpose—I have ever seen. The spirit, the strength of the officer corps in their relationship to the men they led into battle was magnificent."[78]

On January 18, 1968, Rosen was elected to the Cleveland Indians' Board of Directors. James Stouffer, the son of Indians Owner and Chairman of the Board Vernon Stouffer, was also elected to serve on the board.[79]

Through his affiliation with Group 66, Rosen raised money for the Suicide Prevention Center. Rosen, who had an interest in psychology, welcomed the opportunity.

I was glad to help when I was approached by a young psychiatrist who asked me as a member of Group 66 to raise funds for the Suicide Prevention Center that was being formed. A month later I was asked to be president. Very frankly, I'm appalled by the suicide rate throughout the country. If as president I can help the organization solve its budget problems and become more widely accepted in the community.[80]

Perhaps Rosen's interest in psychiatry and suicide was stoked by learning to adapt to life with his wife. Terry Rosen suffered from manic depression, a mental health disease. Tragically, Terry Rosen, at 41 years of age, took her life on May 4, 1971, when she leapt to her death from the 19th floor of the Hotel Warwick in Philadelphia. She left a note saying that she was despondent. Her death was ruled a suicide. Terry Rosen was interred at Memory Hill Cemetery in Dothan, Alabama.

"People ask me if my father was a great dad," said James Rosen. "He was much more than that. He was both mom and dad for us. My mom died when I was 11, and he really raised us three boys. He always had time for us. He was always there. I was born after his playing career and growing up he was just a stockbroker to me. We literally idolized him growing up, and we still do."[81]

On July 24, 1971, Rosen remarried. Flip and the former Rita Loewenstein exchanged vows at Caesars Palace in Las Vegas. She was described as a Detroit socialite.[82] Like Rosen's son, James, Rita did not know about Rosen's past as a baseball star. "He's always been Flip, even to me," said Rita. "But I didn't marry a ballplayer, I married a stockbroker."[83]

Vernon Stouffer purchased the Indians in a stock deal that was worth approximately $8 million in 1966. The deal assured Stouffer that he would have 51 percent of stock ownership.[84] He took the reins from William Daley, the previous chairman of the board, and purchased stock from Gabe Paul, the largest shareholder.[85] The frozen food magnate signed Paul to a 10-year contract to be the president and general manager. But a couple of bad business deals and dwindling attendance did not secure Stouffer a positive return on his investment. Stouffer accumulated debts around $300,000 by 1971 and borrowed money from the team's 1972 television contract.[86]

Rumors being just that, there was talk of the Indians being sold to a group from Washington, D.C., to replace the Senators, who left for Arlington, Texas. Cleveland was also looking at sharing their home schedule with New Orleans. The Indians would play 30 games down in the Big Easy, hoping to improve the attendance figures.

Al Rosen and Rita Loewenstein, shown here circa 1974, were married for 43 years (The Cleveland Press Collection, Michael Schwartz Library, Cleveland State University).

As a member of the Indians' board of directors, Rosen was sickened by the way Stouffer ran the club. To Rosen, Stouffer was a cantankerous old man who drank way too much. Stouffer's personal business dealings and his lack of baseball knowledge made him a liability if the Indians were to be a successful organization.[87]

George Steinbrenner had always dreamed of owning the Indians. When he talked to his Group 66 pals, he would constantly reiterate his intent to purchase the Indians. Steinbrenner and Rosen, knowing of the losses Stouffer was incurring, moved in to purchase the team.[88]

Steinbrenner put together an ownership group that "had more money and more smarts than all the other previous Indians' owners combined," said Rosen. "We had the ability and were prepared to restore the Indians to greatness."[89]

Because Steinbrenner attended Culver Military Academy in Indiana with Stouffer's son, Jim, he was the point man on the discussions. On December 6, 1971, Steinbrenner and Jim Stouffer had a deal. Steinbrenner's group would buy the Indians for $8.6 million as well as absorb all the debt owed by Stouffer. They shook hands on the deal and waited in Steinbrenner's office for Vernon Stouffer to call and accept the terms. Stouffer's affirmation, thought to be a mere formality, turned out to be anything but that.[90]

Shortly after 5:00 p.m. on December 6, Stouffer called Steinbrenner and rejected their offer. "Today a group of Clevelanders, of which I am titular head, made an offer to purchase for cash the Cleveland Baseball Inc. from Mr. Vernon Stouffer," said Rosen. "It has been rejected. I am certain Mr. Stouffer, a civic-minded Clevelander, will continue to exercise his judgment in accomplishing what is best for Cleveland."[91]

"I am going right forward with New Orleans, and I might even sell to Washington," said Stouffer. "This should not have been started ... it did not come from my quarters. I don't know where they got that."[92]

The group was disappointed that the deal did not go through. However, Steinbrenner now had the bug to own a baseball team. He instructed Rosen and Paul to let him know if another team was for sale.

It wasn't long after that Gabe Paul did indeed have a team in mind.

SEVEN

George, Billy, Lem
and a World Championship

During the summer of 1972, Rosen sat next to Gabe Paul on a flight from New York to Cleveland. "Gabe said there was a club for sale, and I asked him who, and he whispered in my ear: 'The Yankees.' I almost fell off my chair, but the Yankees at that time weren't doing well," said Rosen.[1]

Columbia Broadcasting System (CBS) purchased the Yankees in 1964, but it was looking to get out of the baseball ownership business. Rosen relayed Paul's message to Steinbrenner that the Yankees could be bought for $10 million. In 1972, that was quite a sum of money to raise and, in order to do so, Steinbrenner had to reach outside his circle of friends and business contacts in Cleveland. Steinbrenner asked Rosen if he wanted to be included, but the brokerage business took up too much of Rosen's time, so he declined.

Membership in the ownership group numbered 14, including Paul.[2] Steinbrenner owned the largest percentage (11 percent) of the group.[3] Reportedly, Steinbrenner kicked in $168,000 of his personal funds towards the purchase price.[4]

On December 29, 1972, the transaction was complete. The sale price was reported to be $10 million. The deal included two parking garages that New York City had purchased from Steinbrenner for $1.2 million, to make the final figure $8.8 million.[5]

On November 27, 1972, Cleveland traded perhaps its best everyday player to New York. Third baseman Graig Nettles, a star in the making and a left-handed slugger, was part of a six-player deal. Yankee Stadium played to Nettles' strength with its short distance of 314 feet to right field. More than a few eyebrows were raised when Paul, as president of the Indians, engineered a trade of their best player to a team which he joined as part of an ownership group a month later.

Rosen continued to work in the securities business until May 1975. After 19 years as a full-time stockbroker, Rosen made a career change at age 51. He hired on as an executive position in guest relations at Caesars Palace in Las Vegas. "I've known Al Rosen on a professional and personal level for many years," said casino president William S. Weinberger. "He was a great ballplayer, an 'all-star' executive and a gentleman."[6]

"This is a business I know I'm going to enjoy," said Rosen. "It's a people-oriented business ... and one thing I think I've always been able to do is relate to people."[7]

Despite his optimistic outlook on his new job, Rosen was underwhelmed with his career change. Although he was looking forward to playing tennis and golf year-round, the warm weather did little to ease his disdain for his position at the casino. A good part of his job was to be a greeter to the guests of Caesars Palace. In retrospect, it certainly was not the most rewarding job as far as Rosen was concerned.

Over time, Rosen came to loath the city as well. Las Vegas with its glitz and glamour differed greatly from the tree-lined streets and the tranquility of Shaker Heights, Ohio.

On November 5, 1977, Steinbrenner traveled to Las Vegas for the Ken Norton-Jimmy Young prizefight at Caesars. Steinbrenner had dinner with Rosen, who expounded on his unhappiness with his new career. Steinbrenner told Rosen that Paul was leaving the Yankees and returning to Cleveland to run the Indians. He wanted Rosen to replace him as president of the Yankees. "I want you to run the operation, just like Gabe did," said Steinbrenner. "Cedric [Tallis] will remain the general manager, but you'll be the one in charge of the baseball end of it."[8]

Rosen immediately warmed to the idea of returning to baseball. He viewed the president's job as one that would have an impact and one that would matter. In addition to working with his close friend from the Group 66 days in Cleveland, the Yankees were the reigning world champions. "When I was here for the All-Star Game in July," said Rosen, "George raised the idea of my joining the Yankees. I had never given any thought to being in baseball in an active way, but this came along, and you have to be crazy not to jump at it."[9]

"Titles in baseball don't mean that much," said Rosen. "Titles are meaningful only if people fulfill the jobs that are given to them. It's a full circle, I guess. I had always hoped to play for the Yankees but had never made it. Now I'm their president. It's quite a thrill."[10]

The Yankees were the reigning World Champions as well as the

Al Rosen and George Steinbrenner from their Group 66 days. Although they appear to be cordial to each other in this photograph, their time together in the Bronx while running the Yankees could be charitably described as contentious (The Cleveland Press Collection, Michael Schwartz Library, Cleveland State University).

two-time American League Champions. Their team was built with power (Nettles, Chris Chambliss, Reggie Jackson, and Thurman Munson). They had speed (Mickey Rivers and Willie Randolph). New York had veteran leadership (Lou Piniella and Roy White).

Their pitching staff boasted 1977 Cy Young Award winner Sparky Lyle and starters Jim "Catfish" Hunter, Don Gullett, Ken Holtzman, Ron Guidry, and Ed Figueroa.

Jackson and Yankees manager Billy Martin did not get along. Martin piloted the Yankees to their first pennant in 12 seasons in 1976. He did not want the Yankees to sign Jackson, a free agent in 1977. Martin favored Joe Rudi. A decent hitter with a good glove and a terrific throwing arm, Rudi did not have much flash in his game, but he was the consistent, lunch-pail type of player that Martin coveted.[11] Like oil and water, Jackson and Martin did not mix. Of course, Martin probably knew this all along, but he did not have much of a say as to which free agents the club signed. At best, their relationship was on-again, off-again.

Jackson did not make a good first impression with his new teammates when he criticized Munson in an interview in the June 1977 edition of *Sport* magazine. Jackson questioned Munson's leadership ability as the team's captain. He stated that if he were on the club in 1976, the Yankees would never have been swept in the World Series like they were by the Reds.

Besides being a great player, Munson had the respect of his teammates. The article put Jackson in a bad light, and he made enemies of his new teammates right away. The animosity between Jackson and Martin escalated on June 18, 1977, at Fenway Park. Boston was beating New York, 7–4, in the bottom of the sixth inning. Fred Lynn was on first base when Jim Rice hit a double to right field. Martin felt that Jackson gave less than an honest effort chasing after Rice's double. Martin, to show Jackson up, immediately removed him from the game and replaced him with Paul Blair. Jackson jogged to the dugout, a shouting match between Martin and Jackson ensued, and the two had to be separated. The game was broadcast on NBC as its "Game of the Week," and the whole incident was replayed again and again.

Jackson's five home runs in the 1977 World Series, three in a single game, garnered him Most Valuable Player honors as well as the title "Mr. October." For the moment, all seemed forgiven. The New York Yankees were the kings of baseball yet again.

Tallis had been the GM for the expansion Kansas City Royals in 1968. He was awarded *The Sporting News* Executive of the Year Award in 1971 after the Royals finished in second place in the AL West. Tallis built the Royals into a winner, drafting pitchers Steve Busby and Paul Splittorff and third baseman George Brett. Tallis engineered trades that brought Amos Otis, John Mayberry, Cookie Rojas, and Fred Patek to the Royals. But conflict with manager Jack McKeon led to his exit in 1974.

Tallis joined the Yankees as an assistant GM in 1975. Paul hired Tallis to oversee the renovation of Yankee Stadium, which was set to re-open in 1976. "Cedric is a proven baseball man," said Rosen. "The

Yankees are fortunate to have him. His knowledge and strength are very reassuring to me."[12]

On November 22, 1977, the Yankees signed Rich "Goose" Gossage to a six-year, $3.6 million deal. Gossage had led the AL in saves with 26 in 1975 with Chicago. He had 26 saves for Pittsburgh in 1977. Gossage, a right-hander, was now paired with Sparky Lyle. The southpaw pitcher won the 1977 AL Cy Young Award after he went 13–5 with a 2.17 ERA and 26 saves.

But the trio of Yankees executives wanted more pitching for the 1978 Yankees and got it in Hawaii at the winter meetings. On December 7, New York purchased starting pitcher Andy Messersmith from Atlanta for $100,000. Messersmith had signed a five-year contract with Atlanta for $1.5 million in 1976. He posted a 11–11 record for the Braves in 1976. He followed that up with a 5–4 record in 1977 before a batted ball shattered his right elbow, ending his season on July 3 at Houston.

The Yankees also signed right-handed reliever Rawly Eastwick to a five-year deal worth $1.2 million. Eastwick was an important cog in Cincinnati's Big Red Machine, leading the NL in saves in 1975 (22) and 1976 (26). Both seasons the Reds were crowned World Champions.

As the Yankees reported to Fort Lauderdale for spring training, one player who was miserable was Lyle. The signings of Gossage and Eastwick no doubt left a bitter taste in his mouth. He demanded to be dealt to another club. Lyle, whose three-year deal totaled approximately $600,000, was understandably miffed by the new deals given his bullpen mates. "That's why I want to get out of here," said Lyle. "The way things stand now, why shouldn't I go to another club and pitch the way I want to? Then I'll get the money and pitch like I want to. Money is what it's boiling down to. We didn't discuss money, but I don't think he [Steinbrenner] wants to come up with any more money either."[13]

"He [Lyle] has a contract and we expect him to pitch for the Yankees this season and pitch well," said Rosen. "Sparky is too good a competitor to do otherwise."[14]

Another Yankee fought a different kind of battle, as Jim "Catfish" Hunter was diagnosed with diabetes in the off-season. "I talked to the doctor [Dr. Sheldon Nassburg], a specialist," said Hunter, "and he said as long as I take care of myself, I'd be O.K. I got to believe the doctor. He knows more than I do."[15]

Starting pitcher Don Gullett entered his second season with the Yankees in 1978. A starter with Cincinnati most of his career, he signed a six-year, $2 million deal with the Yankees on November 18, 1976. He suffered various injuries in 1977, including spraining his left ankle, pulling a muscle in his neck, and experiencing soreness in his left shoulder that sidelined him for six weeks. Still, the left-hander managed to post a 14–4 record with a 3.58 ERA. He had the distinction of winning a world championship in consecutive seasons with teams in each league.

But in spring training, Gullett felt the same soreness in his left shoulder. Rosen referred to the injury as "the usual Gullett kind of thing." The Yankees brass sure hoped that was not the case. "There's really no problem; otherwise we'd tell you," said Rosen. "You'd be concerned if a fellow couldn't pitch one season, then came in the next year and couldn't pitch. But he was 14 and 4 last year, although he had trouble in the middle of the season."[16]

As spring training wound down in Florida, Rosen was faced with the unpleasant task of trimming the roster. Rosen had experienced this ritual many times as a young player with the Indians. But now, as a club president with New York, it was a complete role-reversal. "It's really tough," said Rosen, "because I've been optioned out. It's a horrible feeling. Now I feel sorry for all the general managers who told me I had to go out. I always thought they didn't give a damn. In those days, no one had to give you any explanations. The general managers didn't even always tell you. The traveling secretary would come up to you and give you a ticket, or a coach would tell you."[17]

Only Boston's Carlton Fisk rivaled Munson as the best backstop in the American League. The Yankees' infield—Chris Chambliss at first base, Willie Randolph at second, shortstop Bucky Dent, and Graig Nettles at third base—was as formidable a unit as there was in the major leagues. Lou Piniella in left field, speedy Mickey Rivers in center, and power hitter Reggie Jackson in right field were as seasoned and as productive a trio of outfielders as one could find.

Starting pitching was the question mark about the New York Yankees in 1978. Injuries to Gullett and Messersmith cast doubt on how much of a contribution they would make during the regular season. The Yankees' rotation as it headed north to begin the season was composed of left-handers Ron Guidry and Ken Holtzman and right-handers Dick Tidrow, Ed Figueroa, and Catfish Hunter.

Of the players listed above, only two players were drafted and developed by the Yankees: Munson and Guidry.

Most of the national tabloids picked the Yankees for first place.

They were not straying too far on the proverbial limb with those prognostications. New York's old rival, Boston, also made moves to keep pace with the Yankees. The Red Sox signed pitcher Mike Torrez (New York) in free agency and traded for hurler Dennis Eckersley (Cleveland) to pair with Luis Tiant and Bill Lee, forming a solid pitching staff. The Red Sox were a tough, veteran club who could go toe-to-toe with New York. A lineup consisting of Carl Yastrzemski, Jim Rice, Fred Lynn, George Scott, and Dwight Evans to go along with Fisk batting in Fenway Park gave nightmares to pitchers around the league.

Martin may have been coy regarding his club's chances, but he did not seem ready to anoint them division champs for the third straight year just yet. Martin preached to anyone who would listen that repeating as division champs, much less as kings of the AL, would be an arduous task. Every other team would be gunning for the Yankees, so the club had to be ready to work hard to remain at the top of the heap. Martin would see to it that they did just that.[18]

After meeting with the players to go over his expectations, Martin reminded them that last season was just that: last season.

> I said, "Quit believing what you read that we've won the pennant already because we haven't won anything yet." Everybody has us winning the pennant and we haven't even won a ball game. Last year they said we bought the pennant, but we won by only 2½ games and the year before, when we didn't buy any players, we won by 10½.[19]

Martin's message to his team may have failed to find its mark when the Bronx Bombers opened the season in Arlington and dropped two of three games to the Rangers. They went on to Milwaukee and dropped two games to the Brewers to begin the season with a 1–4 record before heading home to New York for the opener at Yankee Stadium.

On April 13, the Yankees opened the home portion of their schedule with a 4–2 win over Chicago. Guidry pitched a complete game, which would become a familiar sight in 1978. As part of a promotion for the Opening Day crowd, Reggie Bars were handed out to the fans as they passed through the turnstiles. The circular-shaped confection was a combination of caramel and peanuts, dipped in chocolate.

In the bottom of the first inning, Willie Randolph led off with a walk and Mickey Rivers singled. After Munson struck out, Jackson smacked a home run to right-center off Sox starter Wilbur Wood. It was Jackson's fourth straight home run at Yankee Stadium. He had walloped three off the Dodgers in Game Six of the 1977 World Series, and now one in his first at-bat on Opening Day in 1978. As Jackson headed home, a Reggie Bar came flying out of the stands. Then another, and soon thousands found their way to the field. It took the ground crew ten minutes, using big buckets, to pick up all the candy bars. "This is absolutely horseshit," said Chicago manager Bob Lemon. "But it tells you something about that piece of candy. The fans would rather throw it than eat it."[20]

"It was embarrassing," said Rosen, "but I didn't feel we could call on ballpark security. What were we going to do, arrest the youth of America?"[21]

The next day, the club was required to attend a benefit luncheon at the Americana Hotel to raise money for the Archdiocese of New York. However, five players, Nettles, Lyle, Munson, Rivers, and Roy White, were absent. Rosen had not given permission to the players to skip the luncheon, and he fined each player $500.

"It's lousy what the front office did," said Rivers, who won the second game on April 15 in the bottom of the eighth inning with a two-run, inside-the-park home run. "We're the ones who make things happen. All the front office does is try to destroy the team.

"The timing of the luncheon was bad," said Rivers. "Nobody was settled. It was our first free day here since before spring training. The Yankees aren't doing nothing but for certain guys."[22] Rivers was asked who he was referring to with the "certain guys" reference. "There's a lot of certain guys around here," said Rivers.[23]

"Mickey's all right," said Rosen, who levied the fines. "We're friends. He gets a little worked up sometimes. I know his vocabulary. I'm glad the worst he called me was 'lousy.'"[24]

"The players' rep knew the procedure," said Rosen. "If a player couldn't make it, he had to clear it with me. The players who attended were waiting to see what I'd do. I had no alternative. We don't make these requests too often."[25]

Rosen discussed the differences between baseball players of his day and the current player. He cited the differences in team travel. Rosen believed that it was easier to bond with your teammates over dinner, a game of cards, or a bottle of scotch while riding the rails on a train. However, on a plane, the only teammate you can talk to is the one seated next to you.[26]

Money was also a factor. In Rosen's day, only Bob Feller concerned himself with hiring a financial advisor. Feller was the only player on the Cleveland teams that made enough money to be concerned about financial matters. Today's players were constantly worried about invest-ments and tax structures. Rosen felt that the players of today had a seri-ous problem with money management.[27] "I've often wondered where an owner would cast his lot in a conflict between a superstar and a presi-dent or a GM," said Rosen. "It's like the old joke: It's easy to hire a doctor or a vice president, but where the hell can you find a .300 hitter who hits 40 home runs?"[28]

New York struggled to a 10–9 record in April and trailed first-place Detroit by 3½ games at the end of the month. Three of the Yankees' losses were charged to Hunter. Off the field, the month did not end on a high note. Stewart Thornley, a 22-year-old sophomore at the University of Minnesota, filed a lawsuit that Munson tried to choke him following a game on April 28 at Metropolitan Stadium. Thornley, a member of the Delta Upsilon fraternity, waited outside the Yankees' clubhouse to see if Munson would sign his pledge paddle. Munson had belonged to Delta Upsilon when he attended Kent State University a decade earlier.

Thornley made repeated requests for the Yankees captain's auto-graph but was refused. "I didn't choke him," said Munson, who acknowl-edged that he had his hand behind Thornley's neck. "I just had a hand on him. I just got sick of it."[29]

No charges were filed against Munson, but this was the third occur-rence where he was thrust into the news during the young season. First, a Rangers fan wrote to Commissioner Bowie Kuhn to complain about the catcher's use of inappropriate language during a game on April 10. The fan was sitting with several friends in box seats directly behind the Yankee dugout. The fan wrote:

> During the game, a group of hecklers farther down the left field line got on Thurman Munson. While standing on the edge of the dugout, Munson responded to the group with a very loud, foul, and obscene remark.
> I've heard it before, but I strenuously object to a display in public by an apparently ill-tempered, well paid, professional ballplayer. Subjecting women and children to such invective is totally unnecessary and does little for baseball.[30]

Munson, who could be cantankerous and ornery to those who were not in the clubhouse, boycotted the media. He perceived that he had received unfair treatment from the local press in 1977, and in turn, he gave scribes the silent treatment. "I'd like Thurman to be more outgo-ing, he's our captain, he's a Hall of Fame candidate," said Rosen. "But he leads by performance. As long as he produces, I don't care. And he does produce."[31]

Hunter came back to win two games in a row. But he developed a sore right shoulder after his second win against Minnesota on May 9. The recurring pain shelved Hunter for six weeks. Because of their injuries, Gullett and Messersmith had not yet made their 1978 pitching debuts. Holtzman made two ineffective starts in early April, and Martin moved him to the bullpen. Through May 15, Guidry (4–0, 1.61 ERA) and Figueroa (4–1, 3.14 ERA) were leading the Yankees staff.

But Figueroa disliked the long wait that he was getting between starts. "I asked them to trade me during the World Series," said Figueroa. "They said they need me. Then I asked my agent to ask Rosen to trade me again. I don't want to pitch every seventh day. I want to pitch every fourth."[32] Figueroa was possibly just letting off some steam. The Yankees had won five straight games (May 21–26), but Toronto ruined the victory party on May 27, 1978. The Blue Jays crossed the plate three times in the top of the ninth inning to snatch a 4–1 win. Figueroa took the complete-game loss and pointed to his six-day layoff as the excuse.

"I'm sick and tired of these guys messing up, then asking to be traded," said Martin. "He wants to pitch every fourth day. What am I supposed to do, mess up Guidry and Beattie and Tidrow just to please him? He shows me that he's more interested in himself than he is in the team."[33]

Martin's unhappiness with Figueroa was replaced with glee for Messersmith. The right-hander made his debut on May 29, 1978, at Cleveland. He surrendered just one hit over five scoreless innings but received a no-decision. Eastwick pitched the final four innings to get the win. Nettles eighth home run in the seventh inning delivered the 2–0 win to New York. The Yankees were encouraged by Messersmith's first start in nearly 11 months. Martin played it cool. "I've seen it before," said Martin, "I've seen Gullett do it after being out eight weeks."[34]

Munson had been battling a sore right knee most of the season and played each game with pain. Against Baltimore on May 31, the pain became too much, and Munson had to leave the game. Cliff Johnson, the only other catcher on the Yankees' roster at the time, was moved from designated hitter to catcher. Unfortunately, when this position exchange is executed during a game, the designated hitter becomes null and void and the pitcher is forced to bat.

Orioles starter Mike Flanagan threw a three-hitter as Baltimore won, 3–2. Martin, frustrated enough because of the loss, was incensed when reporters informed him that rookie catcher Mike Heath had been recalled from Class AA West Haven of the Eastern League. Moments later, the phone rang in Martin's office. He listened, said "Thank you" in a biting way, and hung up. The caller, presumably Rosen, informed Martin about the Heath move.[35]

It rankled Martin that he had not been consulted about the personnel move. "I don't bring them up. I don't send them down," said Martin.[36]

Rosen insisted that Martin was fully aware of all the moves that the front office made. Furthermore, Rosen stated that one of his areas of responsibility was to remain in close contact with the field manager.[37]

"Billy Martin is the manager of this ball club," said Rosen, "he has been the manager of this club, he will be the manager of this club. I am sorry that Billy doesn't feel that he doesn't have the same power or whatever, but he certainly does as far as I'm concerned. His purview is that ball field. He's responsible for managing the ball club."[38]

As the month of May ended, the top of the American League East standings looked like this:

Team	Won	Lost	Percentage	Games Behind
Boston	34	16	.680	---
New York	29	17	.630	3
Detroit	26	20	.565	6
Milwaukee	23	22	.511	8½

The June 15 trading deadline was rapidly approaching. The Yankees set their sights on Minnesota's Rod Carew. The six-time batting champion was in the final year of his contract with the Twins. The right deal could possibly wrest away him from the Twins. Both the Royals and Rangers were also in on the bidding for Carew. However, the Yankees had Chris Chambliss and Jim Spencer at first base, and one could be moved. Any deal for Carew coming to the Bronx would almost certainly involve Chambliss. If Carew were dealt to the Yankees, it would be a homecoming of sorts. Carew attended George Washington High School in upper Manhattan after emigrating from Panama with his mother in 1962.

In the end, the Twins were not buying what the Yankees were peddling, which included Spencer, Tidrow, a couple of minor league players, and $400,000. "We elected not to pursue Carew but to go along with our ballclub," said Rosen. "We've got good young ballplayers and we want to follow through on the program we began three years ago."[39]

115

Steinbrenner was a little more direct in his comment. "No way. We are not going to trade Chambliss for anyone."[40]

In spite of not acquiring Carew, the Yankees still made plenty of moves as the trading deadline neared. They dealt Holtzman to the Chicago Cubs on June 10 for a player to be named later. Martin despised Holtzman, and it showed in the few appearances he made. Martin did not think Holtzman had the ability to remain a starting pitcher, and he wanted to use Holtzman in long relief. Holtzman either could not or would not be used in that fashion. In the Yankees; first 48 games, Holtzman appeared in five games, three as a starter. When Gullett was activated on June 3, Holtzman was placed on the 21-day disabled list with a strained back.

On June 12, the Yankees received pitcher Ron Davis to complete the deal for Holtzman.

Second baseman Willie Randolph injured his right knee in a game against Oakland on June 13. He sat out for a few games and then tried to return. But the knee was not cooperating, and Randolph was placed on the DL. It was not known how long he would be absent from the Yankees' lineup. Damaso Garcia and Brian Doyle filled in at second base.

New York then shipped Eastwick to Philadelphia on June 14. Outfielders Jay Johnstone and Bobby Brown were headed New York's way. As with Holtzman, Martin did not care for Eastwick's abilities and showed it by not using him. Eastwick pitched out of the bullpen in eight games. Martin did not warm to him, saying that Steinbrenner signed Eastwick and Messersmith without consulting him. Eastwick and Messersmith were referred to as "George's Boys" by Martin.[41] "The computer never played baseball and neither did the guy who uses it," said Martin about Steinbrenner.[42]

The last move the Yankees made ahead of the trade deadline occurred on June 15, 1978, when they traded two prospects, outfielder Dell Alston and infielder Mickey Klutts, to Oakland for outfielder Gary Thomasson.

On June 17, Guidry threw a four-hit shutout against California. He established a new club record with 18 strikeouts, raising his record to 11–0. Nolan Ryan, who shared the strikeout record of 19 with Steve Carlton and Tom Seaver, watched the game from the Angels dugout. "The kid was overpowering," said Ryan. "Anytime somebody can break that record, I'm all for it. It's just a matter of time. It's going to happen."[43]

The results were not so great on June 21 at Fenway Park. The

Yankees and Red Sox squared off in a three-game series for the first time in the season. After splitting the first two games, the Red Sox were hammering their guests by a 7–2 score heading to the bottom of the eighth inning. Hunter came in to pitch an inning of mop-up and gave up two solo home runs. The treatment he received on his right shoulder did not improve his performance on the field, and he was returned to the disabled list.

After the Boston series, the Yankees dropped to fourth place in the division, eight games behind the front-running Red Sox. The rumors were rampant: Billy Martin was on his way out as manager. Martin had led the Yankees to two consecutive AL pennants. He spoke up:

> I'm sick and tired of hearing about being fired. I give George Steinbrenner 100 percent loyalty and I expect it in return. If he doesn't think I'm doing the job right, he should call Al Rosen and tell him to do something. I'm giving him my best and I'll continue to give him my best. There are managers all over baseball who have never won, and you never hear about them being close to being fired.[44]

One of the problems with Martin centered around his pitching coach, Art Fowler. The two had been together since Martin's first managing position in Minnesota in 1969 (except for 1976). The Yankees brass was not happy with the pitching staff in general, but specifically the development of the club's younger pitchers. Rosen suggested that Fowler go to the minors to work with the young arms down on the farm.[45] Of course, Martin balked at that strategy. Fowler served as a friend and confidante to Martin. The Yankee manager considered Fowler to be the best pitching coach in the big leagues. "If they had told me in spring training that these guys were going to come up with sore arms, I would have traded them for healthy arms. You think if Hunter and Gullett and Messersmith were healthy, they'd have won more than eight games?"[46]

But Rosen was succinct in his appraisal of Martin and his future as manager with the Yankees. "Billy, being a professional manager, knows what happens to managers who are supposed to win [and] don't win," said Rosen. "We're seven games back in the loss column. That's nothing more than a week. But we can't afford to let things get worse. We can't afford to be 12 or 13 games back. You can't let disaster strike you when you're already on the ropes."[47]

Steinbrenner, Rosen, and Martin had a clearing-of-the-air meeting to discuss their issues with the team and each other. Steinbrenner and

Martin, who had had this type of meeting in the past, both felt that the recent meeting had been a productive one. Steinbrenner assured Martin in writing that he would be the manager until the end of the year. Also, Fowler would be retained as the pitching coach. Martin had to agree to let Clyde King assist with the pitchers. Martin also had to pledge his loyalty to his superiors.[48]

The Yankees posted a 14–15 record in June. The month of July did not start off any better. A 3–6 record was punctuated by a three-game sweep at the hands of the Brewers at County Stadium. Even Guidry finally lost a game. "Gator," as he was known by his teammates, lost his first game of the year on July 7. His record on the year stood at 13–1. Gullett pitched his last game on July 9. In two-thirds of an inning, the left-hander gave up four earned runs and walked four. He had surgery to repair a double tear of his rotator cuff at the end of the season, and he never pitched again in the majors.

Just as Randolph and Hunter were getting ready to come off the disabled list, Dent went on the DL with a pulled right hamstring on July 9.

As the league took a break for the July 11 All-Star Game in San Diego, the standings in the top of the AL East stacked up this way:

Team	Won	Lost	Percentage	Games Behind
Boston	57	26	.687	---
Milwaukee	48	35	.578	9
New York	46	38	.548	11½
Baltimore	45	40	.529	13

Seemingly, Boston was pulling away from its division foes with ease. Although the season had nearly half a season to go, the Red Sox were in as comfortable position as a team could be.

If the current standings were to act an incentive for the Yankees to play better ball, they would need another source. The started the second half splitting a two-game series with the White Sox before Kansas City came to Yankee Stadium and swept the Bombers in three straight games.

Nettles was asked what he thought the Yankees chances were at the break. "Our slogan is 'None for all and all for none.' Our only chance is a miracle."[49]

A musical chairs scenario of sorts took place in the Bronx. Munson moved to right field to save wear and tear on his ailing legs. Heath took over at catcher. Thomasson replaced Roy White in left field, and Jackson would DH against right-handed pitchers. The moves were allegedly made by Steinbrenner, and those were not the only ones he thought about making. "I want Cedric to be down there," said Steinbrenner. "I don't want Al bogged down in every detail."[50] Reportedly, Steinbrenner had been disappointed in Rosen for not acquiring a front-line pitcher at the trade deadline. Although Steinbrenner was not willing to part with Chambliss, he was miffed at Rosen's inability to obtain Carew.[51] The fact that Carew hit two triples in the All-Star Game emphasized what a great hitter he was. But the truth was that Rosen did not have the freedom to make trades on his own. Every potential deal had to be cleared by Steinbrenner.[52]

Jackson seethed about his diminished role as a sometimes-DH. It came to a head on July 17, 1978. The Yankees and Royals were tied at five runs apiece as the Yankees came to bat in the bottom of the tenth inning. Munson led off with a single to center field. Jackson stepped into the batter's box, and third base coach Dick Howser flashed him the bunt sign. Royals reliever Al Hrabosky fired one just past Jackson's head. Martin took off the bunt sign because the Royals' infield was now playing in. Jackson defied the sign given by Howser and tried to lay down a bunt, but he was unsuccessful. Howser strolled down the third base line to confer with Jackson, telling him the bunt sign was off. Jackson told Howser he was going to lay down a bunt. And that is what Jackson did. His last attempt was popped up and settled in the glove of Royals catcher Darrell Porter for the inning's first out.

Yankees management served Jackson with a five-day, four-game suspension for defying the manager's orders. Jackson, always the innocent victim, fired back.

> I tried to get a runner over and it looks like I'm defiant. I was trying to move the guy over. Does that make me a bad guy? I figured if I could get the man in scoring position with Lou Piniella coming up, we'd have a pretty good chance of winning the game. If I strike out or pop up, that's not helping us. How can they say I'm a threat to swing the bat? I'm not an everyday player. I'm a part-time player.[53]

"I'm the manager," said Martin. "I don't talk about it. If he comes back again, he does exactly as I say. Period. I'm not getting paid $3 million. I don't disobey my boss' orders. He tells me to do something, I do it. There isn't going to be anyone who defies the manager or management in any way. Nobody's bigger than this team."[54]

Steinbrenner, Rosen, and Tallis all agreed on the suspension for

Jackson. Steinbrenner also acknowledged that there had to be discipline across the board, no matter what the player's status. For Steinbrenner, this may have been especially tough to go along with because he and Jackson were tight friends. Earlier that month, Steinbrenner celebrated his birthday, and Jackson was the only player invited to the bash. Of course, he attended. "I don't know if these people know any of the players other than Reggie," said Rosen, who was said to be livid that Jackson showed up at the party. "He lives in Manhattan; most of the others live in New Jersey. He's associated with them in business. I've seen him at lunch with them at '21.'"[55]

The Yankees won two games in Minnesota without Jackson. They also won the first two of a three-game series in Chicago. Jackson joined the team at Comiskey Park for the last game of the series. Before the game, Jackson told reporters that he felt no remorse over his decision to bunt when he was told to hit away. The slugger did acknowledge that if he had known what the consequences would be, he would have swung away as ordered.

Martin did not insert Jackson in the starting lineup. Martin wanted to use the same lineup that had won the last four games. New York completed the sweep over the White Sox with a 3–1 victory. The Yankees' string of five wins in a row, coupled with four straight losses by Boston, shrank the Yankees' deficit to 10 games.

As the team waited at O'Hare Airport for its plane to Kansas City, Martin was drinking at one of the airport bars with Murray Chass, the team's beat writer from the *New York Times*. Martin had been drinking on the team bus on the way to the airport, and by the time he reached the airport bar, Martin went into a drunken tirade about Jackson.

"I'm saying shut up, Reggie Jackson," said Martin about Jackson's 35-minute pregame interview. "We don't need none of your stuff. We're winning without you. We don't need you coming in and making all these comments. If he doesn't shut his mouth, he won't play, and I don't care what George says. He can replace me right now if he doesn't like it."[56]

Chass was writing at a feverish pace to get it all down, and he assured Martin that the story would be in the *Times* the next day.[57]

Then came the fatal words that Billy Martin became famous for: "The two of them deserve each other," said Martin. "One's a born liar, the other is convicted."[58] Martin was referring to Steinbrenner being convicted for making illegal campaign contributions to Richard Nixon's presidential campaign in 1972. In addition, there was an obstruction of justice charge tacked on against Steinbrenner. He was subsequently pardoned by President Reagan in 1989.[59]

"In view of the events of the past 24 hours," said Rosen, "it was inevitable that as president of the New York Yankees I could not allow a man to make the statements that were made."[60]

Steinbrenner issued a terse "no comment" when reporters asked him for a response to Martin's tirade. But he dispatched Rosen to Kansas City to fire Martin. Tallis had been traveling with the team, and Rosen went to the Crown Center Hotel to meet Martin. Mickey Morabito, the Yankees' P.R. man, was also there. But Martin resigned instead of giving Rosen the pleasure of pulling the plug. Martin was shaking and crying as he read a statement that seemed to contain more lies than Jackson might have ever told. Martin told the press he was resigning for health reasons and his mental state of being. Martin went on to say that he did not say the awful things that were written about Steinbrenner and that the comments about Steinbrenner were not deserved.

Rosen told the gathering that Howser would take over as manager in the interim. But then he placed a call to his old friend Bob Lemon to offer him the Yankees manager job. "The conversation took all of five minutes," said Rosen. "I told him I needed him and he said: 'Where do you want me to be, Meat [Lemon's term of affection for all his friends]?' He never asked me why I needed him or how much he was going to get paid. He just said he'd be on the next plane to Kansas City."[61]

"You kept me out of the Hall of Fame for years because of all the balls you booted behind me and now I have to work for you?" Lemon asked Rosen.[62] Lemon was elected to the National Baseball Hall of Fame in 1976.

Lemon had been the Yankees' pitching coach in 1976 under Martin. He left after one year to become manager of the Chicago White Sox in 1977.

Chicago finished in third place of the AL West in 1977 with a 90–72 record. The club was given the nickname "South Side Hitmen" for their offensive prowess. Big things were expected on the South Side for 1978. But the Sox got out of the gate slowly, posting a 17–28 record through the end of May. Chicago won 12 of 14 games to begin June, but they were still one game under .500. On June 15, the White Sox were 29–30 and in fifth place in the division. They were still in the race, trailing division-leader Kansas City by only 2½ games.

The winning ways did not continue, and the White Sox ended the month with a record of 34–40, 5½ games out of first place. Team owner Bill Veeck made a managerial move on June 30, replacing Lemon with Larry Doby. The selection of Doby, who served as a coach on Lemon's staff, made him the second black manager in major league history. "I have known this man [Lemon] since I first came up to the Cleveland Indians in 1947," said Doby. "Only I will ever be able to know the real problems I faced [as a black man] at that time. I really needed a friend then, and Lemon was it. You don't mind replacing a guy if he was a jerk. But Lemon is my friend, a good friend. And that's why it still hurts deep inside."[63]

"They [the White Sox] just wanted to make a change," said Lemon. "I enjoyed Chicago. We just didn't have a good start this year."[64]

"Billy's a [fan] favorite," Lemon said of Martin, "and he's a tough act to follow. He's been successful. I always considered him my friend. I enjoyed working for him, we had a good year, we barnstormed together, we went to Japan together. I have a high regard for Billy, and I imagine the fans do, too. I imagine there will be some negative reaction."[65]

Old-Timers' Day was scheduled at Yankee Stadium on July 29, 1978. It would be one to remember for a long time. After Martin resigned, Steinbrenner did not feel right about the situation and wanted Martin to return as manager of the Yankees. But he had promised Lemon the manager position for the rest of 1978 and 1979. Martin's agent, Doug Newton, came up with the idea of bringing Martin back on Old-Timer's Day, when the Stadium would be filled with 50,000 Yankees fans.[66] The announcement was kept under wraps. Surprisingly, word did not leak out before the big day.

As Rosen and Lemon stood on the third base line in their Indians uniforms, Yankees greats from decades past were being summoned to the first base line by Yankees broadcaster Frank Messer: Rizzuto, Maris, Berra, Mantle, Ford, and DiMaggio. The microphone was handed over to public address announcer Bob Sheppard:

"May I please have your attention, please, ladies and gentlemen," said Sheppard. "Bob Lemon will be managing the Yankees for the rest of this season and for 1979. In 1980 he will become General Manager." Naturally, a chorus of loud boos reverberated throughout the ballpark. "In 1980, and hopefully for many years to come," continued Sheppard, "the Yankees will again be managed by Number One, Billy Martin!"[67]

The crowd erupted as Martin ran out on to the field, showering him with a loud ovation that lasted seven minutes.

Neither Rosen nor Lemon had been made aware of the plan

hatched by Steinbrenner and Newton. Rosen was incensed. Steinbrenner explained to Rosen that he didn't feel right about how it ended with Martin, and that he had to keep it a secret. "George, what you've done to me, and, more importantly, to Lem, is just unconscionable," said Rosen. "The poor man was booed out there! We've just got everything calmed down around here and you pull a stunt like this! I know why you didn't want to tell me: You knew how I'd react. Well, you're right, George. This is bullshit."[68]

Rosen was not the only person who was upset. It was customary for Joe DiMaggio to be the last player announced. It was a sign of respect. But DiMaggio felt he was upstaged by Martin, and he left the ballpark right after the Old-Timers festivities. Jackson watched the scene unfold on TV from the clubhouse. For once, Jackson sat speechless. Martin called his boss a criminal, and five days later he was rehired. "This means I'm gone," said Jackson. "This means they have to get rid of me, doesn't it?"[69] Bucky Dent was a little more definitive in his response to Martin's probable return: "They better trade me because I ain't playing for him."[70]

"You'd need a psychiatrist to try and figure out George's relationship with Billy," said Rosen. "George always felt Billy was like a wayward son."[71]

"Most kids look forward to being a ballplayer or a member of a circus when they grow up," said Nettles. "Me, I'm lucky. I got both."[72]

Boston came to town and beat New York in consecutive games on August 2 and 3. The August 2 game went 17 innings and had to be completed the next day. But the Bombers rebounded. From August 5–31, the Yankees posted a record of 18–5. Two reasons for the Yankees' successful August were two starters: Catfish Hunter (6–0, 1.64 ERA) and Ron Guidry (4–1, 1.34 ERA). Hunter, who was on the DL more than he had pitched in 1978, was especially inspiring because of all he went through with injuries and the two trips to the disabled list. Three of his victories were complete games, with one shutout.

The standings in the American League East looked like this with one month to go.

Team	Won	Lost	Percentage	Games Behind
Boston	84	48	.636	---
New York	77	54	.588	6½
Milwaukee	76	57	.571	8½
Detroit	73	59	.553	11

But there was a non-baseball story brewing in New York City. On August 9, 1978, a pressmen's strike shut down the three major newspapers: *New York Times*, *New York Post*, and *New York Daily News*. Pressmen, who operate and maintain printing press machines, were striking because of impending job cuts. The three daily newspapers had a combined circulation of 3.3 million subscribers. The newspapers employed 10,000 people who were covered by 11 unions. All 11 of the unions walked off the job in support of the pressmen.[73]

The strike lasted the rest of the season and a total of 88 days into November. With no reporters hanging around the club, combined with Lemon's easy-going personality, there was a sense of calm in the Yankees clubhouse.[74]

The Yankees' deficit of 6½ games, although not a large one, might be settled one way or the other in early September. The Yankees had a four-game series against the Red Sox at Fenway Park beginning September 7. It became imperative that the Yankees, at a minimum, take three games in the series.

New York did better than that. They swept Boston, outscoring the Red Sox, 42–9, in the series. New York and Boston were now deadlocked with identical 86–56 records.

Guidry shut out the Red Sox in the third game, 7–0 to raise his record to 21–2. Figueroa won his fourth game in a row to raise his record to 16–9. Piniella was the hitting hero in the series for the Yankees. "Sweet Lou" batted .625 (10-for-16) with eight runs and five RBI. Randolph also enjoyed a good offensive series, batting .500 (8-for-16) with six RBI.

"No one's going to help, not our wives, not the man in the candy store," said Red Sox first baseman George Scott. "It has to be done by the 25 players, the manager, the coaches. We have to do it ourselves. We have to loosen up and go along and try to have a little fun over the next 20 games."[75]

Boston manager Don Zimmer simplified the outcome of the series in a single sentence. "We took a shellacking," said the skipper.[76]

The following week, Boston headed to the Bronx to take on the Yankees in a three-game series. But before the first game on September 15, Rosen attended a meeting at the office of the American League President, Lee MacPhail. There, with Boston General Manager Lou Gorman, a coin flip would determine the home field advantage for a one-game playoff in the event there was a tie between the two teams at the end of the season. Rosen called heads, and naturally the coin showed tails. When Rosen returned to the office, he phoned Steinbrenner with the news. Steinbrenner wanted to know what Rosen called. When Rosen informed him that he chose heads, Steinbrenner erupted. "Heads? You fucking imbecile! How in the hell could you call heads when any dummy knows that tails comes up 70 percent of the time? I can't believe it! I got the dumbest fucking people in baseball working for me!"[77]Then Steinbrenner hung up the phone.

The Yankees won the first two games of the series. Guidry shut out the Red Sox again, winning the opener, 4–0, for his 22nd win. Hunter pitched a complete-game victory in the second game to raise his record to 10–5. Eckersley won the finale to salvage one win for Boston.

The two teams were done with their season series. New York had the slight edge, winning eight of 15 games. The Yankees were now 2½ games up on Boston, with 14 games left on the docket. The Yankees split a two-game set against Milwaukee. Then they hit the road for the final trip of the season. But they made it hard on themselves, going 3–3 against Toronto and Cleveland, clubs at the bottom of the AL East.

With only seven games left in the season, New York held a slim one-game advantage over Boston. Both teams won their first five games of the final week, setting up the final day of the season. Boston was home to Toronto, while New York was hosting Cleveland. Hunter was opposing the Tribe's Rick Waits. Given the resurgence of Hunter, it seemed like it was a mismatch in the Yankees' favor.

The Tribe pounced on Catfish Hunter, knocking him out of the game after 1⅔ innings. The visitors jumped out to a 6–2 lead and never looked back. "The Waiter," as Waits was referred to, served up a 9–2 win.

The scoreboard flashed the score from the Bronx to the crowd at Fenway: "CLV 9 NY 2 Thank you Rick Waits," much to the delight of the Red Sox fans. They were minutes away from tying their rivals as Luis Tiant was working on a two-hit, 5–0 shutout of the Blue Jays.

> *New York and Boston finished tied*
> *In baseball's roller coaster ride*
> *They played one-hundred-sixty-two*
> *And even that was one too few* [78]

On October 2, 1978, the Red Sox and the Yankees played only the second tiebreaker game in American League history. The Red Sox hosted the first on October 4, 1948, at Fenway Park as well but lost to

Cleveland, 8–3, for the AL pennant. They were hoping for a better result the second time around.

October 2 was also Yom Kippur. Rosen fought a mental battle as to whether attend the game or to observe the Jewish holiday.

> I wrestled with myself about that. It had been a very difficult year. I decided to go to the game. Obviously, I am going to be in the box right next to the dugout. Strange, I only got one comment. A fellow wrote me a letter castigating me for being at the game on the highest Jewish holiday. I wrote him back, "Please accept my apology if I offended you, but I have to wonder how you knew I was at the game if you weren't watching it on television. And if you're watching it on television, don't you think you should have been in temple?"[79]

The game is another chapter in the rivalry between the Yankees and Red Sox and is forever remembered for Bucky Dent's three-run homer in the top of the seventh inning that gave the Yankees a 3–2 lead. "Al called Bucky's home run just before he hit it," said Steinbrenner. "'He's gonna hit one out,' and sure enough he did. It couldn't happen to a finer young man."[80]

The game headed to the bottom of the ninth, with the Yankees clinging to a 5–4 lead. Gossage had come on in the eighth inning, and now was looking to close the door. With one away, Gossage walked Rick Burleson. Up to the plate stepped Jerry Remy. The left-handed batter lined a ball to Piniella in right field.

"I saw the ball leave the bat and that was the last time I saw it," said Piniella. "I knew if the ball got by me, the runner would go to third or maybe score the tying run. I couldn't allow Burleson to see that I lost it in the sun. I kept my composure as I searched for the ball, I kept backtracking as hard as I could. I wanted to give myself more room to find it. Out of the corner of my eye, I saw that damn ball landing a few feet to my left on the grass."[81]

Piniella pounded his glove, like he had a beat on the baseball. When the ball fell a few feet away, Piniella scooped it up and threw a strike to Nettles at third base, freezing Burleson at second base. Jim Rice was the next batter, and he flied out to Piniella for the second out. Carl Yastrzemski popped to third base to end the game.

"It was one of the all-time great plays," said Rosen of Piniella's play on Remy's hit. "Without that play, the game is over. It was just an unbelievably adept play. You could see he fought the sun all the way. I played in that park, and a lot of balls were misplayed. The whole thing happened so rapidly, but it was only because of Lou's character and determination that he made the play."[82]

Guidry (25–3, 1.74 ERA) won the AL Cy Young Award in 1978. He was the fourth Yankees pitcher to be honored. Guidry led the league in wins and ERA and was second in strikeouts (248) to Nolan Ryan (260). Gossage was the league leader in saves with 27. Figueroa (20–9, 2.99 ERA) was the first pitcher from his native Puerto Rico to win 20 games in a season.

Nettles (27 home runs, 93 RBI, and a .276 batting average) and Jackson (27 HR, 97 RBI, and a .274 batting average) had parallel offensive seasons. Chambliss added 12 home runs and 90 RBI.

For the third straight year, New York faced the Kansas City Royals in the ALCS. In 1976 and 1977, the series went the five-game limit. Guidry had started the tie-breaker game in Boston, so his next start would not be until Game Four of the LCS. With the Yankees leading the series 2–1, Guidry picked up right where he left off as he scattered seven hits and held the Royals to one run. Nettles and White both homered and the Yankees won, 2–1. The Yankees were headed to the World Series for the third straight year.

The Los Angeles Dodgers were the NL champions and the Yankees' opponent in the 1978 World Series. Like the Royals, the Dodgers were hoping for history not to repeat itself. The Series opened at Dodger Stadium, and behind Tommy John in Game One and Burt Hooton in Game Two, the Dodgers jumped out to a 2–0 Series lead.

The series shifted to Yankee Stadium, and Guidry again righted the ship, pitching the Yankees to a 5–1 victory in Game Three. Five different players drove in a run for the Yankees. In Game Four, Piniella's single in the bottom of the tenth inning scored White with the winning run, and now the Series was tied. Rookie Jim Beattie beat Hooton in Game Five as Munson drove in five runs and White drove in three more in the 12–2 Yankees spanking of the Dodgers.

The Series shifted back to Los Angeles, but the Yankees were in control. Jackson hit his second home run and Dent had three hits and knocked in three runs to lead the offense. Hunter pitched a strong seven innings as the Yankees wrapped up the World Championship with a 7–2 win. It was the 22nd time the Yankees franchise was crowned world champions. Dent batted .417 (10-for-24) and drove in seven runs in the Series, and he was voted Most Valuable Player.

"If a Hollywood script writer were to try to sell the story of the year," said Lemon, "no one would buy it. It is right there with the Hall of Fame as my most gratifying experience."[83]

Unfortunately, the euphoria did not last long. On October 27, 1978, Lemon's son, Jerry, was in one-car crash on Interstate 10 near Phoenix. He was on his way to visit his brother Jim, who was a baseball coach at Estrella Junior High School. Investigators determined that the car Jerry Lemon was driving was traveling at a high rate of speed. Jerry tried to gain control of the car, causing it to overturn several times. He was ejected from the vehicle. The cause of death was determined to be massive head injuries.[84]

"Losing Jerry," said Lemon, "makes you think if baseball had a drawback, it can only be that you didn't spend enough time with your kids. All of a sudden, you look up and your kids are men. If they turned out to be good men, it's because they were raised that way. I take no credit for it. I give that to their mother. Baseball wives never get the credit they deserve."[85]

The Yankees turned their attention to the 1979 season. They wasted little time in reshaping their pitching staff. Messersmith was waived on November 6, 1978. On November 10, the Yankees and the Rangers made a ten-player deal. The main components were Lyle and Heath going to Arlington and outfielder Juan Beniquez and pitcher Paul Mirabella coming to New York. One of the prospects the Yankees wanted in the deal was Dave Righetti. The Rangers added him to the pot, and although nobody may have realized it at the time, it was probably the best trade Rosen made while he was president of the Yankees. Righetti had a long and productive career with the Yankees, first as a starter, then in the bullpen.

New York signed two veteran starters to help solidify the rotation. On November 13, 1978, they signed Luis Tiant. The right-handed pitcher from Cuba would turn 38 years old on November 23. Tiant had won double-digit games every season since 1972. He went 13–8 with a 3.31 ERA in 1978 with Boston. The two-year, $200,000 deal included 10 more years as a scout. "Sounds like a State Dept. post, doesn't it," said his agent, Paul George.[86]

"We saw a great opportunity to utilize a man who is as well known in Central and Latin America as any man who has played in the majors," said Rosen. "There is an awful lot of talent in those countries and Luis will help us get some of it."[87]

Eight days after signing Tiant, the Yankees added left-hander

Tommy John to their staff. The 35-year-old former Dodger had a record of 17–10 with a 3.30 ERA in 1978.

"Having been beaten by the Yankees two years in a row," said John, "I like playing for a winner. When you look at the Yankee infield, you're talking about the best in baseball. That makes Tommy John a better pitcher. When you're throwing 19 or 20 ground balls a game, you need guys shagging them down. My infielders get a lot of work."[88]

The Yankees brass traveled to Orlando for the annual winter meetings. However, after signing Tiant and John, the Yankees were not expecting to make a major move.

"We'll always be looking," said Rosen, "but we'll be dealing in little pieces. We're not in conversations with anyone for anything big. There's a lot of interest in Juan Beniquez, whom we just got from Texas. And as I said the other day, everybody was asking if it was true that we're making a deal with Minnesota: Beniquez and Chris Chambliss for Carew. We're not."[89]

Carew attracted the most interest at the winter meetings, or at least from the clubs who could afford his salary. He notched his seventh batting title in 1978 and would be a key asset, although an expensive one, to any club. Rosen appreciated Carew's talent, but the Yankees president also knew he had a solid first baseman in Chambliss who was already locked in for 1979.

"You might be surprised if you check a four-year comparison between Carew and Chambliss," said Rosen. "The only category Carew has a large edge is stolen bases. And batting average of course. But Chambliss does not have as many errors and beats him in home runs and doubles, not in triples and Chris strikes out more. But the comparison is not what you might think."[90]

Despite Rosen's attempts to prop up Chambliss, the Yankees were very much involved in the Rod Carew sweepstakes. After Carew declined an offer from the San Francisco Giants, it was down to the Angels and the Yankees as to who would secure the seven-time batting champion. Because the Angels started to negotiate a contract with Carew before a trade was made, Commissioner Bowie Kuhn ruled that a trade must be made before teams could negotiate a contract with Carew.

"We take exception to the commissioner's edict," said Rosen. "I don't know [if] it's aimed at the Yankees, per se, but it's to the detriment of 22 other clubs. For reasons I don't know, the commissioner has changed horses in midstream. It's one upmanship for the California ballclub. It gives them the edge. They worked out an agreement with Carew. Now all they have to do is give the Twins the player they want."[91]

Whether Kuhn's ruling had any impact or nor, Carew was dealt to California on February 3, 1979.

New York began the 1979 season on the road with stops in Milwaukee, Baltimore, and Chicago. The Yankees came out of the trip with a 5–4 record before their home opener against the Orioles on April 17.

On April 19, after the finale against Baltimore, Cliff Johnson and Goose Gossage got into an altercation in the clubhouse/shower room. What began as harmless needling gave way to shoving and punches. The result was Gossage tearing the ulnar collateral ligament in his right thumb when he shoved Johnson, and he would be out for six to eight weeks.[92]

New York ended April and began May on their first trip out west. The results were disastrous, posting a 2–6 record which included being swept in three games by Seattle at the Kingdome. In two games against the Mariners, the bullpen gave up late-inning runs, losing each game by one run. The loss of Gossage, who led the AL in saves in 1978 with 27, would be hard to overcome.

On May 11, the Yankees purchased southpaw Jim Kaat from Philadelphia. The 40-year-old hurler was acquired to help shore up the bullpen. Guidry, in an act of unselfishness and being a good teammate, volunteered to go to the bullpen. "The team comes first," said Guidry. "There's nothing else on my mind. I'm grateful I had one good year."[93] Guidry, the 1978 AL Cy Young Award winner, demonstrated what a leader should be. "Last year, they helped me win the Cy Young Award," said Guidry. "This year maybe it's me who owes them something."[94]

Dick Tidrow was thrust into Gossage's spot as the closer. But he had little success. On May 23, the Yankees traded Tidrow to the Chicago Cubs for pitcher Ray Burris. Paul Mirabella was also given an opportunity as the closer. But he did not fare well in nine games pitched (0–3, 7.24 ERA) and New York optioned him to AAA Columbus.

As May ended, the Yankees were treading slightly over .500, and they were in the middle of the pack in the AL East.

Team	Won	Lost	Percentage	Games Behind
Baltimore	30	18	.625	---
Boston	27	19	.587	2
Milwaukee	28	23	.549	3½
New York	26	23	.531	4½

One of the bright spots for the Yankees was Tommy John. The new acquisition was 9–1 with a 1.79 ERA. John had won his first nine games, losing for the first time at Cleveland on May 26.

The Yankees were 7–7 to start June when Steinbrenner decided to make a move and replace Lemon. Steinbrenner believed that Lemon's heart was not with the club since the death of his son. He also thought that the team had stopped playing for him.[95] He told Rosen on June 15, 1979, that he wanted to make the move and bring back Martin. Rosen knew that Lemon not having Gossage at his disposal was a big reason for the Yankees' losses.[96]

The Yankees were still looking for help and shipped Cliff Johnson to Cleveland for pitcher Don Hood on June 15. They also traded outfielder Jay Johnstone to San Diego for pitcher Dave Wehrmeister.

On June 18, the Yankees made the announcement about replacing Lemon with Martin.

"I think if it can be turned around, he's the guy to do it," said Steinbrenner of Martin. "Last year, I needed someone 180 degrees from what Billy was. This year I need someone who is 180 degrees from what Bob Lemon was. I don't know if it's too late, but I think we can make a run. You have to bury those other things when you're in the position we're in."[97]

Lemon was diplomatic about his dismissal. To his credit, he didn't point fingers or make a big scene. "I might have felt differently if I was 10 games in front," said Lemon. "I know it isn't anything against me. It's just something to get the club going. I think possibly what happened last winter put things in a different perspective for me. I found out there were a lot more important things in the world, in your life."[98]

Reggie Jackson had been out of the lineup since June 2, when he tore a tendon in the calf muscle of his left leg. Jackson was jogging off the field after the top of the ninth inning at Comiskey Park when the injury occurred. After the news broke of Martin's return as manager, Jackson was still unable to play. There were some who questioned if the reason Jackson was not playing was Martin's return or the lingering calf injury. "He is under contract with the New York Yankees and he will play for the New York Yankees and he will do it willingly," said Rosen. "This isn't the first time a player doesn't get along with a manager."[99]

Trading Jackson at this point in the season may not have yielded much value in return. As Rosen said, Jackson was going nowhere. "It sounds like they think I am faking it, and I don't appreciate it," said Jackson.[100]

On June 26, the Yankees traded minor league pitcher Paul Semall to the Chicago Cubs for outfielder Bobby Murcer. It was a return to the Bronx for Murcer, who was a member of the Yankees from 1965--1974. "I feel like a new man," said Murcer. "I've never been more happy in my life. New York is where I feel I belong. It's like coming home again."[101]

Martin wanted to add Murcer, a left-handed batter, to the lineup as a possible replacement for Jackson while he was injured. Rosen didn't want to make the deal and take on Murcer's $320,000 contract. "Much as I was opposed to getting Murcer on principle—I didn't like Billy's motives and I didn't see how he was going to help us—George didn't care about the money and saw it as a popular move with the fans," said Rosen.[102]

Martin had more pull with Steinbrenner than Rosen, and it became a power struggle between the two. The matter came to a head on July 12, 1979. The Yankees were in Seattle when Martin learned that the Yankees' game the next day in Anaheim would start at 5:30 p.m. local time to accommodate ABC. Martin exploded at the news of the time change, mostly because the Angels were starting Nolan Ryan, and Martin knew that Ryan throwing in the twilight would be hard for the Yankees batters. Martin phoned Steinbrenner, complaining about Rosen. "How am I supposed to get this team back in the race when the team president was making decisions like this?"[103] As it turned out, Martin's instincts about Ryan were correct. He carried a no-hitter into the ninth inning in the Angels' 6–1 victory.

Steinbrenner tried to get the game switched back to the original start time. He threatened to instruct the Yankees to not take the field if it wasn't. Both Lee MacPhail and Bowie Kuhn told him the start time was settled months prior. Rosen had indeed made the decision, but he had also sent a memo and a copy of the TV schedule to Steinbrenner months ago.[104] Steinbrenner relented and mentioned to MacPhail and Kuhn that his people had lied to him and he needed to look into the matter.[105]

Rosen heard Steinbrenner's accusation, and he resigned his position as president of the New York Yankees. Nobody called Al Rosen a liar. Although Steinbrenner pleaded with Rosen to stay and threw some money at him, Rosen refused and resigned from the New York Yankees. He grew weary of Steinbrenner's irrational outbursts and saw nothing but stormy waters ahead if Martin stayed on as manager.

Rosen resigned as president of the New York Yankees on July 19, 1979. "I am deeply indebted to George Steinbrenner for giving me the opportunity of becoming the president of the New York Yankees," said Rosen. "I have enjoyed my relationship with the Yankees more than I can ever say. I am resigning to explore other business opportunities that have been offered me. Contrary to speculation, I have not, nor will I, accept any of those business opportunities in the near future."[106]

The players were quiet about Rosen's departure except for Jackson, who took the opportunity to rip Steinbrenner. "The guy was a good guy and he was tired of taking all that crap from George Steinbrenner," said Jackson. "Somebody's got to stand up and say it. You don't put numbers on the board like he [Rosen] did and be a pussycat. It's between Rosen and Steinbrenner. There's not a damn thing he [Rosen] can do for me as a professional because I talk too much."[107]

Dave Anderson of the *New York Times* applauded Rosen for his hiring of Lemon and the moves he made. Anderson wrote:

> Say this for Al Rosen—he left with dignity. Not a word about George Steinbrenner's tyrannical reign. Not a word about Billy Martin's power play. Typically, all of the Yankee players avoided comment on Al Rosen's departure—all except Reggie Jackson who seems to be trying to talk his way into being traded after the season in order to escape Billy Martin, despite their peaceful coexistence so far.[108]

It didn't take Rosen long to find work. He signed on with Bally's Park Place casino hotel as executive vice president. William S. Weinberger, who hired Rosen, was Rosen's boss when he was at Caesars Palace in Las Vegas before joining the Yankees. The $178 million hotel-casino was under construction on the boardwalk in Atlantic City.

Shortly after Rosen's departure, the New York Yankees may have suffered their biggest loss in franchise history. On August 2, 1979, Thurman Munson was practicing takeoffs and landings with a Cessna Citation airplane he had just purchased weeks before. The Yankees had an off-day as Munson, and two companions, were at the Akron-Canton Airport. Munson, who had flown mostly prop planes, was now flying a jet.

"I told him that he was jumping too fast from a prop plane to a jet, that a Cessna Citation was harder to fly than a Lear," said Steinbrenner. "I think he was only checked out in it for 10 days but he had nothing but problems with it. Somebody over at Teterboro told me he had problems with it and then Thurman told me he had to return it to Wichita to check out the problems."[109]

Munson was on his third practice run when the plane went into a sudden descent as it approached the runway. It hit the ground about 1,000 feet before the runway and skidded through a bunch of small trees. The plane began to catch fire and the right wing struck a tree, spinning the jet around. It came to a stop on a roadway outside the airfield. Loss of power was given as the initial cause of the crash. His two friends were able to escape the burning plane. Munson died in the cockpit.

At the time of the crash, the Yankees were in fourth place in the AL East with a 58–48 record, 14½ games behind front-running Baltimore. The loss of Munson on the diamond hurt the Yankees immeasurably. Losing a person just as invaluable to his teammates off the field was a tragedy. Thurman Munson's death resonated throughout the Yankees family, and among baseball fans everywhere.

The Yankees played a little better in the final two months of the season. But they were too far behind the Orioles to make a serious run. New York ended the season in fourth place with an 89–71 record, 13½ games off the pace.

Later that year, news broke that Denver oilman Marvin Davis had made an offer to purchase the Oakland A's and move them to Denver. Davis planned to hire Rosen and Tallis to run the organization. But Oakland owner Charlie Finley had eight years remaining on his stadium lease in Oakland. Like many stories, this one had more smoke than fire.

But it would not be long before Al Rosen received another opportunity to work for a major league team.

EIGHT

The Houston Mediocres

The August 7, 1980, edition of the *New York Daily News* ran a story that Al Rosen was headed back to baseball. The San Diego Padres were hiring Rosen to run their organization. *News* sportswriter Dick Young broke the story, which he had heard from a third party. He called Rosen for confirmation, and their conversation went like this, according to Young:

> "I hear you're going back to baseball," said Young.
> "Who told you that?" asked Rosen.
> "I can't tell you, Al," replied Young.
> "Of course. I shouldn't have asked. What club did you hear?"
> "San Diego."
> "Okay, you have it. I've had two talks with [Padres President] Ballard Smith. I think we understand each other. I would have complete control of the baseball operation."[1]

The article indicated that Rosen would suggest to the Padres that they hire Bob Lemon as their manager.

Reached in San Diego, Ballard Smith denied the validity of the entire story. Neither Rosen nor Lemon was being considered by the Padres for the GM job or the manager post. "No one has been offered either job, there's no basis for the story at all," said Smith. "In fact, I just had a call from Al saying he was embarrassed about the story, that it was untrue, that he had nothing to do with it."[2]

Rosen could not be blamed if he closed all the open doors that led back to an executive position in major league baseball. After how his tenure ended in New York, the old saying "once bitten, twice shy" may have come to his mind. But when the opportunity came about to leave Bally's Park Place Casino in Atlantic City to go to Houston to run the Astros, the baseball bug had bitten Rosen quite hard. "When I left the Yankees, it was with deep regrets," said Rosen. "But the time had come.

It was best for everyone concerned. Almost from the moment I left, though, my fervent desire was to get back into baseball. Anytime you've walked between those white lines, you never get it out of your system."[3]

In 1962, the National League expanded from a league of eight teams to a league of 10. The NL welcomed the New York Mets and the Houston Colt .45s into the fold. The year prior, the American League also grew by two teams. A new version of the Washington Senators (the original Senators moved to Minneapolis in 1961) and the Los Angeles Angels joined the junior circuit. Thus, major league baseball grew to 20 teams.

The first three seasons were as typical for the Colt 45s as for any other expansion team. They tussled with the Mets as cellar dwellers in the standings. On December 12, 1964, at the winter meetings, the Houston franchise announced that it was rebranding itself as the Houston Astros. Their new home would be the Astrodome, the first indoor, all-purpose stadium in the country. The new team insignia was circular, bore a replica of the domed stadium, and featured "Astros" in block letters underneath the dome.[4] "We feel the new insignia encompasses all aspects of the Houston baseball scene, the dome, the new nickname, baseball and the space age connotation," said club president and owner Roy Hofheinz. "We feel the insignia will be one the fans can be proud of."[5]

"The name and insignia will help dispel the image of Texas as a land of cowboys and indians and it behooves every citizen in this area to call to attention the twentieth-century aspects of Texas and Houston."[6]

The Astrodome, dubbed the "Eighth Wonder of the World," was the crown jewel in a developing complex called Astrodomain. Also part of the 260-acre compound were an amusement park called Astroworld, four hotels, the Astroarena and The Livestock Exposition Building, commonly known as Astrohall.[7]

The stadium, the team name, and the uniforms may have changed, but the Astros' losing tradition continued for years. After 10 losing seasons, the Astros completed their first winning season in 1972. Houston finished with a record of 84–69 as they finished second to Cincinnati in the NL West division

Tal Smith began his career as a baseball executive in 1958 with the Cincinnati Reds. Smith worked for Gabe Paul, then the Reds' general manager, and Paul served as a mentor for Smith while in Cincinnati. When Houston was awarded a major league franchise in the fall of 1960,

Paul was offered and accepted the GM job. Smith, the young protégé, went with him to Houston.

Paul's stay in Houston was a short one. Months after accepting his position with the Astros, he took a similar position with Cleveland in 1961. Smith was all set to join Paul. But Hofheinz interceded and offered Smith the job of being a liaison and project manager for the Houston Sports Association (HAS) during the construction of the Astrodome.[8] Although Smith's background had mostly been in player development, he accepted the offer made by Hofheinz and oversaw the construction of the Astrodome. Houston hired Paul Richards as the new general manager.

Richards lasted through the 1965 season. After the completion of the Astrodome, Tal Smith was named personnel director, and he also assumed some of the general manager duties. Astros manager Grady Hatton and business manager H. B. "Spec" Richardson also assumed some of the GM duties. Richardson was named the full-time GM on July 27, 1967. Smith served as the Astros' personal director from 1967–1972.[9]

Meanwhile, Hofheinz had assumed deep debt by 1975, owing creditors $38 million for the Astrodomain complex. The notes were held by three creditors: Ford Motor Credit Company, the General Electric Credit Company, and HNC Reality. The creditors assumed ownership of Astrodomain, the Astrodome, and the Astros pending payment of principal plus interest. Eventually, Ford singularly took ownership of the entire monopoly board known as Astrodomain. Astrodomain directors Sidney Shlenker and T. H. Neyland were chosen to oversee the day-to-day operations of the Astros and Astrodomain.

The official date when George Steinbrenner purchased the Yankees was December 29, 1972.[10] His ownership group of ten included Paul. This time Paul got his man, and Smith left the Astros to join Paul, this time in the Bronx, before the 1973 season. They worked together to rebuild the once-proud Yankees franchise. Smith was not around to see the final product, as he returned to Houston to take the reins of the Astros in August 1975.

Shlenker and Neyland now had control over the Astro company and voted 2–1 over Hofheinz in most important matters. For instance, the two directors voted to oust General Manager "Spec" Richardson, a Hofheinz loyalist. Shlenker and Neyland hand-picked Smith to become Houston's new GM.

"The Yankees are one of the outstanding organizations in sports and New York is an exciting city," said Smith. "But I believe basically that it is easy for anyone to understand that when you have been in baseball 18 years, you would like to run your own organization. That is why I am returning to Houston, a place we enjoyed when we were here before and to an organization that has an excellent future."[11]

When Smith took over the Astros on August 7, 1975, the club occupied last place in the NL West with a 40–75 record. They were 35½ games behind first-place Cincinnati. "To make the team into a contender is going to take a long time," said Smith, stating the obvious.[12]

Smith wasted no time getting to work. Bill Virdon was a star center fielder for the Pirates in the 1960s and managed the Pirates in 1972–1973. Smith and Virdon crossed paths when Virdon took over the helm of the Yankees in 1974. He was fired in 1975. Steinbrenner, no fan of Virdon, didn't think he brought enough flare to the Yankees. Although Virdon was a good tactical manager, "he didn't put asses in the seats," said Steinbrenner.[13]

Within three weeks of Virdon getting the heave-ho from the Bronx, Smith hired him to replace Preston Gomez as the Houston manager. Gomez skippered the Astros to an 81–81 record in 1974. In seven seasons managing in the big leagues, it was the only season a team managed by Gomez reached .500.

In 1975 the attendance at the Astrodome was the lowest (858,002) in the Astros' brief history.[14] To the average fan, the Astros may not have been a competitive club. But there were pieces that were in place in 1975 that would prove to be cornerstones to future success. Cesar Cedeno (center field) and José Cruz (right field) gave the Astros two veterans in the outfield who were both capable hitters. Enos Cabell came over from Baltimore in a multi-player deal in 1974. After playing most of his early career in the outfield and first base, Cabell settled in at third base in 1976. Like Cedeno and Cruz, Cabell was an excellent hitter. First baseman Bob Watson batted cleanup, bringing power to the Astros' lineup.

J. R. Richard, Ken Forsch, and Joe Niekro were solid starting pitchers Smith could use as a foundation for a strong staff. Although the Astros may have had some pieces to the puzzle in place, there was a long way to go to compete with the bullies of the West: Cincinnati and Los Angeles.

Smith acquired some key pieces via trades (second baseman Art Howe, catcher Alan Ashby), promoted a few promising players from the minors (shortstop Craig Reynolds, outfielder Terry Puhl, reliever Joe Sambito) and signed a free-agent (pitcher Vern Ruhle) over the next few seasons. The acquisitions, combined with the pieces that were already in place, resulted in a team primed to challenge for a division title.

The Astros got out of the gate fast in 1979, winning 15 of 21 games in April. The fans were beginning to come out of the heat and into the air-conditioned Astrodome to catch some MLB action. They were not disappointed. On July 4, Houston held a record of 52–31 and led Cincinnati by 10 games. However, the Astros faltered as the season wore on. As August ended, the Astros trailed Cincinnati by a half-game.

The Astros posted a 13–15 record in September, and the Reds went 13–13 to close out the season. Cincinnati (90–71) edged Houston (89–73) by 1½ games. But the Astros had arrived and were recognized as a force in the NL.

A development materialized off the field in 1979 when the Astros were purchased by John McMullen. The new owner shelled out $20 million to Ford to purchase the Houston club. Astrodomain was also part of the purchase package. McMullen resided in Montclair, New Jersey, and he had his business office in Manhattan. But for the sale to go through, Ford insisted that a local presence account for at least 51 percent of the ownership group.

The former United States Naval officer had been a minority owner of the Yankees. McMullen also sat on the board of Steinbrenner's American Shipbuilding Company. But McMullen often clashed with Steinbrenner regarding matters regarding the Yankees as well as the shipbuilding business. "There's nothing more limited than [being] a limited partner of the New York Yankees," said McMullen.[15]

McMullen owned half a dozen companies, all of them related to naval operations. John J. Mullen Associates was a naval architectural and transportation consultation firm, while Norton, Lily and Company was a steamship agency.[16] McMullen ultimately purchased approximately 33 percent of the Astros, while partner David LeFevre, a Wall Street lawyer, bought 10 percent. Local investors made up the rest of the ownership group.

Two additions in the off-season heightened the excitement of Astros fans for the 1980 season. On November 19, 1979, Houston signed free agent pitcher Nolan Ryan to a four-year, $4.5 million contract.[17] The deal reportedly made him the highest-paid athlete in a professional team sport, and the first player in MLB history to earn $1 million in a season.

On January 31, 1980, Joe Morgan signed a free-agent deal with the Astros. "Little Joe" broke in with Houston in 1963 and was a solid player with Houston before being dealt to Cincinnati in November 1971. Both Ryan and Morgan were seasoned veterans who one day would be enshrined in the National Baseball Hall of Fame. Also, they were both Texas natives, Ryan from Refugio and Morgan from Bonham.

Bob Watson was traded to Boston the previous season, and the Astros had failed to find another power hitter. It was an area of their offensive lineup they surely lacked as the Astros hit only 49 home runs in 1979 and no player totaled more than nine.

In 1980, the Astros carried their dreams of a postseason berth to the final day. They tied Los Angeles with records of 92–70. A one-game tiebreaker was held at Dodger Stadium on October 6. Joe Niekro went the distance to win his 20th game of the season as the Astros topped the Dodgers, 7–1, earning them their first division title and a trip to the NLCS.

The Astros faced the Philadelphia Phillies in the LCS. The Phillies won their fourth NL East title in 1980 and were by far the more playoff-savvy club. Nonetheless, both clubs battled in an extremely competitive series. Four of the five games went into extra innings as the Phillies came out on top to advance to the World Series.

One significant factor that may have prevented the Astros from advancing farther was the sudden departure of pitcher J. R. Richard. The flame-throwing right-hander led the NL in strikeouts in 1978 (303) and 1979 (313). On July 14, 1980, in a home game against Atlanta, Richard exited the game because he felt nauseous. Richard also had a difficult time seeing the signals from the catcher, and he heard a constant ringing in his ears. "I felt a little nauseated, and I knew if I felt that way I shouldn't stay out there," said Richard.[18]

But there was more to Richard's illness then just nausea. He was experiencing fatigue in his right arm which was caused by a circulatory problem. He was placed on the 21-day disabled list. At times, the Houston media as well as the Astros fans ridiculed Richard, labeling him as being lazy and a quitter.[19] It was soon discovered that surgery was needed to remove a clot from an artery above his right collarbone. The surgery was successful, but it left Richard paralyzed on the left side of his body.

While the outcome of the 1980 playoffs was disheartening, the news on October 26 that Smith had been fired shocked most people.

Smith had built the Astros into a playoff team, and attendance in 1980 was 2,278,217. It was an increase of 1,420,000 fans since he assumed the GM job in 1975.[20] In the five seasons that Smith presided over the franchise as GM, the team went from averaging 97 losses in a season to 93 wins. *The Sporting News* named Smith as its MLB "Executive of the Year" in 1980 after his dismissal.[21] Virdon was voted Manager of the Year by the sports weekly paper.[22]

The reason for Smith's firing was never disclosed publicly. In an article that appeared in *The Sporting News* on November 15, 1980, Smith offered this explanation: Because of an attendance bonus clause in Smith's contract, the owner couldn't afford to pay Smith anymore.[23] Smith indicated that the bonus that was to be paid to him in 1980 was more than his base salary. In essence, Smith did his job so well, building a competitive club that went to the postseason and filled the seats at the ballpark, that he was let go. "Mr. McMullen represented to me yesterday that my contract was a problem to some degree," said Smith. "But to me that was a lame duck excuse."[24]

Moments before McMullen fired Smith, he sent a letter to the minority owners stating his intentions. In it, McMullen wrote, "For reasons that are obvious, I do not feel it appropriate to consult my partners prior to the decision,"[25] LeFevre countered by saying what would be obvious was the minority partners revolting against a short-sighted move.

"I'm sick. I'm saddened," said pitcher Ken Forsch. "Tal has always been around and always so close to us. Right now, I'm looking to get traded or move on or whatever—just to go somewhere else. This isn't the kind of ballclub I want to be with anymore. This is a heck of a way to repay loyalty, ability and anything else that goes along with getting the job done."[26]

LeFevre also criticized McMullen for signing Nolan Ryan. "John went out totally on his own to sign Ryan," said LeFevre. "Nolan is a nice guy, but there are a lot of 11–10 pitchers [Ryan's record in 1980] you could get for $120,000 a year," said LeFevre.[27] McMullen may have been counting on Ryan to fill the seats in the Astrodome, no matter how the team fared. However, on days when Niekro pitched, the attendance (32,840) outdrew the days Ryan took the hill (27,237). Richard and Forsch were the closest behind Ryan in terms of drawing the crowd to the Dome.

McMullen chose Rosen to succeed Smith as president and general manager of the Astros. "Making this move, hiring Al Rosen, was something I feel had to be done," said McMullen. "And it had to be done now, because as an owner, I only have about one month after a season to make a move. I don't believe in making changes in the middle of the year. It disrupts things too much. I wanted to make the change and give Al the time to prepare for next season."[28]

McMullen felt that there was a difference in interpretation between Smith and himself. He knew that there would be a lot of backlash when he fired the popular Smith. But despite the criticism he knew that would be coming his way, McMullen felt he had the courage to make an unpopular move. McMullen said there was a limit on a team's effectiveness. If a man has not gotten the job done in five years, surely, he won't get the job done in ten years.[29]

The limited partners of the Astros took a vote to dissolve the partnership with McMullen. The results came back with 60 percent of the vote to dissolve the partnership agreement. McMullen went from being a general partner to a shareholder like the other partners. Furthermore, the limited partners brought a suit against McMullen, charging him with "engaging in acts of mismanagement that have brought great damage to the interest of the partners" and having "breached his fiduciary [trust] obligation to the limited partners by misuse of partnership assets."[30]

With the partnership no more, an executive committee of three was created to act as a corporation to operate the club. The triumvirate included McMullen, Jack Trotter, and T. H. Neyland. The possibility of undoing Smith's firing existed since McMullen would be outvoted 2–1 on almost anything of importance.

On November 16, 1980, the news broke of Rosen's involvement in a scandal back in Atlantic City. A credit scam of up to $3 million came to light as crooks hit three casinos on the boardwalk. Bally's, where Rosen worked as the executive vice president in charge of credit operations, approved credit payouts totaling $2.5 million. As many as 90 people, from Staten Island, Brooklyn, and Venezuela, may have been involved in the caper, and several had ties to organized crime. The thieves were known as the "Staten Island Group" and were led by Vito Internicola, 54, of Staten Island. As an example of the scam, Rosen authorized up to $136,000 in credit to Internicola, whose bank account never rose to more than "low three figures" on deposit.

"At this juncture, I feel like a complete idiot," said Rosen. "It's very embarrassing. But at the time, the procedures were not set in place [in the credit department], and had they been, this never would have happened."[31]

It may be hard to believe that given Rosen's deep background in finances, not to mention his casino experience, he could be taken in so easily. Still, Rosen was not charged in the crime, and he said that his decisions were the result of poor judgment.

Despite the rumors that his stay in Houston would be only a temporary one, Rosen rolled up his sleeves and got to work. Rosen and McMullen, with their front office team, made the short trip to Dallas for the Winter Meetings. The Astros signed right-handed starter Don Sutton on December 4, 1980, to a four-year deal estimated at $3.5 million.[32] They made two more moves on December 8, when they traded third baseman Enos Cabell to San Francisco for southpaw starter Bob Knepper and outfielder Chris Bourjos. They also released Joe Morgan. On December 10, the Astros signed utility player Dave Roberts.

Sutton was the big haul, although he would turn 36 just before the season began.

"I probably wouldn't have signed with the Astros except for these two men (McMullen and Rosen)," said Sutton. "They convinced me they not only want to bring a West Division championship but a World Series championship to Houston. I've never wanted to be a star, just a good player on a good team. If Bill Virdon wants me to pitch every seven days, I'll do it. [Virdon] is a very stable, patient manager I'll enjoy playing for."[33]

It later became known that Rosen had taken ill. It was a little more serious than ill when he entered Houston's Methodist Hospital to have open-heart surgery on January 5, 1981. The operation was a success, but Rosen remained hospitalized for a couple of weeks. Since he arrived in Houston in late October, the man who hired him was facing a mutiny by his partners and the fans. Both factions wanted to see McMullen exiled from Houston. If that did not keep Rosen awake at nights, there were constant rumors that the man he replaced would be coming back to lay claim to his old, and Rosen's new, job. Media members reminded Rosen almost every day that his time in Houston was to be a short stay, as Smith's return was imminent. Piled on top of it all was the story regarding the credit scam in Atlantic City.

While Rosen recuperated in the hospital, he received some welcome news. McMullen dragged his feet in signing the papers to transfer the ownership of the Astros from one of a partnership to that of a corporation. In essence, McMullen held up the deal until he knew for certain that Tal Smith would not return to the Astros. The partners sacrificed Smith for a new ownership structure. "I'm not going back to the Astros," said Smith. "The decision was made last Thursday at a partnership meeting, and I was informed by Herb Neyland Friday."[34] In the end, Neyland voted to reinstate Smith, while Jack Trotter sided with McMullen.

"McMullen is a fighter," said a source. "He already had been beaten and hurt by the revolt [of his partners], but the one thing he could do was try his best to keep Tal Smith from coming back. That was his victory."[35]

Rosen was thrilled by the news. Reading articles every day that you were going to be fired and that Tal Smith was returning could not have done much good for his health. Or his self-esteem. Still, Rosen had been around the game a long time, and he knew the media was just doing their job. But now he could concentrate on getting to his first spring training with the Houston Astros. And so could the sportswriters.[36]

"I accept the situation that because the club did so well last year, I'm in a can't-win position," said Rosen. "If we win, the obvious reaction is it's Tal Smith's team. Tal put the team together. And if we don't win, it's going to be my fault. But I know knowledgeable people don't feel that way. And all I can do is my best."[37]

Rosen recovered for a few weeks before heading to spring training at Cocoa, Florida. J. R. Richard had made a remarkable recovery, and the left side of his body became operational. But his reflexes were not what they were, and his lack of motor skills told the tale. Richard never pitched again in the big leagues.

Before the season started, Rosen made a couple of moves to strengthen his infield. On April 1, he traded the disgruntled Forsch to the California Angels for shortstop Dickie Thon. On the same day, he sent Bourjos to Baltimore for infielder Kiko Garcia.

On April 20, Rosen sent little-used outfielder Jeffrey Leonard and utility player Dave Bergman to San Francisco for first baseman Mike Ivie. But the trade turned out to be a bust as Leonard found his stroke with the Giants and became a starting outfielder. Bergman eventually landed in Detroit, where he became a solid bench player for the Tigers.

For Houston, Ivie played in a grand total of 26 games for the Astros in 1981 and 1982. When he refused to be sent down to AAA Tucson, the Astros waived him on April 30, 1982.

"I feel good about our team," said Rosen of the 1981 Astros. "Bill Virdon and I were analyzing our 25-man roster last week trying to see if we could make improvements. Admittedly, we don't have an All-Star at every position, but we have better depth than anyone in our division, we have more versatility, we have the best starting pitching, the best middle relief and the best short relief."[38]

There was a saying about winning and losing that Rosen liked to recite: A club is never as good as it is when it's winning and is never as bad as it is when it's losing.[39] This adage would prove true time and again during his tenure in Houston.

The Astros broke out of the gate with a 3–12 record. Because of their lethargic beginning, the Astros were in the cellar of the NL West on April 26. But they rebounded, winning eight of nine games, and inched their way up to fourth place, just five games back of the first-place Dodgers.

As May ended, the Astros were playing .500 ball, but the season was still young. Or was it?

Team	*Won*	*Lost*	*Percentage*	*G.B.*
Los Angeles	33	15	.688	---
Cincinnati	27	20	.574	5.5
San Francisco	25	25	.500	9.0
Houston	24	24	.500	9.0
Atlanta	22	23	.489	9.5
San Diego	19	29	.396	14.0

The black cloud of a players' strike had settled over baseball beginning in 1980 and carried over to the 1981 season. The players union and management disagreed over free-agent compensation. There were three cases that management used to make their point. Each case involved a high-profile player signing a free-agent contract with a new team. The Yankees signed Dave Winfield, formerly of San Diego. St. Louis signed Kansas City catcher Darrell Porter, and the Astros inked Sutton. The Padres, the Royals, and the Dodgers received nothing in return for the player who departed their team.

Management wanted to change that system. In a nutshell, the Yankees would be able to protect a set number of players, and the Padres would be able to select a player from the remaining roster to replace Winfield. "If George [Steinbrenner] is so concerned about compensation, let him sell one of his players to San Diego for one dollar," said

Marvin Miller, the union's chief negotiator. "He signed Dave Winfield. Let him volunteer. If his heart bleeds for the Padres, let him do something unilaterally. We won't object."[40]

Negotiations went nowhere, raising tempers instead of hope that a settlement might magically occur. The players voted to strike on May 29, 1981. When that date came around, two more weeks of talks were scheduled with the goal of avoiding a work stoppage. With no agreement in sight, the players walked out on June 12, 1981. Indeed, the balance of the season hung in the balance.

Just before the strike, the Astros pulled off a deal. Houston dealt pitcher Joaquin Andujar (2–3, 4.94 ERA) to St. Louis for center fielder Tony Scott (2 HR, 17 RBI, .227 batting average). "Sitting on the bench, I knew something was going to happen," said Scott. "But when you get in your option year, you've got to expect anything."[41]

After 49 days and 713 canceled games, the two parties reached a settlement on July 31. If a club lost a "premium" player to free agency, it would receive compensation by selecting a player or players from a pool of players that were left unprotected from all of the clubs and not just the club who signed the free agent. Players needed to accumulate six years of service in the major leagues before they were eligible for free agency. The agreement would expire on December 31, 1984. Miller wrote on his copy of the agreement, "Significance? Not anxious to do battle again."[42]

Baseball returned as clubs held a mini-spring training for just over a week before resuming the season. The season was split into two halves. The teams that occupied first place on June 12 were declared winners of the first half of the season. Each winner from the first half would play the winner of the second half, which created an extra layer of playoff action. The "second season" commenced after the All-Star Game.

The All-Star Game, originally scheduled for July 14, 1981, took place at Cleveland Stadium on August 9. A sold-out park of 72,086 fans may have given the indication that they were welcoming baseball back with open arms. Interestingly, two of the moves Rosen made were on display at the mid-summer classic. Ken Forsch (9–3, 2.27 ERA) was named to the AL squad, and Bob Knepper (5–1, 1.15 ERA) and Nolan Ryan (5–3, 1.37 ERA) represented the Astros as the NL won, 5–4.

Despite a clean slate and a chance at the postseason for each club, attendance suffered in the second half. In the AL, average attendance for the first half was 20,865. That figure decreased to 17,751 in the second half. The NL saw a similar drop at the turnstiles, from 21,015 to 19,034 patrons per game.[43]

Major league clubs were given a second chance to make the postseason. The Astros did not squander the opportunity. They posted consecutive winning months in August (13–8) and September (18–10).

The Astros did acquire a player who unquestionably helped their team in 1981 and several seasons beyond. On August 31, the Astros shipped three minor-league players to Pittsburgh for second baseman Phil Garner. The second base position had resembled a revolving door in a department store, as four players were given the opportunity to start at the keystone position. Garner, a three-time All-Star, solidified the Astros' infield.

Although Rosen landed a quality player in Garner, his acquisition did not come without a price. Among the three minor leaguers sent to Pittsburgh was Johnny Ray. The Astros ranked Ray as their number one prospect. *The Sporting News* selected Ray as their National League Rookie of the Year in 1982.

On September 26, Ryan tossed his fifth career no-hitter as Houston defeated Los Angeles, 5–0. Ryan had been tied with Sandy Koufax for the most no-hitters with four. Ryan whiffed 11 Dodgers and walked three in front of 32,115 fans at the Astrodome. "Something like this doesn't get me real emotional," said Ryan. "I know I'll enjoy it more in the morning."[44]

Even though they showed a vast improvement from the first half, the Astros held a precarious lead in the NL West heading into October. Houston had four games remaining on its schedule, and the top of the NL West looked like this:

Team	Won	Lost	Percentage	G.B.
Houston	31	18	.633	---
Cincinnati	30	18	.625	.5
San Francisco	27	21	.563	3.5

Houston could only muster a 2–2 record in its final four games. Cincinnati went 1–3 and the Giants 2–2. The Astros were the second-half winners and faced off against the Dodgers in the first round of the playoffs. But the playoff appearance cost the Astros dearly. Making his last start of the regular season against the Dodgers on October 2, Don Sutton suffered a fracture of his kneecap. Sutton, batting in the top of the third inning, squared to bunt with men on base when the pitch from Jerry

147

Reuss plunked him squarely on the kneecap. Sutton's injury not only knocked him out for the season, but it halted a hot streak. Sutton had won seven of eight decisions before his last start against L.A.

Because of the playoff format, the St. Louis Cardinals (59–43) and the Cincinnati Reds (66–42) would have made the playoffs under the traditional system. Each team had the best overall record in its division. Reds skipper John McNamara said that he hoped "this thing would end up on Halloween in Montreal [which won the NL East in the second half] with the baseball powers that be up to their butts in snow."[45]

In a best-of-five series against Los Angeles, the first two games were played at the Astrodome. The Astros won both games behind a two-hit, complete-game effort by Ryan and a combined shutout by Joe Niekro, Dave Smith, and Joe Sambito in Game Two.

The Dodgers turned the tables in Los Angeles. The Astros' pitching wasn't enough to carry the day as Houston totaled only six runs on the road. Los Angeles won all three games at Dodger Stadium, ending the Astros' 1981 season.

Houston's power numbers reverted to its 1979 numbers, totaling only 45 home runs in 1981. José Cruz led the way with 13. Art Howe replaced Cabell at third base, and he led the team with a .296 batting average. Tony Scott, who only had 225 at-bats, batted .293.

Ryan (11–5, 1.69 ERA) and Knepper (9–5, 2.18 ERA) were first and second, respectively, in ERA in the NL in 1981. Knepper also tossed five shutouts, and Sutton added 11 victories.

It had been a trying year for Rosen. With a full season under his belt, he began preparations for the 1982 season. Although the winter meetings brought little movement to the Astros, Rosen did complete one trade before the end of the year. On December 18, Rosen shipped outfielder Cesar Cedeno to Cincinnati for third baseman Ray Knight. Cedeno had been a Houston Astro since 1970, but his power numbers had declined in recent years.

Knight would play third base for the Astros, moving Howe across the diamond to first. "He joins with [second baseman] Phil Garner to give us tremendous leadership in our infield," said Rosen. "He's a hard-nosed guy who walks out there and gives his best every day."[46] For Howe, he was just looking for an indication of how he fit into the Astros plans.

"I don't want to sound like I'm complaining, but to a certain extent, I'm confused," said Howe. "I really haven't had a chance to talk with

Al Rosen since the trade was made, but I want to see what they have planned for me. I mean I did lead the team in hitting last year. But after my performance last year, I don't think I have to worry about playing."[47]

As spring training opened, Sutton made it known that he wanted to be traded. Sutton said all the right things about the Astros, Rosen, McMullen, his teammates, and the city. He wanted to be traded close to home. The California Angels were Sutton's prime target. "Top to bottom, it's [playing in Houston] as good a situation as a ballplayer could ever hope to find. Except for one thing—it's not my home. And I want to stay at home."[48] Sutton had thought that Houston would be the place he wanted to settle down with his family. But that ultimately changed, and Anaheim became the destination of choice for the Sutton clan.

It is a wonder why Sutton didn't sign with the Angels when he entertained offers after the 1980 season. In any event, Rosen had no plan to trade Sutton or any of his pitchers. "I did talk with Houston a couple of months ago about pitching, but they said they wanted to keep their pitching intact," said Angels V.P. Buzzie Bavasi.[49]

"I think there just aren't enough toys in the world for Don Sutton," said Rosen. "He just keeps wanting more and more."[50] Rosen and Sutton exchanged words through spring training, especially when Rosen said, "you get the Sutton mentality when you get Sutton."[51]

As it turned out, Howe did not need to be concerned. Virdon moved Knight to first base and Howe remained at the hot corner. However, as in 1981, the 1982 Astros got off to a slow start, posting losing records in April (9–14) and in May (12–14), which landed Houston in fourth place, seven games behind first-place Atlanta.

June showed no improvement, as the Astros went 10–16. The Astros' record prompted Rosen to give the kiss-of-death to Virdon. "Bill is one of the best managers in baseball," said Rosen. "He runs a club as well as any manager. And in terms of tactics, he has no peers. The problems experienced by our club are not Bill's fault. It's a lot easier to blame the manager than it is the players. But I can't fault Bill."[52]

As the losing continued, Virdon's record (49–62) showed that the Astros were giving a lackluster effort. The Astros fired Virdon and replaced him with coach Bob Lillis on August 10, 1982. As expected, Virdon took the high road. "I have no bitterness toward anybody in the organization," said Virdon. "They paid me for my services. You can't question a man's right to make a change if he is running an organization. I'd want that right, too."[53]

Lillis had been with the Astros since the birth of the franchise. Lillis was an infielder (1962–1967), a scout and special assistant (1968–1972) and as a coach (1973–1982), and he was taking his first stab as a manager when he was appointed to the job permanently on November 2, 1982.[54]

The Astros' starting pitching had been the key to their success. But three of the starters were aging. Ryan (35), Niekro (37) and Sutton (37) may have been getting a bit long in the tooth, but they were still hurling well. However, the younger starters, Knepper and Vern Ruhle, were not making the grade. Joe Sambito, the closer for Houston, injured his left elbow. He only appeared in 10 games in 1982, the last one on May 5. His replacement, Dave Smith, battled back pain most of the year.

Perhaps because of the age factor, plus the fact that they were not going north in the standings, the Astros decided to deal Sutton (13–8, 3.00 ERA) on August 30. However, the Milwaukee Brewers acquired Sutton, not California. In exchange, the Astros received three prospects: pitchers Frank DiPino and Mike Madden and outfielder Kevin Bass. "I've been working on it for two months," said Rosen. "If I've had one telephone conversation with [Brewers General Manager] Harry Dalton, I may have had 100 conversations."[55]

Houston finished the 1982 season in fifth place in the NL West, with a 77–85 record. Their offense was abysmal, batting .247 as a team. Knight led the team with a .294 batting average. "I've given a lot of thought as to whether I should recommend shortening the fences [at the Astrodome]," said Rosen. "I wonder how much our hitters are affected by the dimensions, and whether some adjust their stroke in the Dome and thus, are not as effective on the road. I'm convinced that we've got better hitters than some showed last year."[56]

The Astros hit the free agent market during the winter meetings in Honolulu, signing center fielder Omar Moreno to a five-year pact worth $3.2 million. The fleet-footed Moreno, who had spent his entire seven-year career with Pittsburgh, was an ideal leadoff hitter as well as an accomplished base stealer. Moreno swiped 412 bases as a member of the Pirates.

Houston also sent reserve outfielder Danny Heep to the New York Mets for right-handed pitcher Mike Scott. But the Astros left Hawaii without securing their biggest need, a right-handed power hitter.

"Our main goal when the convention began was to find a right-handed power hitter," said Rosen. "We tried. The right-hander with pop just isn't available. So we accomplished the 'fall-back' position in that we increased our speed and defense. [Free agent Steve] Garvey is 34, his best years may be behind him and he's never hit well in the Astrodome. It's hard to justify paying him more than $5 million, which is what it would take."[57]

During spring training in Cocoa, Rosen gave his prediction on how the Astros would fare in 1983. "Even though we finished in fifth place, we were only 12 games out of first place," said Rosen. "And we lost 28 games in which we [led] or were tied as late as the seventh inning. We obviously missed Sambito, and Dave Smith had back trouble most of the year which hurt his effectiveness. If we have a healthy Sambito and Smith this year, I think we will win our division."[58]

Spring training turned into a disastrous situation, as storms and a poor drainage system prompted the Astros to incorporate makeshift conditions for their training. They ran on city streets, exercised in parking lots, and worked out in covered cages.

When the club could finally practice on the field at Astrotown, it resembled more of a swamp, and several players came down with colds. With Cocoa in the northern part of Florida, the forecasts called for chilly conditions and offered no breaks of warm weather. The club took the high road, but they lost 16 of 19 games in the Grapefruit League.

Sambito, still rehabbing his left elbow, sat out the entire 1983 season and set his sights on 1984 for a possible comeback. The Astros continued their recent tradition of breaking out of the gate slowly. Houston dropped the first nine games, including five to the Dodgers. It led to an 8–14 overall record in April.

Ryan began the season on the disabled list with a swollen prostate. He made his season debut on April 17. When he returned to the rotation, Ryan posted a 9–1 record through mid–July.

Howe, who had off-season surgery on his right elbow, missed the whole 1983 season. He had a second surgery on the elbow in May, and the Astros placed him on the 60-day disabled list. Lillis moved Garner from second base to third, making room for rookie Bill Doran to man the keystone position.

Moreno, a left-handed batter, became unhappy with Lillis when the Houston skipper benched him against certain left-handed pitchers. Moreno balked and threatened not to play at all. But after a meeting between Moreno, his agent Tom Reich, Rosen, and Lillis, Moreno agreed to follow Lillis' strategy. But Moreno sulked, did not communicate with his teammates, and outwardly displayed his unhappiness.

Moreno asked to be traded, and on August 10, he got his wish. Houston dealt Moreno to the Yankees for Jerry Mumphrey. Lillis may have pushed for the move, as he was a proponent of Bill Doran being moved to the leadoff spot.

"I know that Mumphrey was unhappy," said Rosen. "The pressure of playing in New York is tremendous. As a result, the Yankees were unhappy with him. They seemed to think he didn't play center field very well. We had talked to the Yankees about Mumphrey in the past. And when you've got a player who is unhappy and wants to be traded, it's best to see what other talented players may be in a similar situation."[59]

The Astros improved in the summer months, posting a 48–34 record from June through August. Going into September, the Astros (70–62) trailed first-place Los Angeles (77–55) by seven games. The Astros finished the season in third place with a record of 85–77.

Houston did improve its power numbers, belting 97 home runs. They were led by shortstop Dickie Thon, who had career highs in home runs (20) and RBI (79). Jose Cruz led the team in hitting with a .318 average. Ryan (14–9, 2.98 ERA), Niekro (15–14, 3.48 ERA), and Scott (10–6, 3.72 ERA) led the pitching corps.

McMullen gave Rosen a new three-year contract. Rumors circulated that Rosen was the leading candidate to replace Lee MacPhail as the American League President. MacPhail was stepping down to become director of the owners' Player Relations Committee. "I don't know if I was formally offered the American League Presidency," said Rosen, "but I got the idea the job was mine if I wanted it. It was flattering, but I prefer to be in Houston. Building the Astros into a yearly contender is our goal, and I want to be part of it when we succeed."[60]

At the winter meetings in Nashville, the Astros re-signed Denny Walling. Houston had granted the first baseman-outfielder free agency at the end of the season. But the Astros had every intention of bringing him back into the fold. Walling, a left-handed batter, had value as a pinch-hitter. His career batting average as a pinch-hitter was .266. However, it was also his willingness to learn the ropes at third base that made him valuable to the Astros, according to Rosen.[61]

The three-year deal netted Walling $1.025 million. "He's the best we've got as a left-hander off the bench, and I feel we really need to sign him," said Lillis.[62] To get Walling to sign on the dotted line may have been a priority for the Houston front office, but the search for a right-handed slugger continued. The viable candidates were either aging, carried a high price tag, or were not deemed a good fit for the Astros.

Relief pitcher Frank LaCorte and Howe were also granted free agency, and neither player returned to the Astros. Just as spring training got underway, Enos Cabell signed a two-year deal worth $375,000 per year with Houston. The former Astros third baseman batted .311 for Detroit in 1983, while playing mostly at first base.

Houston also reached out to Ryan to restructure his contract. Even though Ryan had one year remaining on his contract that called for $1 million, the Astros were asking that he take a pay cut in 1983 and sign a two-year extension. The deal would call for Ryan to make between $700,000 and $800,000 in 1984 and 1985.

Under the Basic Agreement, no player can have his contract cut by more than 20 percent over one year and 30 percent over two. The most that could be sliced from Ryan's contract was $200,000. Although Rosen pointed out that Ryan would come out ahead, Ryan declined the Astros' offer. "I don't feel there is any reason for me to take any cut because that contract was signed a long time ago. I'm open to discussion about whatever amount of money the club suggests for future seasons, but as for this season, I feel there is some principle involved."[63]

As the MLB players' contract approached expiration at the end of the year, drug-testing became a hot topic around the league. Numerous players, including Vida Blue, Jerry Martin, Willie Aikens, Willie Wilson, Ferguson Jenkins, and Darrell Porter, had been charged as chemical abusers, specifically cocaine.

Ken Moffett, the union chief negotiator, agreed that random drug testing should be a part of the Basic Agreement. However, the players were not on board and fired Moffett. Donald Fehr, his replacement, took a harder stance against players getting tested for drugs. Some players called it a violation of their civil rights.

Rosen was liked and respected by the players of the teams he worked for because he was a star player and he understood the daily life of a baseball player. Billy Martin may have been a "players' manager" because he understood not only what was inside a player, his heart, but also his character and his talent. Rosen could be labeled as a "players' general manager." Rosen understood people, and that quality came through in his dealings with agents and players.

But on the topic of drugs, Rosen stood with the owners. He knew the dangers of the rampant use of drugs among big league ballplayers. In his mind, owners had the right to protect their investment, and if that meant drug testing, he was all for it.

> Any time there is an open dialogue, some benefits will be achieved. I hope both sides are able to work closely because everyone knows the problem exists. It is horrifying to think sane people can't sit down and reach conclusions on how to deal with it. What gripes me, though, is that some of my players have volunteered to take random drug tests, but then they start getting hit with peer pressure and back off.[64]

The Astros were hoping for a different start to the season from the previous few years. It was not to be as the Astros, who came to be known as the "Lastros" in some circles, lost their first nine games. They ended April with a record of 8–14. Indeed, the 1984 season seemed to be a carbon copy of 1983, at least at the outset.

The Astros again incurred a high number of injuries. Thon, a favorite of Rosen's, got hit in the eye by a pitch by New York's Mike Torrez on April 8. Thon's season ended after five games. He was replaced at shortstop by Craig Reynolds.

Alan Ashby suffered a broken toe when he was struck with a foul ball on April 24 at Los Angeles. He was replaced in the lineup by rookie Mark Bailey.[65] Mumphrey joined Ashby on the DL with back spasms. Terry Puhl, the Astros' right fielder, missed three weeks with a sprained right elbow. Ray Knight had multiple ailments to overcome, including a sore right shoulder, bouts of vertigo, and kidney stones. "Now I know how Custer felt when he looked up and saw all those Indians," said Rosen.[66]

Members of the Astros' disabled list "were going to get together, have a party, cook some barbecue, pop some popcorn and watch our games on television. And I understand it's going to be a pretty big party," said Ryan.[67]

The month of May brought a 12–14 record. It was a slight improvement, but the Astros were in fifth place of the NL West with a 20–28 record. Yet they trailed the front-running Dodgers by only 6½ games. A winning streak of any type would be a beneficial boost to the Astros to get back in the race.

But the offense continued to be the albatross around the Astros' neck. Houston scored three runs or less in 30 of their first 48 games. The Astros went 9–4 in a 13-game homestand against their NL West foes in mid–June. But their offensive offense shackled the team from escaping their losing ways. "Absolutely, no changes are planned," said McMullen.

"My main function as an owner at this point is to be supportive of Al, Bob and the players."[68]

The Astros played better baseball in August. Even though they were in second place with a 68–65 record on August 28, they were nine games behind the San Diego Padres. Lillis benched Knight and his .233 batting average. Cabell took over at third base, and Garner received most of the playing time at first base. "Al has talked to me like a son," said Knight. "I think the world of him. I respect Al Rosen as much as any man I know. And he's told me he has no desire to trade me. But he's also told me he'll do his best to move me elsewhere, and I think it would be best for all concerned if it came quickly."[69]

Knight got his wish when he was dealt to the New York Mets on August 28 for three minor league players.

The Houston Astros finished the 1984 season with an 80–82 record. They tied Atlanta for second place in the division, 12 games behind San Diego. Cruz (.312), Cabell (.310) and Puhl (.301) were the leading hitters on the club. Cruz led the Astros in home runs with 12. Of the club's 79 home runs, only 18 were hit at the Astrodome.

"We do have a game plan," said Rosen. "We've always had a game plan. We haven't deviated. We don't plan to deviate. We believe the proper way to build a ball club is through the farm system. John McMullen has invested a lot of money into that farm system, and we're making progress. We've had some good drafts in recent years, but every player needs time to develop. The long-term answer is in the farm system."[70]

Rosen noted that unlike football and basketball, where a number one or number two draft pick can make an immediate impact, baseball had to develop their players. Often it took three or four years to bring a prospect along to the big league team.[71]

One change that occurred for the 1985 season took place at the Astrodome. The outfield fences were shortened. The distance down the line was curtailed by 10 feet, 340 to 330. The power alleys were brought in by 10 feet from 390 to 380. In straightaway center field, the new distance was 400 feet, shortened from 406. The dimensions reverted to what they were from 1972–1976.[72]

Pitchers Vern Ruhle and Mike LaCoss were granted free agency. Neither hurler re-signed with Houston. The Astros had high expectations for Manuel Lee. The young infielder from the Dominican Republic had been one of the minor leaguers obtained from the Mets in the Ray Knight deal. However, Toronto claimed Lee in the Rule 5 draft.

In 1985, the Astros were still looking for the right-handed power hitter that they had craved for several years. Perhaps bringing in the outfield walks would alleviate that hole in their lineup.

The Astros opened their new spring training complex in Kissimmee, Florida. The $5.5 million facility featured four fields with lights that surrounded a two-story building that served as offices and a clubhouse. An observation deck allowed club officials to keep tabs of what was happening on the diamonds. "I can't help but believe the new facility will have a positive effect on player attitude and performance and will go a long way toward helping us avoid another bad regular-season start," said Rosen.[73]

Just before the season began, the Astros waived Joe Sambito. The relief pitcher made a comeback of sorts in 1984, but after three surgeries on his left elbow, he lost some zip on the ball. The Astros asked Sambito to accept a demotion to AAA Tucson, but he declined. One of the more popular players in Astros history, he saved 72 games for the club.

Kevin Bass, who came over to the Astros in the Don Sutton deal with Milwaukee, received his first opportunity as a full-time player. He had been the Astros fourth outfielder in 1984, and now Mumphrey moved to right field and Bass took over in center.

For the first time since 1980, the 1985 Astros did not have a losing record in April. They finished with a record of 10–10, a slight improvement. Houston treaded water to finish one game over .500 in May and June, but an 8–18 record in July sank the team for good. At the end of July, the Astros (46–55) trailed Los Angeles (58–41) by 13 games.

Through it all, the Astros finally found their right-handed slugger through the farm system. Glenn Davis moved into the first base position in June and stayed there for good. Houston drafted Davis in the January draft, secondary phase in 1981, making him the fifth pick overall. Davis showed power at all levels in the minors, and he also hit for average.

For a team hungry for power, Davis provided it with 20 dingers to lead the team in his first full season. Bass, a switch-hitter, swatted 16 home runs. Houston clubbed 121 home runs as a team, their highest total since 1973 (134). Mike Scott (18–8, 3.29 ERA) was the bright spot in the rotation, while Ryan (10–12) and Niekro (9–12) posted losing records in 1985.

Houston finished the 1985 season tied with San Diego for third place with 83–79 records. Division champion Los Angeles finished 12 games ahead of them.

On September 13, Rosen and McMullen parted on mutual terms. The *Houston Chronicle* reported that Rosen and McMullen parted ways amicably and that McMullen even urged Rosen to look for another job while he still ran the Astros.[74] Dick Wagner, who was an executive in Cincinnati for 17 seasons, replaced him.

Rosen did not remain unemployed for long. He accepted a similar position with the San Francisco Giants. He was off to the "City by the Bay."

Ed Fowler of the *Houston Chronicle* summed up Rosen's tenure this way: "What we have here is a case of addition by subtraction. The absence of Al Rosen is a positive. Under Rosen, the Astros were going from bad to worse, and no number of meaningless victories in September after the race is over will change that condition."[75]

It would be hard to dispute Fowler's capsule review of Rosen's time in Houston. The team that won a division title in 1980 was on the verge of big things. The Astros had many injuries during Rosen's tenure. Al Rosen would be the last person to use injuries as an excuse for a team's losing records. However, after Tal Smith's dismissal and during Rosen's term, the team wallowed in mediocrity.

NINE

A Pennant by the Bay

The New York Giants relocated to San Francisco after the 1957 season. Together with the Brooklyn Dodgers moving out to Los Angeles, the two National League titans extended Major League Baseball's footprint to the West Coast.

The Giants were one of the great franchises of the big leagues. New York triumphed over the Philadelphia Athletics in five games of the 1905 World Series. It won 13 more pennants and four world championships before leaving Gotham behind and heading to northern California.

Since unpacking their bags in 1958, the Giants had won only one pennant. In 1962, the Giants flew the National League flag at Candlestick Park, but they were defeated in seven games in the World Series by the New York Yankees. In 1969, the big leagues realigned, and each circuit was halved into divisions. San Francisco claimed their only division title in 1971, taking the NL West with a 90–72 record, edging out the rival Dodgers by one game. Pittsburgh ousted San Francisco in four games in the NLCS, ending the Giants' 1971 campaign.

Tom Haller served as the Giants' GM from 1981–1985. In that time, San Francisco finished with a record north of .500 twice. In the strike-shortened season of 1981, the Giants posted a 56–55 record. In 1982, the Giants were 87–75 and finished third in the NL West. The Giants did not build on that success, finishing in fifth place in 1983 (79–83). That year was followed by successive seasons of occupying the basement of the West Division in 1984 (66–96) and 1985 (62–100). The 100 losses in 1985 remains the only 100-loss season in franchise history.

Haller was fired on September 17, 1985. The Giants were 56–88 and staggering their way to that 100-loss season. Haller was a former catcher of the Giants, then a bullpen coach at San Francisco for three years (1977–1979) before rising to the position of farm director in 1980. He was named vice president of baseball operations (general manager) for the Giants in 1981. Indeed, Haller's rise to becoming a baseball executive was a curious one. His resume did not indicate that a GM position would come his way that quickly.

Meanwhile, San Francisco Giants owner Bob Lurie and Rosen had become friends over the years at various baseball meetings. Lurie valued Rosen's opinion because of his background as a player and an executive and because Rosen had worked in private business. When Rosen became available because McMullen was cleaning house in Houston, hiring Rosen seemed to be a natural fit for Lurie. Together, they sought out Roger Craig to take over as the field manager job from Jim Davenport.

Lurie termed the hirings of Rosen, and Roger Craig as "a major turning point in the history of the San Francisco Giants."[1] Rosen vowed that the Giants would "definitely be competitive next year. There will be some changes made, I promise you that."[2]

Craig, a former NL pitcher for 12 seasons (1955–1966), had previous managing experience as the pilot of the San Diego Padres (1978–1979). "I made a mistake in San Diego—I thought I could get everybody to like me," said Craig. "With 25 different personalities, not everyone is going to like you."[3] Craig's record with the Padres was 152–171. Craig added Lillis to his coaching staff as the Giants' bench coach. Lillis served in this capacity for the next 11 years.

Lurie considered Rosen as the only viable candidate for the vacant GM job. Rosen was asked how the hiring went down. "Bob heard they were going to make a clean sweep in Houston, and asked permission to speak to me. He came to Houston and we spoke for a week or so. Haller sat in on the second day. We had breakfast together at my place and went until 2:30. Tom wanted to go down on the field [be manager, but I felt the gamble was too great for San Francisco at this stage."[4]

Many thought that Lurie was taking a gamble in hiring Rosen. Judging from his recent tenure in Houston, it may not be surprising that Lurie's selection for GM had been met with skepticism. Rosen went on the offensive. He pointed out that he had been tested under extreme conditions in New York. The decision to hire Bob Lemon demonstrated Rosen's business acumen. The acquisitions of Ron Davis and Dave Righetti showed Rosen's ability to judge talent. Although Lemon added a calmness to the clubhouse after replacing Billy Martin, some of that serenity must be attributed to the New York newspaper strike. Rosen liked to point out that the Yankees pitching staff resembled a triage ward. However, Ron Guidry and Ed Figueroa each won 20 games, and Goose Gossage led the league in saves. The cupboard was not completely bare when it came to pitching.

> At Houston, I lost J. R. Richard, a future Hall-of-Famer, and Joe Sambito and Dickie Thon, the best all-around shortstop in baseball. Players like those don't grow on trees. The Astros were still over .500 when I was there. We didn't win. That's the bottom line. I accept that. In my mind, I don't believe I failed.[5]

Richard suffered his stroke in 1980, when Tal Smith was still the GM. Although Richard did attempt to make a comeback, he never pitched for the Astros while Rosen was the GM. Rosen was always talking Thon up as one of the great shortstops in history, partly because he caught a lot of heat from the fans for trading Ken Forsch to California in 1981 for Thon. Although the deal eventually worked out well for the Astros, labeling Thon as the "best all-around shortstop in baseball" might have been a reach.

> I have a mandate to resurrect this franchise. Before I do anything, I'll tell Bob [Lurie] as a courtesy to my boss, but if I want to do something, I'll do it. Some general managers have responsibility without authority. I'll have both. I'm convinced we need to make changes on this club, to bring in new faces. We've got a real attitude problem, and we've got to change that.[6]

Running the Giants would be a much different experience for Rosen. Lurie gave him free rein to make the decisions that were needed to turn the Giants into a competitor. Unlike his previous tenures in New York and Houston, Rosen would not have anyone looking over his shoulder. Steinbrenner and McMullen had the final say in all the transactions and decisions that Rosen made. The micro-managing in New York and Houston was all in the past, and San Francisco indeed was a fresh and invigorating beginning under Lurie.

It didn't take long for Rosen to make good on his promise. On October 7, Rosen traded pitchers Eric King and Dave LaPoint and catcher Matt Nokes to Detroit for catcher Bob Melvin, pitcher Juan Berenguer, and minor league pitcher Scott Medvin.

In the "Voice of the Fan" section of *The Sporting News* of October 28, 1985, a reader gave his opinion of the multi-player deal:

> *If Al Rosen intended to reverse the record of ineptitude of the San Francisco Giants under Tom Haller's stewardship, his first trade represents an inauspicious beginning.*

Nine—A Pennant by the Bay

Before the '85 season, the Giants gave up their best hitter, Jack Clark, to acquire pitcher Dave LaPoint. LaPoint pitched well this season and is of proven ability. Yet, he now is traded along with a promising young catcher with power, for a pitcher and catcher of much lesser ability.[7]

Rosen was not bashful about reshaping the Giants. He made six trades, signed four free agents, and released or granted free agency to four more players. Like most trades, some hit the mark, and some proved to be busts. On December 11, 1985, he traded backup catcher Alex Trevino to the Los Angeles Dodgers for outfielder Candy Maldonado. Trevino never blossomed into a first-string backstop, while Maldonado started in right field for three years with the Giants.

On December 18, Rosen sent outfielder Rob Deer to Milwaukee for two minor league prospects. Deer was one of the more prolific sluggers in the American League. He hit 23 or more home runs for seven straight seasons (1986–1992) with both the Brewers and Tigers. The two prospects (Dean Freeland and Eric Pilkington) never made the big leagues. "Before this year is over, I'm going to take it on the chin for this," said Rosen in September 1986. "It's one of the phenomenal stories of our time. Who would realize he would go from a utility player traded for two minor leaguers to leading the league in home runs?"[8]

The hiring of Roger Craig began the "Humm Baby" era of Giants baseball.

"Roger was always using the phrase whenever there was a good play or a good effort, a humm baby hit, a humm baby catch, a humm baby slide, a humm baby throw," said second baseman Robby Thompson. "And it even referred to players, so-and-so was a humm baby. Once in spring training, he spotted a good-looking girl in the stands and he called over to me, 'Hey Thompson, that's a humm baby sitting over there behind third.'"[9]

Lingering over the organization was the future of Candlestick Park. Attendance had dropped to 818,679 paid patrons in 1985. The National League average was 1,857,680.[10] The 100-loss season did not help draw people to the ballpark in 1985. But the Giants consistently drew under the league season average.

The Giants had called Candlestick Park (named because it was built on San Francisco Bay's Candlestick Point) home since 1960.[11] The stadium project was in trouble from the beginning, as various disagreements between the architect, the builder, and the city did not make for a harmonious working partnership. Many of the amenities that were planned for the park were either cut back or altogether eliminated.[12]

The ballpark was in a remote site, 10 miles from the downtown City Center. There was enough seating for over 40,000 fans, and the parking lot was big enough to accommodate approximately 10,000 vehicles.[13] Buses and railway lines were also offered for those fans who wanted to avoid the congested highways.[14] However, the temperature at Candlestick Park dropped to near-frigid degrees in the evening. It was often described as not having any character as well as being a cold and bleak venue.

When Rosen arrived in San Francisco, he found out that Lurie was adamant about not playing the 1986 season at Candlestick. Even though there was a lease agreement in place between the Giants and the city of San Francisco until 1994, Lurie wanted out. A native son of San Francisco, Lurie also had served on the Giants Board of Directors under the previous owner, Horace Stoneham. He desperately wanted to keep the club in his hometown, but he was through with Candlestick. Or so he thought.

The Giants sent a contingent to Colorado to meet with the Denver Baseball Commission about the possibility of playing at Mile High Stadium for three years. At the end of the three years, the Giants would return to San Francisco when a new downtown stadium was completed.

Rosen and club vice president Corey Busch were part of the Giants' traveling party.

"Denver had been mentioned as a temporary home, so we went there for no other reason than a fact-finding mission," said Busch. "We cannot continue to hemorrhage money at Candlestick. We'll lose between $5 million and $10 million this year. It will take at least three years for a new stadium, so we're talking about further losses of between $15 million and $30 million. That's not an option—that's economic suicide."[15]

At least one national sportswriter was critical of the Giants and their plan. Bill Conlin wrote in his "National League Beat" article on February 3, 1986, in *The Sporting News*:

> Less than a month before pitchers and catchers report to Phoenix for spring training, the Giants have virtually guaranteed that the new front office headed by Al Rosen and the new field operation under Manager Roger Craig are doomed to fail. Even if the Giants manage to slither out of sixth place in the National League West, another financial bloodbath is guaranteed.[16]

Conlin added that as of January 22, not a single ticket had been sold for the 1986 season. Furthermore, the Giants had not put together a yearbook or a media guide, as they were unsure where they would be playing their home games.[17]

Despite their misgivings about Candlestick Park, the Giants did return there for the 1986 season. On the field, Rosen knew that an upgrade to the right side of the infield was imperative. In 1985 David Green manned first and Manny Trillo was the second baseman. Both had been dispatched during the winter meetings. Those moves meant that veteran first baseman Dan Driessen and utility infielder Brad Wellman were the incumbents to start for the Giants.

But both players were supplanted in spring training as rookies Will Clark and Robby Thompson beat out Driessen and Wellman, respectively. "I'm out of options, so they must not care too much about me," said Wellman. "Hopefully, I won't clear waivers and I'll get a chance to play somewhere else in the majors."[18]

Clark was a college sensation at Mississippi State. After his junior year, he was named to Team USA for the 1984 Summer Olympics, when baseball was played as a demonstration sport for the summer games. He returned to Mississippi State for his senior season and batted .420 with 25 home runs and 77 RBI. The Giants selected him in the first round, the second overall pick, in the June draft. He played one year at Fresno of the Class A California League. In his first major league at-bat on April 8, 1986, Clark homered off Nolan Ryan in the first inning at the Astrodome. "Will Clark is the type of player who comes along only now and then," said Rosen. "Some guys are born to play. Will is a natural."[19]

Thompson took a little bit longer to get to the majors, as he was drafted by the Giants in the June 1983 draft, secondary phase, out of the University of Florida. In 1985, Thompson started at second base for AA Shreveport of the Texas League, and he batted .261. The Giants promoted Thompson the following spring, and like Clark, he made his MLB debut on April 8, 1986.

Rosen was not forgotten in Houston. *Houston Chronicle* reporter Ed Fowler, no fan of Rosen's body of work in Houston, took another shot at him. "Certainly Al 'Round Heels' Rosen, when he showed up for the opener Tuesday night, couldn't have recognized the club he bequeathed to [Houston Dick GM] Wagner. Players [and agents] who once walked all over Rosen at contract time now click their heels when Wagner enters the room."[20]

Both the Giants and the Astros broke out of the gate with strong play on the diamond. At the All-Star break (the Astrodome hosted the All-Star Game in 1986), the Giants had a slim lead over Houston. The division looked this way:

Team	Won	Lost	Percentage	Games Behind
San Francisco	48	40	.545	---
Houston	47	41	.534	1.0
San Diego	45	43	.511	3.0
Atlanta	42	46	.477	6.0
Cincinnati	40	44	.476	6.0
Los Angeles	40	48	.455	8.0

But the Giants could not keep their advantage over their divisional foes. After faltering in July (a record of 12–14), they followed it up with a 12–16 record in August.

As the schedule concluded on Labor Day, September 1, the Giants had slipped to third place in the NL West with a 65–66 record and trailed the Astros (74–57) by nine games.

It was bittersweet for Rosen as his old team was cruising into the postseason. "I'm rooting against players I regard as my own kids," said Rosen. "It was like I wet-nursed a lot of them. I watched them play in places like Asheville and Columbus. I spent five years buoying their spirits."[21]

The Giants finished in third place in 1986 with an 83–79 record. It was a 21-win improvement from the previous year. There were enough positives pieces in place for the fans to have restored hope in the Giants. Clark put up decent numbers despite missing two months with a hyper-extended left elbow, batting .287, with 11 home runs and 41 RBI. Candy Maldonado led the club in home runs (18), RBI (85), and doubles (31). Catcher Bob Brenly also provided some power with 16 home runs.

Thompson was named NL Rookie of the Year by *The Sporting News*. He batted .271 with seven home runs and 47 RBI. Thompson led all NL Rookies in hits (149) and games played (149).[22] Thompson and Clark shared the lead in doubles (27) among freshmen. It was a remarkable season for Thompson, considering he was promoted from Class AA to start at second base for the Giants. He played many games despite his aching right knee. Thompson had arthroscopic surgery after the season to remove some torn cartilage.

Mike Krukow anchored the staff, hurling the only 20-win season of his 14-year career. Krukow went 20–9, with a 3.05 ERA. Scott Garrelts was a combo starter—reliever in 1986. The right-hander went 13–9 with a 3.11 ERA. Vida Blue, in the final season of his career, posted a 10–10 record with a 3.27 ERA.

A "Who's Who" of free agents were available for the plucking for the Giants in the off-season. Reggie Jackson, Tim Raines, Andre Dawson, Jack Morris, and Lance Parrish were among the bigger names looking for the big contract. Despite the star power, players' union chief Don Fehr charged the owners with collusion. "They're not going to sign any free agents because they have a conspiracy not to," said Fehr. "All you have to do is look at last year. No free agent got more than an offer from his former club until his former club was out of it and then a couple of them moved. But he only had one club to bargain with at a time."[23]

Rosen was not biting on Fehr's collusion charges. Instead, he laid out his plan for building a contender. "I don't believe that's the way to build an organization," said Rosen. "It's better normally to build within and establish continuity. That's the way the Giants are going to go. We set the stage last year."[24]

Rosen did not make any big additions to his club. As Fehr predicted, the Giants signed two of their own free agents, pitcher Mike LaCoss and utility player Harry Spilman. The Giants had also released Atlee Hammaker in the off-season but re-signed the southpaw hurler before spring training.

The lack of movement in the off-season did not mean the Giants front office was content with their team. With the right side of the infield cared for, Rosen went to work on the left side. José Uribe started at shortstop for the Giants in 1986. He played in 156 games and showed some wear down the stretch. San Francisco turned to a familiar face, signing Chris Speier as insurance at shortstop. Speier broke in with the Giants in 1971 and played there for seven years before moving on to Montreal. Rosen said, "Speier can back up all three infield positions, and if we have to pinch-hit for Uribe, I feel very comfortable with Speier at shortstop."[25]

Third baseman Chris Brown had been under criticism by the media, the fans, and his teammates for telling Rosen that his season was over on September 1, 1986 (Brown did make one more start, on October 1). It was the second straight season that Brown had ended his season, prematurely to some, instead of playing through nagging injuries. But Brown wanted his left shoulder examined, which had caused him pain since July. Rosen noted that Brown had not been the same player since the All-Star break. "This is a tough thing for everybody. But if a player says he's hurt, I believe him."[26]

Teammates pointed to Thompson, playing with a sprained thumb and a sore right knee, as an example of a teammate who went all-out, despite the lingering injuries.[27] Although he was labeled as a malingerer and a quitter, Brown stood by his assertion that he was in pain. The Giants medical staff could not find anything wrong with Brown. Dr. Frank Jobe, the Dodgers team doctor, examined Brown and found a partially detached biceps tendon. "In my mind, this certainly vindicates Chris Brown," said Rosen.[28]

Rosen acquired outfielder Eddie Milner from Cincinnati for pitcher Frank Williams and two minor league prospects. An average batsman, Milner's game centered around his defensive ability as well as stealing a few bases.

Another addition was Matt Williams. The Giants drafted the slick-fielding infielder with the third pick overall in the MLB Amateur draft on June 2, 1986. The former University of Nevada–Las Vegas star began the 1987 season in Phoenix of the AAA Pacific Coast League. But an injury to Uribe early in the season brought Williams up to the Giants. However, the long-range plan for Williams was to develop him into a third baseman at Phoenix.

San Francisco won its first five games of the 1987 season and 11 of its first 14. But the euphoria of a 16–7 record in April quickly faded. The Giants staggered through May and June, compiling a 22–31 record.

As the sun set on June, the Giants were still in the thick of the NL West race:

Team	Won	Lost	Percentage	Games Behind
Cincinnati	42	34	.553	---
Houston	40	35	.533	1.5
San Francisco	38	38	.500	4.0
Atlanta	36	40	.474	6.0
Los Angeles	36	40	.474	6.0
San Diego	27	51	.346	16.0

On July 5, 1987, Rosen made a blockbuster deal with San Diego that involved seven players. The trade turned the season around for the Giants and gave them the shot in the arm they needed. Rosen sent Chris Brown plus relief pitchers Mark Grant, Keith Comstock, and Mark

Davis to San Diego. In exchange, the Giants received third baseman Kevin Mitchell, starting pitcher Dave Dravecky, and relief pitcher Craig Lefferts.

"I don't view this as anything but a deal for now and the future," said Rosen. "Dravecky is only 31, Lefferts 29 and Mitchell 25. They're here to help us win beyond this year too. Mitchell can play positions besides third base, and we know we got Matt Williams coming. The key is Matt Williams. I'm not saying Mitchell won't be our third baseman. But he can also play the outfield and shortstop."[29]

Mitchell, a member of the New York Mets' World Championship team in 1986, was traded to San Diego as part of a multi-player deal on December 11, 1986. Now he was being shipped off to San Francisco. "I don't understand why they got me and then traded me," said Mitchell. "They got me from the Mets, then they got rid of me. And the part I don't understand is why they traded for another third baseman."[30]

Mitchell may have been upset that he was leaving his hometown of San Diego. But if he was a bit sour, it did not seem affect to his play on the field. In his first game in a Giants uniform, Mitchell clubbed two home runs off Les Lancaster at Wrigley Field on July 5, 1987. The Giants were victorious, 7–5.

The Giants finished a game over .500 at 14–13 in July. They were now in second place, only looking up at Cincinnati in the standings. The Reds (55–48) held a slim three-game lead over San Francisco (52–51).

Rosen knew he needed additional starting pitching. He made two deals with Pittsburgh that netted him two veteran hurlers. On July 31, Rosen sent catcher Mackey Sasser and $50,000 to Pittsburgh for right-hander Don Robinson. Three weeks later, Rosen and Pittsburgh general manager Syd Thrift did business again. On August 21, pitchers Jeff Robinson and Scott Medvin were sent to the Pirates for pitcher Rick Reuschel.

Reuschel had to clear waivers for the deal to happen since it was made after the July 31 trading deadline. If he had been claimed, the Pirates would have pulled him back. Allegedly there is a gentlemen's agreement among the general managers that if a good player such as Reuschel appeared on the waiver wire, teams were to pass on picking him up. It is preferred that two teams make a trade. It was frowned on for a team to claim a player specifically to block a potential deal.[31]

The moves by Rosen were celebrated as if the Giants were now shoo-ins for the NL pennant. One of the reasons was that the Giants outbid, or outhustled, rival Cincinnati for Reuschel. Cincinnati manager Pete Rose did not agree with those who said the Giants could start taking payments for playoff tickets.

"I would have liked to have had him," said Rose, "but evidently they [Pittsburgh] didn't like what we offered. I think our offer to Pittsburgh was better than what they got. I heard Roger Craig said this would give his team the pennant. They've still got to beat us; they've still got to beat Houston. If Roger wants a ticket to the playoffs, I'll send him one—and right behind home plate."[32]

But the Giants pulled away from the Reds in August. San Francisco went 18–11, while Cincinnati went 9–20. The Reds dropped to third place, and the race was on between the Giants and the Astros. But just like the Reds in August, Houston had a horrific September. The Astros went 9–18, while the Giants posted an 18–8 record.

On September 28, 1987, the Giants clinched their first division title since 1971 with a 5–4 win over San Diego. The hero of the day was Don Robinson. He relieved Dravecky after four innings with the score tied, 3–3. He held the Padres to one run over the final five innings, and he also hit a solo home run in the top of the eighth inning that turned out to be the game-winner.

San Francisco won the NL West in 1987 with a record of 90–72. Cincinnati finished in second place, six games back with a record of 84–78.

Of the three pitchers Rosen acquired, Robinson brought the highest return. Pitching out of the bullpen, the veteran right-hander went 5–1 with a 2.74 ERA. Dravecky (7–5, 3.20 ERA) and Reuschel (5–3, 4.32 ERA) also pitched well. For all the griping Mitchell did at the time of the deal, he provided solid offensive numbers (15 HR, 44 RBI, and a .306 batting average).

Will Clark was the offensive force for San Francisco, slamming 35 home runs, driving in 91 runs, and batting .308. Maldonado had one of the best seasons of his career with 20 home runs, 85 RBI, and a .292 average.

Two members of the Giants, outfielder Chili Davis and catcher Bob Brenly, heaped praise on the job Rosen had done to rebuild the Giants. Both Davis and Brenly broke in with the Giants in 1981 and had seen some lean seasons by the 'Frisco bay.

"Rosen could really be considered our MVP, if you really think about it," said Davis. "This is the best blend of players we've had since

I've been around. And this is his team. Rosen's deals gave us the pitching we needed."[33]

"There was no way to assume Bob Lurie and Al Rosen would go crazy making deals when we needed them most," said Brenly. "The trades demonstrated a commitment to winning the division."[34]

An interesting development occurred shortly after the regular season concluded. Rosen's counterparts in Cincinnati (Bill Bergesch) and Houston (Dick Wagner) were both fired. Rosen's ability to land Dravecky and Reuschel, while Bergesch and Wagner did not, was believed to be the reason why they were both dismissed from their positions.[35]

The St. Louis Cardinals opposed the Giants in the NL Championship Series. The Cards won the NL East with a 96–67 record and thus earned home-field advantage in the best-of-seven series.

The Giants and Cardinals split the first two games at Busch Stadium. In Game Two, Dravecky pitched a complete-game, two-hit shutout as the Giants won, 5–0. "Basically, the thing Dravecky did today was pitch his butt off," said Craig. "To beat this club, in this ballpark, that's something. You just can't pitch any better than that."[36]

As the series moved on to Candlestick Park for Games Three, Four and Five, the Giants won two of three games. A record crowd of 59,363 crammed into Candlestick to see the Giants' 6–3 victory in Game Five.[37] The Giants were one win away from the World Series, but that win would have to come in St. Louis. Craig felt the jubilation as the Giants took the lead in the series. "The momentum is going our way,"[38] said Craig. Asked who would start in Game Seven, Craig replied, "It might not go that far."[39]

Game Six was a matchup of Dravecky and John Tudor of the Cardinals. It was a classic duel, but this time Dravecky came out on the other end of a shutout. Tudor combined with Todd Worrell and Ken Dayley to shut out the Giants, 1–0. The solo run came on a sacrifice fly by José Oquendo in the bottom of the second inning. Unfortunately for San Francisco, their bats did not wake up for Game Seven. The Cardinals' Danny Cox hurled the complete-game shutout as the Cardinals won Game Seven, 6–0, and the series.

About 1,000 fans greeted the Giants at San Francisco International Airport when they returned home. "This is incredible," said Craig. "We want to thank all the fans, and for all the strength they've given us. You guys haven't seen anything yet."[40]

"I'm not known for being too considerate about fans," said Chili

Davis. "But I feel sorry for the fans—and Bob Lurie, Al Rosen and Roger Craig. I don't feel angry. I feel like my wife-to-be left me at the altar and ran away with another guy. The door was open; all we had to do was step in."[41]

Rosen was named the 1987 Executive of the Year by *The Sporting News*. He is the only person to be named MVP as a player and recognized as Executive of the Year. His name was chosen on 25 of the 42 ballots cast.[42] United Press International (UPI) and *Baseball America* also honored him as their choice for Executive of the Year.[43]

"If Al Rosen isn't Executive of the Year, the award is rigged," said Dodgers manager Tom Lasorda. "Roger Craig has done a great job, too, but the key guy is Rosen for getting pitchers when he really needed them."[44]

"It's always been my thought that when you're in a real pennant race, pitching makes the difference," said Rosen. "I saw the way the Pirates were heading. They were going with youth."[45]

Lurie did not give up easily in finding a new home for the Giants. He turned to the voters to seek public funding to build a new stadium for the Giants. He first tried San Francisco in 1987 and 1989, then Santa Clara County in 1990, and finally San Jose in 1992. Each time the vote for funding a new ballpark was defeated.[46]

Rosen was busy in the off-season. Free agency was granted to Davis, Hammaker, LaCoss, Milner, pitcher Joe Price, and outfielder Joel Youngblood. Except for Davis and Milner, the rest of the players re-signed with San Francisco.

On December 1, 1987, the Giants signed free agent center fielder Brett Butler. Butler had spent the previous four seasons with Cleveland, leading the team in stolen bases each season, and he batted .295 for the Tribe in 1987. On the same day, Chili Davis signed with California. It was uncharacteristic for Rosen to dip his toe into the pool of free agency. However, this time, he made a big splash with the signing of Butler.

"If you wanted to say we traded Chili Davis for Brett Butler," said Rosen, "we are giving up some power but we get more speed. Butler is an excellent outfielder. As for Chili, he was never a problem here at all. I don't think he's a .250 hitter [what he hit in 1987] but I don't think he's a .290 hitter either."[47]

On March 23, 1988, the Giants made a deal that at the time barely caused a ripple. In a trade of minor league pitchers, the Giants sent Charlie Corbell to Oakland for Rod Beck. It took a couple of years for

Beck to reach the major leagues. But when he did, he was one of the great closers in Giants history.

The Giants took a big hit to their starting rotation when a sore left shoulder sidelined Dravecky early in the season. He returned to pitch at Philadelphia on May 28, 1988, and made a strong start. However, he was experiencing more pain and made a return to the disabled list.

The Giants made a rather surprising move on June 8 when they shipped outfielder Jeffrey Leonard to the Milwaukee Brewers for infielder Ernie Riles. Leonard, who had been a leader in the clubhouse, saw his playing time diminished with the emergence of Mike Aldrete. At the time of the deal, Leonard was batting .256, while Aldrete was hitting .295. "We wanted him [Aldrete] to be an everyday player and, unfortunately, somebody, something, had to give,"[48] said Rosen.

"Candy Maldonado and Aldrete have to play every day, I understand that," said Leonard. "Hopefully I can play every day in Milwaukee—wherever that's at."[49]

"We feel fortunate to get Ernest Riles," said Rosen. "He's a left-handed hitter, has above-average speed. Plays infield positions and outfield. [He] is the kind of player Roger's been after me to acquire since spring training. He balances our team very well."[50] Riles was in his fourth season in the big leagues. Primarily stationed at third base, Riles was batting .252 with one home run and nine RBI. Leonard was in the last year of a five-year pact. The last year of the deal called for him to make $900,000.[51] Though the company line may have been that the Giants wanted to play Aldrete, it may have also been a case of getting something for Leonard in case he left the Giants via free agency.

Art Spander, sports columnist for the *San Francisco Examiner*, took shots at Rosen for trading Leonard.

> It wasn't a trade. In a trade, you give something and get something. This was an athletic version of Publisher's Clearing House. Check your mailbox. The Giants are giving away ballplayers. What Giants president Al Rosen did was give away the heart of the team for a utility infielder. Hey, Al, the patient is supposed to be dead before you donate organs for a transplant.[52]

As June ended, the Giants sported a 39–37 record and were in third place in the NL West. San Francisco trailed first-place Los Angeles by 5½ games. Besides Dravecky, Mike Krukow was also sidelined with capsulitis. "There's no hurry," said Craig. "We've found another starter in Don Robinson, and I'll keep starting him until after the break, and Big Daddy [Rick Reuschel] said he'd pitch every fourth day until the break."[53]

The Giants ended July by sweeping Atlanta in a four-game series and won eight of their last 10 games that month. Their July record was 17–11 as they pulled into a tie with Houston with identical records of 56–48. Both clubs trailed Los Angeles by 4½ games with two months to go.

But the Giants could not keep their momentum going and registered two losing months, going 26–30 through August and September. The Giants finished the season in fourth place with a record of 83–79, 11½ games behind the first-place Dodgers.

Reuschel (19–11, 3.12 ERA) led the club in wins. He lost three times at the end of September in a bid for the second 20-win season of his career (1977). Kelly Downs (13–9, 3.32 ERA) and Don Robinson (10–5, 2.45 ERA) also pitched well.

Butler led the team in stolen bases with 43. It was the highest total for a Giant since Bill North swiped 45 in 1980. Will Clark was the league leader in RBI (109) and smacked 29 home runs while batting .282. Kevin Mitchell contributed 19 home runs and 80 RBI, while taking over for Aldrete in left field. The switch came in mid–August as Aldrete's batting average dropped to .267 with three home runs and 50 RBI.

The season concluded on a most sobering note as news came on September 21 that Dravecky had a 2x3 centimeter tumor on his left bicep. Dravecky traveled to the Cleveland Clinic, where a biopsy was performed.[54]

The results of the biopsy showed that the tumor was cancerous. Because the tumor was close to the bone in his upper arm, radiologists took a bone scan to see if any of the bone would need to be removed and a bone graft performed.[55] The surgeons also cut away half of the deltoid muscle in his left arm. Dravecky was told he would never pitch again.

On December 8, the Giants shipped Aldrete to Montreal for outfielder Tracy Jones. The right-handed-swinging Jones split the 1988 season between Cincinnati and Montreal. Jones was primarily a backup outfielder who batted .295 with three home runs and 24 RBI between the two clubs.

On January 24, 1989, the Giants and the Baltimore Orioles swapped catchers. Bob Melvin went to the Orioles for Terry Kennedy. Mickey Tettleton and Kennedy shared the catching duties in Baltimore, with each player starting 75 games behind the plate. But Kennedy hit a career-low .226, and the Giants were hoping that a change of scenery might reenergize his play. Kennedy's father, Bob Kennedy, was Rosen's top assistant and a former teammate with the Indians.

The Chicago Cubs released Goose Gossage during spring training in 1989. Gossage's role as one of the best stoppers in the game was behind him. Still, the Giants signed him to a free-agent deal on April 14, 1989. Gossage cited teams not giving him enough work so that he could stay sharp. "The last couple of years I haven't gotten the kind of work I need to stay sharp," said Gossage. "Roger said I'll be starting in a middle-relief role. I'm just looking to redeem myself."[56] In 43⅔ innings of work for Chicago in 1988, Gossage went 4–4 with a 4.33 ERA and 13 saves.

However, the Giants were unable to use Gossage as much as they planned. The New York Yankees claimed Gossage on waivers from the Giants on August 10, 1989. "Al told me that Gossage just needed to pitch more, something the Giants couldn't do with him," said Yankees GM Syd Thrift.[57]

Scott Garrelts, primarily a reliever, was moved into the rotation to join Reuschel, Robinson, and LaCoss. Except for Kennedy being named the starting catcher, the rest of the Giants' lineup stayed intact from the previous season.

The Giants started the 1989 season playing .500 ball in April and improved in May with a 17–10 record. Rosen turned to the Steel City again for personnel help, obtaining third baseman Ken Oberkfell from Pittsburgh for relief pitcher Roger Samuels. Oberkfell had been a starter in St. Louis and Atlanta and was a capable batsman, hitting .270 or more in nine different seasons.

Oberkfell and Riles were keeping the spot at third base warm for the long-awaited arrival of Matt Williams. Although the converted shortstop broke camp with the varsity, he did not show much at the plate. Williams was sent to AAA Phoenix for more seasoning. The youngster showed some power at the plate and great hands while manning the hot corner. It was just a matter of time before the third base duties were turned over to Williams on a full-time basis. The time came on July 24, 1989, when Williams was inserted into the Giants' starting lineup. Williams was there to stay for the next several seasons.

Apparently, Tracy Jones was not what the Giants were looking for in a spare outfielder. San Francisco dealt him to Detroit for outfielder Pat Sheridan on June 16, 1989. Two days later, Rosen made another move that paid immediate dividends. Rosen sent pitchers Terry Mulholland

and Dennis Cook and third baseman Charlie Hayes to Philadelphia for relief pitcher Steve Bedrosian and a player to be named later.

All three players the Giants sent to the Phillies were young and not receiving much of an opportunity. They were not dealt for any other reason than the Giants needing a boost in their bullpen, with Garrelts in the rotation. Bedrosian, an established reliever, led the National League in saves with 40 in 1987, and he had 28 saves in 1988.

Rosen was showing his aggressive nature, a quality he also had as a player. Although he recognized that Cook, Hayes, and Mulholland were all talented players who might be solid contributors down the road, he dealt them for what the Giants needed today. It is always a risk to trade tomorrow's prospects. However, whenever Rosen saw a weakness in his team, he worked to make it a strength.

"This gives us the anchor to the bullpen we haven't been able to find," said Rosen. "He's a quality right-handed pitcher, the type of guy who wants the ball in tough situations. We think that coming to a club that's in the race will stimulate him. Look, you're always reluctant to give up players like that. It's tough to give up players you've nurtured through your system."[58]

The Giants went 18–10 in June and sat atop the Western Division standings.

Team	Won	Loss	Percentage	Games Back
San Francisco	47	32	.595	---
Houston	45	34	.570	2.0
Cincinnati	41	37	.526	5.5
San Diego	39	41	.488	8.5
Los Angeles	37	41	.474	9.5
Atlanta	32	46	.410	14.5

Over the next two months, San Francisco sputtered a bit, playing just over .500 (28–26). But their opponents could not make up any ground. Houston in the same period was 26–28 and fell four games behind the Giants heading into September.

Dave Dravecky battled back from his surgery to pitch for Class A San Jose and Class AAA Phoenix. He was 3–0 with an ERA of 1.80. It was an amazing comeback, and the Giants believed that Dravecky was ready to complete his rehabilitation with a start in the big leagues.

On August 10, 1989, Dravecky faced Cincinnati and pitched a strong eight innings on his way to his first win. Dravecky gave up three earned runs, struck out five, and walked one in the Giants' 4–3 win. Five days later in Montreal, Dravecky was pitching a shutout through five innings. Damaso Garcia led off the bottom of the sixth inning and homered, slicing the Giants' lead to 3–1. Andres Galarraga followed, and he was hit by a pitch. Tim Raines was at the plate when Dravecky threw a pitch. A snap could be heard around the diamond. Dravecky went down, withering in pain as the training staff and players rushed to his aid.

Part of the treatment for Dravecky's tumor was to "freeze the bone," which killed the cancerous cells, but it also killed the healthy cells that strengthened the bone.[59] "I was certainly aware that the freezing would weaken the bone," said Dravecky. "And over a period of time the bone would have time to heal. I don't think there was any talk of it after we passed through the danger zone, four to six months."[60] Dave Dravecky's career ended that day in Montreal.

The Giants pulled away from the rest of the teams in the West, posting a 17–11 record and finishing the season with a 92–70 record. San Diego finished in second place, 6½ games behind San Francisco at the end of August. The Padres made a run at the Giants with a 19–8 record in September. But the Giants' lead proved to be too much for the Padres to overcome.

The offense was anchored by Clark (23 home runs, 111 RBI, and a .333 batting average). Matt Williams, in 84 games, smacked 18 home runs with 50 RBI. Combined with the 26 home runs he cracked at Phoenix; Williams tallied 44 round-trippers for the season. Butler batted .283 and led the team in stolen bases with 31.

But the big man in the lineup was Kevin Mitchell. The Giants' left fielder belted 47 home runs and drove in 125 runs, leading the league in both categories. Mitchell also batted .291. He was named the National League's Most Valuable Player, the first Giant so honored in 20 years (Willie McCovey 1969).

Reuschel (17–8, 2.94 ERA) once again led the pitching staff in wins. Garrelts (14–5, 2.28 ERA) also turned in a fine season in his first as a full-time starter. Craig Lefferts led the team in saves with 20, while Bedrosian totaled 17.

The Giants' opponent in the NLCS was Chicago. The Cubs (93–69) won the East by six games over the New York Mets (87–75). The seven-game series started in Chicago, and the teams split two games at Wrigley Field. Garrelts topped Greg Maddux in the opener as the Giants pounded out 13 hits and 11 runs. Clark touched Maddux for two home runs, one a grand slam. Mitchell also homered, a three-run shot.

As the action moved to San Francisco, the Giants used some late-inning magic to win the series. In Game Three, Thompson smacked a two-run homer in the bottom of the seventh inning to lead the Giants to a 5–4 win. In Game Five, Cubs starter Mike Bielecki walked the bases loaded in the bottom of the eighth inning. Chicago manager Don Zimmer brought in closer Mitch Williams. Clark greeted him with a single to bring home two runs and break a 1–1 tie. The Giants won Game Five, 3–2.

Clark was named Most Valuable Player of the series. He went 13-for-20 at the plate for a .650 batting average. He homered twice, doubled three times, drove in eight runs, and scored eight runs.

San Francisco made its first trip to the World Series since 1962. Their opponent was their neighbor from across the Bay, the Oakland Athletics. The A's had it all: power (Mark McGwire, Jose Canseco, Dave Parker), speed (Rickey Henderson), starting pitching (Dave Stewart, Mike Moore, Bob Welch, and Storm Davis), and stellar relief pitching (Dennis Eckersley, Rick Honeycutt).

The A's were a formidable outfit, and the Giants certainly had their work cut out for them in the Series that was initially given the name "Bay Ball."[61] The odds makers agreed, making Oakland 9–11 favorites to win the Series.[62]

"I think Al's done an extraordinary job," said Oakland general manager Sandy Alderson. "He's taken a team that lost over 100 games and in short time turned it into a winner. He has great report [sic] not only with the rest of the organization but, obviously, with the manager. What's very important is that he's put together a club that's not only good but fits the manager's style."[63]

Alderson was not the only one to take notice of the job Rosen had done with the Giants. Peter Pascarelli heaped praise on Rosen in his weekly column in *The Sporting News* on October 23,1989.

> The Giants, who won the National League Pennant, are a monument to Rosen's shrewd operation of a franchise he was given free rein to operate by Giants owner Bob Lurie, one of the genuinely nice people to own a sports franchise. Rosen, with Craig, has made the Giants' baseball operation a model for detail. At the same time, Rosen has made Candlestick livable by pushing for various improvements to the fading mistake by the Bay.[64]

Rosen changed the culture of the Giants. The franchise was once considered a joke, but no more. Winning division titles and league pennants play a part in an organization feeling good about itself and wanting to project a new image. This new attitude by the Giants could be attributed to Al Rosen. Although he was not the self-promoting type, he did not have to be. Others like Pascarelli took note.

The first two games of the Series were played at Oakland-Alameda County Coliseum. The A's won both contests, 5–0 and 5–1.

The Series shifted to San Francisco for the next three games. Just before the start of Game Three on October 17, tragedy hit. And it hit hard. The Bay Area was struck by the Loma Prieta earthquake. The result was violent tremors spreading through Oakland and San Francisco, causing heavy destruction across the region. Journalists from around the world, who were in the Bay Area to cover the series, now turned their attention to reporting on the destruction of bridges, freeways, and buildings. Baseball was put on hold, and "Bay Ball" became known as the "Earthquake Series."

The earthquake registered a 7.0 on the Richter scale. An aftershock the following morning at 3:14 a.m. registered a 5.0.[65] Damage was reported in seven counties:

- 264 people died
- 972 people injured
- 250 buildings damaged
- 4 buildings collapsed
- 1,300 homes in Oakland damaged, 10 collapsed
- Power lines and water resources were cut[66]

During the break, the Giants ended a workout on October 20 to visit a shelter that provided housing for families that were left homeless because of the earthquake.

"It's a small thing, and I don't know if it is going to have any real significance," said Rosen. "But the players, like everybody else, felt great compassion for the people hurt by this thing and we wanted to find out what we could do. This visit, and the others we're planning to make, came out of talks with city officials."[67]

Rosen's youngest son, James, lost his Marina District home because of the earthquake. James had started to collect memorabilia from his father's playing days. "They're only things," said Rosen. "After something like that, you see how little they matter. It was just baseballs, scrapbooks, trophies, unimportant things. He got all the belongings out he needed."[68]

"I don't care what happens," said Terry Kennedy. "The intensity isn't going to be there. Things have changed. This just doesn't mean the same anymore."[69]

Twelve days later, on October 27, 1989, the Series continued at Candlestick Park. Kennedy was right in his assessment. Given how close the destruction was to the World Series, the last two games had an anti-climactic feeling. And that is exactly how they were played as Oakland steamrolled the Giants in Game Three, 13–7, and Game Four, 9–6. Oakland swept San Francisco in four games straight.

"It's not easy to lose four straight," said Rosen. "You can't make light of it. I feel badly for everyone. It was a disastrous loss and you can't minimize its impact. But you can't go jumping to conclusions after four games. We're the National League champions, so my spirits aren't dampened."[70]

Outfielder Kevin Bass, who was with Rosen in Houston, inked a three-year, $5.25 million free-agent deal on November 16, 1989. Nine players on the Giants filed for free agency heading into 1990. Those players included Maldonado, Oberkfell, Kennedy, Lefferts, Krukow, and Sheridan. Two catchers signed on with the Giants. Kennedy re-upped with a one-year deal worth $850,000. His deal also included an option year for 1991. Gary Carter also joined the Giants. Carter, known as "The Kid," was a teammate of Mitchell's on the Mets' World Championship team in 1986. His playing time dwindled due to a sore knee that limited him to 50 games for the Mets in 1989. He signed a one-year, non-guaranteed deal, worth $250,000 including incentives.[71]

Will Clark became the highest-paid player in history when he signed a four-year deal worth $15 million. The deal also included a no-trade clause and a $2 million signing bonus. "Will Clark is the premier player in the game, and he earns every cent," said Rosen. "He plays like a Hall of Famer, and he should be paid like one."[72]

San Francisco also signed reliever Dan Quisenberry to a two-year deal on January 28, 1990. Quisenberry had been one of the top relief pitchers in the majors when he was with Kansas City (1979–1988). He led the AL in saves in five seasons. He had 244 career saves to his credit.

The collective bargaining agreement expired on December 31, 1989. The owners locked the players out of spring training. Both sides worked to come to an accord on the two biggest issues: free agency and arbitration.

Commissioner Fay Vincent worked with both sides, and an

agreement was reached on March 19, 1990. The minimum salary was raised from $68,000 to $100,000 a year. The owners wanted to implement a revenue-sharing plan with the players. But this idea was tabled when it was agreed that both sides needed to do more thorough research and have more discussion.

The lockout lasted 32 days and essentially wiped out the entire spring training. The start of the season was pushed back a week to enable some semblance of spring training to take place. Three games were added on to the end of the schedule so that a full 162-game season would be played.

Just before the season, the Giants added one more free agent. Outfielder Mike Kingery, who was out of options with Seattle, signed with the Giants when the Mariners tried to send him down to Calgary, their AAA affiliate.

Perhaps the Giants had a bit of a hangover from their pennant-winning season in 1989. Or maybe the lack of a proper spring training caused the Giants to play poorly early in the season. The Giants stumbled through April with a record of 8–12. On April 29, Quisenberry (0–1, 13.50 ERA) announced his retirement. "It's time to go," said Quisenberry. "I had the first sore arm of my career in San Diego, and at my age [37], I'm not interested in rehabilitation, cortisone shots, post-natal blues and all that. I never went on the D.L. before, and I just knew it was time."[73]

The month of May was no better, and the Giants had a 19–29 record two months into the season.

Injuries to key players contributed to the Giants' losses. Bass underwent arthroscopic surgery to repair fractured cartilage in his left knee. San Francisco recalled Kingery from AAA Phoenix to take his place. Reuschel twisted his left knee in a 5–2 loss to Pittsburgh on May 27. He was placed on the 15-day disabled list, although the Giants feared that he might need surgery and be lost for the season.[74] Garrelts could not use injuries as an excuse for his miserable performance. He carried a record of 1–6 and a 6.88 ERA through May.

Rosen favored developing young players in the Giants' minor league system instead of building a team through free agency. In June, Rosen's strategy began to pay off as the Giants won 16 of their first 17 games. They finished June with a 19–8 mark. Starting pitcher John Burkett (3–1, 2.68 ERA), reliever Jeff Brantley (1–0, 1.82 ERA, five saves), and Matt Williams (7 home runs, 29 RBI, and a .336 batting average) were all products of the Giants' farm system. They were not the sole reasons for the Giants' turnaround, but they certainly contributed to it.

On August 31, 1990, the Giants signed Mitchell to a four-year deal worth $15 million, plus a $1 million signing bonus.[75] His contract, which he was lobbying for much of the season, matched Clark's. "Kevin Mitchell is one of the outstanding power hitters in the game today," said Rosen. "He has put great numbers on the board, especially in the last two years. He has produced for us, and he deserves to be compensated."[76]

The 1990 NL West title belonged to the Cincinnati Reds. They won the West with a 91–71 record. Los Angeles (86–76) finished in second place, and the Giants (85–77) were in third, six games out. If the Giants were looking for a reason to pinpoint their fall from first place, they could look to their record against the East. San Francisco was 32–40 against those East clubs, posting a losing record against every team but St. Louis (9–3).

The three-headed monster of Clark (19 home runs, 95 RBI, .295 average), Mitchell (35 home runs, 93 RBI, .290) and Williams (33 home runs, 122 RBI, .277) were toughs out in the middle of the Giants' lineup.

Garrelts rebounded from a rough start to finish with a 12–11 record and a 4.15 ERA. However, it was Burkett who led the club in wins, 14–7, and an ERA of 3.79.

Rosen was busy in the off-season. Carter, who backed up Kennedy in 1990, was granted free agency. On November 9, 1990, the Giants signed free-agent pitcher Bud Black to a four-year, $10 million deal. The left-handed starter spent the 1990 season with Cleveland and Toronto. He turned in a record of 13–11 record with a 3.57 ERA. "We felt that left-handed pitching was an area we wanted to strengthen this season," said Rosen, "and with the addition of Bud Black, we think we have done just that."[77]

The signing of Black to a lucrative contract brought out some critics. "It would have not been a surprise if one pitcher had jumped out there quickly and been signed big early, a [Mike] Boddicker or [Tom] Browning," said one American League GM. "But Bud Black? All this does is raise the price of every other pitcher even more."[78]

Brett Butler, who had two years remaining on his contract, was termed a "new look" free agent. Essentially, Butler signed his deal in 1987, and the major league owners were judged by an arbitrator to be in collusion that spring. Based on that ruling, and when an agreement between the players and owners was ratified, Butler was declared a free agent despite of his current contract with the Giants.[79]

Butler's demands, which matched the contracts given to Clark and Mitchell, were deemed too steep a price for the Giants. "Once I heard that number [Butler's request] and felt that number was inviolate, I just felt I had to do something else,"[80] said Rosen.

Instead, they turned to the free-agent market at the winter meetings in Rosemont, Illinois. San Francisco came away with Willie McGee as its new center fielder. The fleet-footed outfielder signed a four-year, $13 million pact. "We were just determined not to leave here without a center fielder," said Rosen. "Brett represents everything it means to be a Giant. He is a fine player and a fine person, and I will miss him."[81]

McGee, who spent 8½ seasons with St. Louis, was traded to Oakland in 1990. He was thrilled to return to the senior circuit. "There are a lot of plusses coming back to the National League," said McGee. "I know the league, and I know most of the players. It will be easier for me to adjust to a new team in the National League."[82]

Rosen was far from finished. On December 4, 1990, Rosen plucked Dave Righetti off the free agency list. Righetti, a southpaw closer for the New York Yankees, saved 36 games in 1990. New York (67–95), uncharacteristically, finished in last place of the AL East in 1990. Righetti had a direct hand in 55 percent of the Yankees' wins. Like Bud Black, Righetti signed with the Giants for four years at $10 million.

Also, on December 4, the Giants shipped infielder Ernest Riles to Oakland for minor league outfielder Darren Lewis and a player to be named later. The Giants received minor league pitcher Pedro Pena on December 17, 1990. Lewis had appeared in 25 games for Oakland in 1990, making his major league debut on August 21, 1990. He began the 1991 season with AAA Phoenix.

On December 5, Rosen sent relief pitcher Steve Bedrosian to Minnesota for two minor league prospects: pitchers Johnny Ard and Jimmy Williams.

"If you add it all up, you'll find the only increase in our salary structure is because of the free-look [free agency] situation,"[83] said Rosen. The recent signings seemed to go against the grain for Rosen and the Giants. There was a sense of urgency to get back into contention for a National League West division title and a pennant. The quickest way to accomplish that goal was to sign free agents. Bob Lurie bought into the idea, opening up his wallet so that Rosen could sign the players he felt he needed. The Giants' payroll for 1991 was approaching $30 million.

Players' salaries were skyrocketing, and those who could afford to pay, did so and then some. "For 100 years we couldn't find a way to destroy this game, but now I think we've found the key. It's disastrous,"[84] said Rosen with regards to the high-priced salaries.

Just before the season began, the Giants dipped into the free-agent market once again, signing outfielder Mike Felder. The six-year veteran was released by Milwaukee a week earlier. "The main reason for getting him was his speed off the bench," said Craig. "He can also play all three outfield positions."[85]

There were high hopes that the winter activity conducted off the field would yield successful results on it. But they did not. The Giants posted a 16–32 record in April and May, which landed them in last place in the West, 11½ games off the pace. They never got back in the race.

Reuschel and Garrelts both began the season in the starting rotation. But injuries to Reuschel (left knee) and Garrelts (elbow) damaged the pitching staff. Together, they appeared in a total of 12 games, with one win between them. Knee and wrist injuries contributed to a shortened season for Mitchell. Right fielder Kevin Bass (left knee) and shortstop José Uribe (left leg laceration) also missed a considerable amount of time. "We do not have a great pitcher on this staff," said Rosen. "We do have fellows who are very capable of being four or five games over .500, but right now we're not even getting that."[86]

Just as in 1990, the Giants in 1991 showed some life in the middle of the season during June and July but fell back in the standings during August and September. San Francisco finished the year in fourth place with a 75–87 record.

Despite the poor record, the Giants did get a solid season from Clark (29 home runs, 116 RBI, .301 average), Williams (34 home runs, 98 RBI, .268) and McGee, who batted .312. Mitchell, despite playing in only 113 games, clubbed 27 home runs and drove in 69 runs. Felder led the team in steals with 21.

Bud Black led the league in losses in 1991 (12–16, 3.99 ERA). Trevor Wilson (another product of the Giants' farm system) pitched well (13–11, 3.56 ERA). Righetti led the club in saves with 24.

Rosen insisted through the season that despite the disappointing year the Giants were having, Craig would not be fired. "He will not lose his job," said Rosen. "He's here to stay. That's in bold print."[87]

True to Rosen's word, Craig was again the pilot of the Giants in 1992. However, the team was on a downward spiral. Part of the problem was a lack of solid starting pitching. Reuschel and Garrelts were released, while Don Robinson filed for free agency. With Dravecky out of baseball, their staff from just three years prior was gone. The Giants had to find some arms. And hopefully those arms were attached to players who were good pitchers.

Their greatest bargaining chip heading to the winter meetings was Mitchell. The power-hitting outfielder did not endear himself to his teammates or the front office. There were enough instances of Mitchell missing flights, showing up late for pre-game activities, and not playing due to questionable injuries. Mitchell became a headache to everyone in the Giants organization. Even the traveling secretary was subjected to Mitchell's inconsiderate behavior. After the travel itinerary was sent out to the club, Mitchell would reject it and then make his own plans.

Mitchell was arrested on November 30, 1991, on charges of rape and battery. But the woman who filed the charges did not pursue the case. "The decision the deputy district attorney made today in choosing not to prosecute does vindicate Kevin in our eyes and in the eyes of the legal system, and for that we are delighted,"[88] said Rosen.

When Mitchell produced the high numbers on the diamond, a lot of his shenanigans were overlooked. But when the production dropped, like in 1991, his antics were harder to swallow.

On December 11, 1991, the Giants dealt Mitchell and pitcher Mike Remlinger to Seattle for pitchers Dave Burba, Mike Jackson, and Bill Swift. The trade did not go over well with the Giants fans who felt that the Giants dealt Mitchell much too early and did not receive enough in return.

Rosen gave an interview on Mitchell and the trade to the *San Francisco Chronicle* on December 18, 1991. "Roger [Craig] and I built up this aura about Mitchell, this tough, hard-playing guy," said Rosen. "Well, it's just the contrary, absolutely a 180-degree difference. It had reached the point where we had to stroke this guy just to get him in the lineup."[89]

One such incident occurred in Los Angeles when Mitchell, who tied one on the night before, told Craig he had to sit out the game because of a headache. When Rosen came to the clubhouse, he found Mitchell sleeping on the trainer's table. Rosen and Mitchell had it out.

For someone like Rosen, who played with broken noses and blood streaming down his jersey, the maladies that allegedly affected Mitchell were laughable. Rosen certainly did not think the Giants were getting value for the millions they shelled out every year for Mitchell. Craig felt that if he pushed Mitchell to change his ways, Mitchell would just leave the team. It would be a fair assumption that his legal problems were also a factor when the Giants traded him to Seattle (Besides the rape charge that was dismissed, Mitchell was also harboring a known fugitive who was wanted for killing a policeman.) And of course, there was the question about Mitchell's conditioning. He seemed to be gaining weight at an incredible rate.[90]

But the ultimate reason for unloading Mitchell, besides the need to replenish a depleted pitching staff, was that the Giants simply were not winning with Mitchell in the lineup.[91] "I'll tell you one thing: we'll win more than 75 games [last year's total] without Mitchell, and we'll have a better time doing it. Write that down."[92]

Giants fans and many in the media took Rosen to task for trading an everyday player for three pitchers. And a productive everyday player at that.

> "After the Mitchell trade, nearly every television sportscast carried the frenzied cries of the Giants' management extolling rhapsodically the virtues of their three newest pitching sensations," wrote J. R. Horne from Paradise, California. "I haven't heard such unrestrained euphoria since the wily, crafty Horace Stoneham stiffed the Cardinals with Orlando Cepeda for Ray Sadecki."[93]

The Giants signed two outfielders to free agent deals before the season. Cory Snyder signed a minor league contract on January 13, 1992; Chris James came to terms on a one-year deal on January 15, 1992.

Another new face on the 1992 Giants was the shortstop, Royce Clayton. He was drafted by the Giants in the first round (15th pick overall) in the June 1, 1988, MLB amateur draft. Clayton won the starting job over José Uribe, who had held the starting shortstop since 1985. Kirt Manwaring, a backup at catcher for a few seasons, was getting a chance to be the everyday backstop of for the Giants.

Rosen's prediction of over 75 victories for the 1992 Giants fell flat. San Francisco suffered through its worst season in the Al Rosen era with a record of 72–90. The offensive production dropped considerably as cornerstones Clark (16 home runs, 73 RBI, .300 average) and Williams (20 home runs, 66 RBI .227) combined for 139 RBI in 1992. The year before, they drove in 214 runs. Robby Thompson and Snyder (14 home runs each) were the only other players to reach double-digits in round-trippers.

The bright spot of the pitching staff was Swift (10–4, 2.08 ERA), who led the NL in ERA. Burkett (13–9, 3.84 ERA) also threw well. The big mystery of the Giants' pitching staff was Righetti. He started the season as the Giants' closer but gave way to Rod Beck when it was estimated that he had lost almost 10 MPH on his fastball. Righetti started four games but then returned to the bullpen. For Righetti (2–7, 5.06 ERA, three saves), it marked the beginning of the end of his career.

There were other distractions the players had to deal with in 1992, and these came from ownership. Bob Lurie realized that after his failed attempts to secure funding for a new stadium via the voting polls, it was time to sell the franchise. Taxpayers were being asked to foot the bill for a new stadium for a team owned by a man of enormous wealth. Indeed, the proposition of paying for a new stadium did not appeal to the taxpaying public.

Although San Francisco Mayor Frank Jordan had a plan in place to build a new stadium downtown, Lurie had heard that story before and listened politely, and half-heartedly, to the proposal.

Lurie, Rosen, and VP Corey Bush flew to New York to meet with Commissioner Fay Vincent and National League President Bill White to discuss the "Giants situation" and possible relocation of the franchise.[94] Vincent laid out a plan in 1990 that consisted of four criteria for a franchise to consider relocation. If a franchise met all four of these points, the door to possible relocation would be opened. The criteria included:

- The organization has been losing money over a substantial period
- There has been declining attendance over a period of three years
- The stadium is inadequate or unsuitable for baseball
- The team resides in a community that has demonstrated a lack of interest in baseball or otherwise.[95]

"I think the history of transfers leads one to the conclusion that baseball ought to be careful," said Vincent, "but I think there are circumstances under which I am prepared to acknowledge that a transfer should be looked at. San Francisco has my permission to look at these options."[96]

While nobody locally stepped forward to offer to buy the Giants, there was outside interest. Bush traveled to St. Petersburg, Florida, to measure the interest in moving the Giants to the Tampa-St. Petersburg region. Voters had approved a bill to fund a new stadium in the area; the Suncoast Dome (now known as Tropicana Field), was built in 1990 and had a capacity of 43,000.

Lurie and Rosen followed up with a trip to Florida to talk terms of an agreement with the prospective buyers of the Giants franchise. On August 6, 1992, they reached an agreement, and the Giants were moving to Tampa—St. Petersburg. The front page of the *Tampa Bay Times* trumpeted the headline "A Giant leap" on its August 8 editions.

The reality was that Tampa had seen this act before. In 1989, the Illinois legislation approved a deal to build a new stadium for the Chicago White Sox when it looked as if the South Side club would be heading to Tampa—St. Petersburg. In 1991, the ownership group was approved for an expansion team, but the owners were rejected when they came up short of cash.

"I hope we're not getting our hopes too high, too early," said Frank Morsani, the car dealer who unsuccessfully tried to buy the Minnesota Twins and the Texas Rangers in the past. "There are a lot of bridges to be crossed, and I hope we're not going to be hurt again."[97]

Indeed, Morsani was correct. The deal, worth a reported $110 million, needed to be approved by the league. Lurie agreed not to "accept or consider" any other offers during a two-week review process.[98]

St. Petersburg assistant city manager Rick Dodge told a cheering crowd of several hundred a quote he had heard from Rosen: "The greatest thrill in the world is the end of the game, to end it with a home run and watch everybody else walk off the field while you're running the bases on air," Dodge quoted Rosen as saying. "Everybody in Tampa Bay should feel like they're running the bases on air today."[99]

Of course, the city of San Francisco was not going to just lie down and let the Giants leave town. Mayor Jordan put together a local ownership group led by Peter Magowan, the CEO of Safeway, Walter Shorenstein, a real estate magnate, and Charles Schwab, among others.[100] The San Francisco ownership team put together a counteroffer to trump the one made by the St. Petersburg group.

Lawsuits began flying. San Francisco filed one against Lurie for breaking his stadium lease. The St. Petersburg ownership group sued San Francisco, claiming their bid was the only legitimate one. St. Petersburg was sued for interference with the contract Lurie held with Candlestick Park.[101]

The San Francisco offer topped out at $100 million and carried with it certain concessions. Two of these concessions were to waive the rental fee and let the city of San Francisco assume all utility and field management costs.[102]

On November 10, 1992, the National League owners voted against the Tampa–St. Petersburg ownership bid, 10–4. This vote freed Lurie from his obligation with the Florida group, and he was able to listen to other offers.

The San Francisco group, with Magowan as the chief operating officer, took ownership following a unanimous vote by the owners to accept their ownership bid at the winter meetings. Hitting coach Dusty Baker replaced Craig. Rosen resigned on November 19, 1992. The new ownership group named Bob Quinn as the new General Manager.

"I've felt that my hands have been tied since September," said Rosen. "One way or the other, there would be different ownership, and I didn't want to commit new owners by making decisions they may not have made."[103]

"It's been a great seven years," said a teary-eyed Rosen. "Obviously, I'm not very good at resigning. Bob Lurie has no peer as an owner. He's absolutely the best man I ever worked for."[104]

After Rosen's resignation, Glenn Dickey of the *San Francisco Chronicle* wrote an article expressing his thoughts on the departing GM.

"I'll miss Al Rosen," wrote Dickey. "I'll miss our talks in his office on baseball past and present; with his playing background, Rosen had a perspective that is rare among general managers. He's an old-fashioned man in the best sense of the phrase, extremely loyal to Lurie and honest to everybody. There have been times when he said he couldn't comment, but he has never lied to me or misled me."[105]

Two months after submitting his resignation, Al Rosen turned 69 years old. He retired from the game he loved so much. In his 13 years as a team president/general manager, Rosen's teams made four playoff appearances, won two pennants, and one World Series. It was a solid record that any front office executive would be proud to put on his resume. Baseball was not the same game anymore. Money, escalating salaries, free agency, and arbitration dampened the enthusiasm for many who loved the sport of baseball.

Rosen's MVP Award as a player in 1953 and his selection as the Baseball Executive of the Year in 1987 are his legacy. As of 2021, Rosen is the only person in history to win both awards.

He had goals to win championships in Houston and San Francisco as he had in New York. He failed to do so, but Rosen did not fail due to lack of effort. It shows how hard it is to win one world championship, much less to win multiple ones.

Rosen will always be remembered as a fierce competitor and an ideal teammate on the field. As an executive, Rosen was said to be a "players' GM." A former player who respected the players and dealt with them in a fair and impartial manner.

Epilogue

After Rosen's retirement in 1992, he and Rita settled in Rancho Mirage, California. Rosen did some consulting work for a few major league teams to keep himself busy. But as he neared 70 years of age, Rosen was focused on those activities related to one's retirement ... golf, bridge, and the challenge of crossword puzzles. He served on the boards and committees of various organizations in and around Rancho Mirage.

Rosen returned to Cleveland several times. He was present for the final weekend in 1993 as the final chapter was written in the history of Cleveland Stadium. The Indians were moving to a new baseball-only stadium in 1994. The organization held several commemorative events during its last season at the stadium. Rosen participated in an Old-Timers game on October 2, 1993.

In 2001, the Indians celebrated their 100th anniversary by naming the top 100 players in franchise history. They honored those players on July 21, 2001, before a Tigers-Indians game at Jacobs Field. Rosen was one of nine third basemen named to the list. "I always collected baseball cards," said former Indians catcher Ray Fosse. "I have Al Rosen's card, probably all the cards of all the guys in here. I started collecting cards in the '50s."[1]

On July 13, 2003, in a special "Turn the Clock Back" celebration, the Indians honored the 50th anniversary of Rosen's MVP season. One of the promotions clubs have for children is to "run the bases" after the completion of a game. The Indians put a twist on it for Rosen's day, and adults were invited to "walk the bases" after the White Sox–Indians game. "What a class act Al Rosen is," said Bob Emling of Cleveland. "He stood at home plate and greeted everyone as they made their way around the bases. He had a handshake and a kind word for everyone."[2]

On July 29, 2006, the Cleveland Indians inducted seven members into its Hall of Fame. Rosen was included in a class enshrined in the Hall along with Herb Score, Rocky Colavito, Addie Joss, Al Lopez, Sam McDowell, and Ray Chapman. The Indians had not hosted a "Hall of Fame" celebration since 1972. The event in 2006, and in subsequent years, was an effort to connect fans with the team's history.

The Cleveland Indians Hall of Fame was just the latest Hall of Fame of which Rosen was a member. In 1971, Rosen was inducted into the University of Miami Hall of Fame. Although Rosen never played baseball at Miami, he was recognized for being "UM's Greatest Professional Baseball player to that time" of his induction.

Rosen was inducted into the Jewish Sports Hall of Fame on July 27, 1980, in Beverly Hills, California. The event was called an "Evening of Jewish Pride II." Los Angeles Dodgers general manager Al Campanis presented Rosen for induction. "At no time have I been so deeply moved as I have been this evening to be recognized as a Jew by Jews," said Rosen.[3]

On June 5, 1988, in Irvine, California, Rosen was inducted into the International Jewish Sports Museum. Proceeds from the event went to the Howard Cosell Center for Physical Education at the Hebrew University of Jerusalem.

On January 11, 2000, Rosen's dear friend Bob Lemon died. Flip often called Lem his favorite teammate and served as the Eulogist at Lem's funeral. "With Lem, you never felt you were in the presence of a great player," said Rosen. "He was always just Lem, a Huckleberry Finn type. He could pitch a shutout the same day he'd been out to 5 a.m."[4]

In 2010, a film was released titled *Jews and Baseball: An American Love Story*. The film was produced by Will Hechter and directed by Peter Miller. "It's not about baseball," said Miller. "It's a story about how a people found their way into a mainstream. And there's nothing more mainstream than baseball."[5]

Rosen, along with many other Jewish players and writers, was featured in the movie. "A lot of people are going to see this movie and not recognize the exploits of people like Hank Greenberg and Sandy Koufax," said Rosen. "It's going to be something new for them, and they're going to take it with great pride, because both of these men were so exemplary in everything they did."[6]

As for his playing career, Rosen was quite candid.

> My career, to sum it up, was short but an awfully good one. I suspect—at least I'd like to think—that if I was not hurt I would have played longer. Longevity is important when talking about the greats, which is proper. I led the

league in home runs and RBI twice. I never thought of myself as one of the all-time great third baseman because I wasn't. But I had some good years. I was as good as an offensive player as there was.[7]

In Cleveland, Rosen is remembered for being an outstanding baseball player who was the last Indians player to be selected MVP. In San Francisco and New York, he may be remembered as a top baseball executive who helped create winning teams. When his name is mentioned in baseball circles, he is described as competitive, honest, friendly, passionate, and trustworthy.

I know who I am. What I represent to anybody else, I don't know. I'm very comfortable with what I've done in my life, the way my life went. Would I change things? Of course, you would change some things. You don't get a second chance, so you become self-satisfied with things you've done. I don't think that I've accomplished things worthy of note—they may be to my kids and to close friends of mine who say I have. But I haven't done anything differently than anybody else. I chose sports as a career, and I had success as a player and an executive. Did I retire too soon from the executive branch? Probably. But it's just my life. It's just like any other life. I've been very lucky.[8]

Al Rosen passed away on March 13, 2015, from natural causes. He was survived by Rita, his three sons (Robert, Andrew and James), two stepchildren (Gail Evenari and David Loewenstein), four grandchildren, and one great-grandchild.

"During his time as Yankees president in the late 1970s, Al was not only a trusted member of the Yankees' front office, but someone my father relied on," said Yankees owner Hal Steinbrenner. "Al left an imprint on baseball and we are grateful a portion of his time was spent with the Yankees."[9]

"We lost a cherished member of the Indians' family," said Indians owner Larry Dolan. "Watching Al play was a true joy and something Indians fans of our generation still cherish."[10]

Cleveland Jewish News ran this headline for Rosen's obituary on its March 20, 2015, edition: "Rosen, AL MVP, recalled as 'Hebrew Hammer.'"

Indeed, he will be for many, many years.

Appendix

Appendix

Indians 3B Offense Stats

Player	Years	Games	Plate App.	At Bats	Hits	Doubles	Triples
Ken Keltner	1937–1949	1,513	6,284	5,655	1,561	306	69
Brook Jacoby	1984–1991, 1992	1,240	4,804	4,314	1,178	192	24
Bill Bradley	1901–1910	1,231	5,196	4,648	1,265	238	74
Al Rosen	1947–1956	1,044	4,374	3,725	1,063	165	20
Buddy Bell	1972–1978	987	4,089	3,712	1,016	155	27
Max Alvis	1962–1969	951	3,864	3,514	874	140	22
José Ramírez	2013–2021	980	4,028	3,545	987	245	28
Casey Blake	2003–2008	810	3,358	2,981	794	183	9
Toby Harrah	1979–1983	712	3,060	2,577	725	111	14
Larry Gardner	1919–1924	673	2,653	2,306	693	128	36
Travis Fryman	1998–2002	602	2,425	2,184	600	116	11
Willie Kamm	1931–1935	522	2,094	1,785	507	105	18

MLB 3B Offense Stats

Player	Years	Games	Plate App.	At Bats	Hits	Doubles	Triples
Eddie Mathews	1952–1968	2,391	10,101	8,537	2,315	354	72
Eddie Yost	1944, 1946–1962	2,109	9,177	7,346	1,863	337	56
Bob Elliott	1939–1953	1,978	8,207	7,141	2.061	382	94
George Kell	1943–1957	1,795	7,529	6,702	2,054	385	50
Willie Jones	1947–1961	1,691	6,718	5,826	1,502	252	33
Billy Cox	1941, 1946–1955	1,058	4,081	3,712	974	174	32
Al Rosen	1947–1956	1,044	4,374	3,725	1,063	165	20
Randy Jackson	1950–1959	955	3,549	3,203	835	115	44
Andy Carey	1952–1962	938	3,221	2,850	741	119	38
Hank Thompson	1947–1956	933	3,570	3.003	801	104	34

Names in bold indicate Hall of Fame members

Appendix

Home Runs	RBI	Walks	Strikeouts	Batting Avg	Slugging Percent	On Base Percent	On Base + Slugging
163	850	511	474	0.276	0.441	0.337	0.778
120	524	428	738	0.273	0.412	0.338	0.750
27	473	242	435	0.272	0.317	0.373	0.690
192	717	587	385	0.285	0.495	0.384	0.879
64	386	297	332	0.274	0.382	0.328	0.710
108	361	257	642	0.249	0.393	0.305	0.698
163	540	404	491	0.278	0.504	0.354	0.855
116	424	292	681	0.265	0.451	0.337	0.787
70	324	403	265	0.281	0.417	0.383	0.799
10	401	223	99	0.301	0.400	0.365	0.765
74	343	212	438	0.275	0.440	0.339	0.779
4	239	255	115	0.284	0.370	0.375	0.745

Home Runs	RBI	Walks	Strikeouts	Batting Avg	Slugging Percent	On Base Percent	On Base + Slugging
512	1,453	1,444	1,487	0.271	0.509	0.376	0.885
139	682	1,614	920	0.254	0.371	0.394	0.765
170	1,195	967	604	0.289	0.440	0.375	0.815
78	870	621	287	0.306	0.414	0.367	0.781
190	812	755	541	0.258	0.410	0.343	0.753
66	351	298	218	0.262	0.381	0.318	0.698
192	717	587	385	0.285	0.495	0.384	0.879
103	415	281	382	0.261	0.421	0.320	0.741
64	350	268	389	0.260	0.396	0.327	0.722
129	482	493	337	0.267	0.453	0.372	0.825

Appendix

Indians 3B Defense Stats

Player	Years	Games	Innings	Chances	Put-Outs	Assists	Errors	Fielding Percentage
Ken Keltner	1937–1949	1,492	13,169.0	4,798	1,568	3,060	170	0.964
Bill Bradley	1901–1910	1,173	10,502.0	4,231	1,490	2,489	212	0.941
Brook Jacoby	1984–1981, 1992	1,109	9,295.1	2,836	735	1,980	121	0.957
Max Alvis	1962–1969	935	8,260.2	2,701	947	1,638	116	0.957
Al Rosen	1947–1956	933	8,081.2	2,855	970	1,773	112	0.961
Buddy Bell	1972–1978	843	7,374.0	2,782	752	1,918	112	0.960
José Ramírez	2013–2021	673	5,653.1	1,579	469	1,051	59	0.963
Toby Harrah	1979–1983	680	5,776.0	1,774	501	1,208	65	0.963
Larry Gardner	1919–1924	600	5,232.0	2,004	622	1,294	88	0.956
Travis Fryman	1998–2002	592	5,058.0	1,368	338	981	49	0.964
Willie Kamm	1931–1935	522	4,427.0	1,588	569	980	50	0.975
Casey Blake	2003–2008	520	4,420.1	1,399	354	973	72	0.976

MLB 3B Defense Stats

Player	Years	Games	Innings	Chances	Put-Outs	Assists	Errors	Fielding Percentage
Eddie Mathews	1952–1968	2,181	19,010.1	6,664	2,049	4,322	293	0.956
Eddie Yost	1944, 1946–1962	2,008	17,294.1	6,285	2,356	3,659	270	0.957
George Kell	1943–1957	1,692	14,455.2	5,294	1,825	3,303	166	0.969
Willie Jones	1947–1961	1,614	14,050.0	5,171	2,045	2,934	192	0.963
Bob Elliott	1939–1953	1,363	11,802.2	4,428	1,448	2,744	236	0.947
Al Rosen	1947–1956	933	8,081.2	2,855	970	1,773	112	0.961
Andy Carey	1952–1962	881	6,951.0	2,650	847	1,692	111	0.958
Randy Jackson	1950–1959	844	7,298.2	2,716	868	1,725	123	0.955
Billy Cox	1941, 1946–1955	699	5,675.2	2,012	668	1,273	71	0.965
Hank Thompson	1949–1956	655	5,499.1	2,055	592	1,341	122	0.94

Names in bold indicate Hall of Fame members

Chapter Notes

Introduction

1. Danny Peary, ed., *We Played the Game* (New York: Hyperion, 1994), 270.
2. Larry Ruttman, *American Jews & America's Game: Voices of a Growing Legacy in Baseball* (Nebraska: University of Nebraska Press, 2013), 70.
3. David Colker, "Al Rosen, 1924–2015: MVP and Exec of the Year," *Los Angeles Times*, March 15, 2015: B7.
4. Roger Kahn, *How the Weather Was* (New York, Harper & Row Publishers, 1973), 77.

Chapter 1

1. https://www.visitspartanburg.com/a-briefhistory-of-spartanburg/ Spartanburg Convention and Visitor Bureau website, Accessed April 1, 2020.
2. 1920 United States Census.
3. 2010 United States Census.
4. Harry T. Paxton, "That Clouting Kid from Cleveland," *Saturday Evening Post*, August 11, 1951, 87.
5. Larry Ruttman, *American Jews & America's Game: Voices of a Growing Legacy in Baseball* (Lincoln: University of Nebraska Press, 2013), 69.
6. *Ibid.*
7. 1930 United States Census.
8. Ralph Berger, "Al Rosen," Society for American Baseball Research Bio Project: https://sabr.org/bioproj/person/40d66568, Accessed April 2, 2020.
9. Peter Ephross, with Martin Abramowitz, *Jewish Major Leaguers in*

Their Own Words (Jefferson, NC: McFarland, 2012), 74.
10. https://www.history.com/this-day-in-history/the-u-s-acquires-spanish-florida, Accessed April 10, 2020.
11. Paxton, "That Clouting Kid," 87.
12. Roger Kahn, *How the Weather Was* (New York: Harper & Row, 1973), 75.
13. Harold U. Ribalow and Meir Z. Ribalow, *Jewish Baseball Stars* (New York: Hippocrene Books, 1984), 135.
14. Kahn, *How the Weather Was*, 76–77.
15. Hank Greenberg, with Ira Berkow, *Hank Greenberg: The Story of My Life* (New York: Random House, 1989), 218.
16. Kahn, *How the Weather Was*, 76.
17. *Ibid.*
18. Greenberg with Berkow, *Hank Greenberg*, 218.
19. Ruttman, *American Jews & America's Game*, 70.
20. Paxton, "That Clouting Kid," 87.
21. *Ibid.*
22. Peter Ephross, with Martin Abramowitz, *Jewish Major Leaguers*, 74.
23. *Ibid.*
24. *Ibid.*
25. Cynthia J. Wilber, *For the Love of the Game: Baseball Memories From the Men Who Were There* (New York: William Morrow, 1992), 98.
26. *Ibid.*

Chapter 2

1. Peter Ephross, with Martin Abramowitz, *Jewish Major Leaguers in*

Notes—Chapter 2

Their Own Words (Jefferson, NC: McFarland, 2012), 76

2. *Ibid.*

3. *Ibid.*

4. Gordon Cobbledick, "They Love Al Rosen in Cleveland," *SPORT Magazine*, May 1952, 68.

5. Peter Ephross, and Martin Abramowitz, *Jewish Major Leaguers*, 77.

6. *Ibid.*

7. *Ibid.*

8. *Ibid.*

9. *Ibid.*

10. Larry Ruttman, *American Jews & America's Game: Voices of a Growing Legacy in Baseball* (Lincoln: University of Nebraska Press, 2013), 72.

11. Harry T. Paxton, "That Clouting Kid From Cleveland," *Saturday Evening Post*, August 11, 1951, 88.

12. Cynthia J. Wilber, *For the Love of the Game: Baseball Memories From the Men Who Were There* (New York: William Morrow, 1992), 100.

13. "Minor League Class C Highlights," *The Sporting News*, July 24, 1946, 31.

14. John M. Flynn, "Electrics Win First Game, 7- 2 and Drop Second 11–6," *Berkshire Evening Eagle*, June 21, 1946, 18.

15. John M. Flynn, "Rosen's Terrific Triple in Ninth Scores Two Men To Beat Oneonta," *The Berkshire Eagle*, July 5, 1946, 18.

16. "Minor League Class C Highlights," *The Sporting News*, September 25, 1946, 31.

17. "Texas League," *The Sporting News*, July 16, 1947, 31.

18. John Cronley, "Rosen Homers as All Stars' Power Topples Buffs, 4–2," *The Daily Oklahoman*, July 11, 1947, 22.

19. Alex Zirin, "Scribe Calls Rosen, Indian Farm Hand, Natural Hitter," *Cleveland Plain Dealer*, August 15, 1947, 17.

20. John Cronley, "Player Prizes Won by Rosen and Beers," *The Sporting News*, September 10, 1947, 29.

21. "Al Rosen Rides Roughshod to Sweep Texas Bat Honors," *The Sporting News*, October 22, 1947, 20.

22. Peter Ephross, with Martin Abramowitz, *Jewish Major Leaguers*, 77–78.

23. Ruttman, *American Jews & America's Game*, 70–71.

24. Hank Greenberg with Ira Berkow, *Hank Greenberg: The Story of My Life* (New York: Random House, 1989), 219.

25. Peter Ephross, with Martin Abramowitz, *Jewish Major Leaguers*, 78.

26. Luther Evans, "Shorter Training Season to Help Most Players, Says the Splinter," *The Sporting News*, January 28, 1948, 8.

27. Cynthia J. Wilber, *For Love of the Game*, 100.

28. "Bill Veeck and the Orioles Make Up After Rosen Row," *The Sporting News*, April 28, 1948, 20.

29. https://www.history.com/this-day-in-history/state-of-israel-proclaimed#:~:text=State%20of%20Israel%20proclaimed.%20On%20May%2014%2C%201948%2C,establishing%20the%20first%20Jewish%20state%20in%202%2C000%20years, Accessed September 29, 2020.

30. Ruttman, *American Jews & America's Game*, 69.

31. "American Association: Kansas City," *The Sporting News*, June 2, 1948, 19, 22.

32. "Flip Rosen on All-Stars," *Miami Herald*, July 28, 1948, 10.

33. "Lemon and Gromek Face Browns Today," *Cleveland Plain Dealer*, September 11, 1948, 15–16.

34. Harry Jones, "Pitcher Black in Critical Condition," *Cleveland Plain Dealer*, September 14, 1948, 1.

35. Al Rosen, "World Champs—What a Feeling for Rosen," *Miami Herald*, October 12, 1948, 5-B.

36. "$6,772 for Each Injun Sets Series Mark," *The Sporting News*, October 27, 1948, 16.

37. "Indians Al Rosen Weds," *Akron Beacon Journal*, October 18, 1948, 4.

38. "Tribe May Put Rosen at First," *Miami News*, September 12, 1948, 2-C.

39. University of Miami Hall of Fame website: http://www.umsportshalloffame.com/al-rosen.html, Accessed May 10, 2020.

40. Gordon Cobbledick, "Spring Slumps Stump Rosen," *The Sporting News*, March 23, 1949, 25.

41. "Spring Training Averages," *Cleveland Plain Dealer*, April 18, 1949, 22.

42. "Mrs. Rosen Files Divorce Suit," *Miami News*, May 12, 1949, 6-B.

43. "Barrett, Savage, Win Two for The Padres," *San Diego Union*, July 5, 1949, B-5.

44. Mitch Angus, "Padres Get Draw in Hitting Bees," *San Diego Union*, July 18, 1949, B-3.

45. John McMullan, "'Third Time He's In,' Rosen, Back Home, Looks to Staying with Tribe," *Miami News*, October 26, 1949, 5-C.

46. *Ibid.*

47. *Ibid.*

Chapter 3

1. Hal Lebovitz, "Move Into Office 'Eye-Opener' to Greenberg," *The Sporting News*, March 1, 1950, 7.

2. Harry Jones, "Keltner Ready to Battle For Job, Lou says," *Cleveland Plain Dealer*, March 1, 1950, 22.

3. Hank Greenberg, with Ira Berkow, *Hank Greenberg: The Story of My Life* (New York: Random House, 1989), 221.

4. Harry Jones, "Here's Form Chart As Tribe Nears Post Time," *Cleveland Plain Dealer*, April 9, 1950, 42.

5. Staff Reports, "Keltner Hopes to Line Up Major League Job," *Cleveland Plain Dealer*, April 13, 1950, 23.

6. Jim Schlemmer, "Keltner Released; Rosen to Open Up at 3d," *Akron Beacon Journal*, April 12, 1950, 33–34.

7. Ed McAuley, "Keltner Reaches End of Trail as an Indian," *The Sporting News*, April 19, 1950, 13.

8. Gordon Cobbledick, "They Love Al Rosen In Cleveland," *SPORT Magazine*, May 1952, 51.

9. Charles Heaton," Rosen Willing to Trade First Big League Homer for Tribe Victory," *Cleveland Plain Dealer*, April 19, 1950, 26.

10. "Rosen's Homers Threaten Good Neighbor Policy," *The Sporting News*, November 1, 1950, 16.

11. Harold U. Ribalow and Meir Z. Ribalow, *Jewish Baseball Stars* (New York: Hippocrene Books, 1984), 125.

12. Harold Sauerbret, "Rosen Tries Bunt After 2 Homers," *Cleveland Plain Dealer*, July 2, 1950, 2-B.

13. Joseph Thomas Moore, *Larry Doby: The Struggle of American League's First Black Player* (Mineola, NY: Dover Publications, 2012), 92–93.

14. Hal Lebovitz, "Indians Blast Stengel's All-Star Snub of Rosen," *The Sporting News*, July 12, 1950, 31.

15. Terry Rosen with Hal Lebovitz, "My Guy Flip," *Baseball Digest*, October 1954, 31.

16. *Ibid.*, 32.

17. Cleveland Indians website, http://cleveland.indians.mlb.com/stats/sortable.jsp?c_id=cle#playerType=ALL&elem=%5Bobject+Object, Accessed November 12, 2018.

18. "Davis, Seltzer, Witt Join Some Exclusive Clubs," *The Sporting News*, August 10, 1987, 26.

19. Hal Lebovitz, "News Came to Cleveland Like Bomb," *The Sporting News*, November 22, 1950, 6.

20. Ed McAuley, "New Skipper Will 'Stick to Best Lineup,'" *The Sporting News*, November 22, 1950, 6.

21. Jimmy Burns, "'Greatest Day of My Life,' Says Slugger of Reception," *The Sporting News*, November 1, 1950, 16.

22. Hal Lebovitz, "Rosen Takes Kiner Advice, Asks Hank For Batting Advice," *The Sporting News*: March 21, 1951, 18.

23. *Ibid.*

24. Harry Jones, "Mitchell-Simpson Battle For Tribe Job Gets Hot," *Cleveland Plain Dealer*, March 1, 1951, 24.

25. *Ibid.*

26. *Ibid.*

27. Gordon Cobbledick, "Boone Finally Coming Into His Own After Three Years of Living in Shadow of Peerless Boudreau," *Cleveland Plain Dealer*, March 1, 1951, 24.

28. *Ibid.*

29. Charles Heaton, "Easter Opposes Kiner In Homer Duel," *Cleveland Plain Dealer*, June 11, 1951, 23.

30. Gordon Cobbledick, "They Love Al Rosen In Cleveland," *SPORT Magazine*, May 1952, 68.

31. *Ibid.*

32. Frank Gibbons, "Rosen's Injury

Pays Off in New Batting Stance," *Cleveland Press*, June 13, 1951, 66.

33. *Ibid.*

34. Harry Jones, "Rosen's Grand Slam Homer Gives Indians 9–4 Victory Over Browns," *Cleveland Plain Dealer*, August 16, 1951, 13.

35. Charles Heaton, "Indians Break Loose After Simpson's Inside-the-Park Homer Erases Tension," *Cleveland Plain Dealer*, September 3, 1951, 59.

36. Gordon Cobbledick, "They Love Al Rosen In Cleveland," *SPORT Magazine*, May 1952, 68.

37. Ed Sullivan, "Little Old New York," *New York Daily News*, September 22, 1951, 22.

38. Stan Isle, "Caught on the Fly," *The Sporting News*, April 16, 1984, 22.

39. Ed McAuley, "Indians Off to Fast Start in Trade Talks," *The Sporting News*, October 10, 1951, 16.

40. Doc Goldstein, "Share of Blame For Tribe's Flop Accepted by Doby," *The Sporting News*, December 19, 1951, 21.

41. Hal Lebovitz, "All Star Game 'Just Nonsense' Feller Denies He Said It That Way'" *The Sporting News*, October 31, 1951: 2.

42. Jimmy Burns, "Ted Moves Into Home Near Miami," *The Sporting News*, November 28, 1951: 15.

43. Ed McAuley, "Pre-Camp Batting School for Five Tribe Slumpers," *The Sporting News*, January 23, 1952: 21.

44. Hal Lebovitz, "Bat School Makes Big Hit With Tribe," *The Sporting News*, March 5, 1952, 16.

45. Oscar Ruhl, "From the Ruhl Book," *The Sporting News*, March 19, 1952, 16.

46. Hal Lebovitz, "Rosen Fires Back at Critic Hornsby, Asserts 'Those Old Guys Like To Knock'," *The Sporting News*, April 9, 1952, 8.

47. "Baseball Preview for '52," *SPORT Magazine*, May 1952, 87.

48. Hal Lebovitz, "Upswing in Changes of Batting Stance," *The Sporting News*, April 2, 1950, 5.

49. *Ibid.*

50. Charles Heaton, "Casey Starts Kuzava After Tribe Fails To Hit Lopat," *Cleveland Plain Dealer*, June 16, 1952, 18.

51. *Ibid.*, 17.

52. Hal Lebovitz, "Rosen an All-Star After Two All-Star Misses," *The Sporting News*, July 9, 1952, 7.

53. "Al Rosen To Marry Miss Terry Blumberg," *Dothan Eagle*, July 27, 1952, 17.

54. "Evening Parties at Cleveland Honor Miss Blumberg and Fiancé Mr. Rosen," *Dothan Eagle*, August 11, 1952m 6.

55. Terry Rosen, with Hal Lebovitz, "My Guy Flip," *Baseball Digest*, October 1954, 32.

56. Harry Jones, "Westlake Will Prove Big Help, Cuccinello says," *Cleveland Plain Dealer*, August 8, 1952, 14.

57. Harry Jones, "Wilks and Strickland Will Join Indians in Boston Today; Needed Reliefer, says Lopez," *Cleveland Plain Dealer*, August 19, 1952, 14.

58. Hal Lebovitz, "Rosen Benched: Majeski on Third," *Cleveland News*, August 20, 1952, 25.

59. Hy Hurwitz, "Sox Tie Game on Fluke, Beat Indians in Ninth 6–5," *Boston Globe*, August 20, 1952, 6.

60. Hal Lebovitz, "Rosen Benched: Majeski on Third," 25.

61. Robert L. Burns, "Brownie-Indian Feud Flames in Downpour," *The Sporting News*, September 10, 1952, 5.

62. *Ibid.*

63. Ed McAuley, "What Happened to Tribe? Better Team Won," *The Sporting News*, October 8, 1952, 11.

Chapter 4

1. Hal Lebovitz, "Rosen Asks to Attend Batting School; 17 Other Injuns to Take Early Drills," *The Sporting News*, January 21, 1953, 6.

2. Hal Lebovitz, "Indians Scorch, Calls Them 'Chronic Quitters'," *Cleveland News*, April 13, 1953, 20.

3. Hal Lebovitz, "Maglie Calls Indians Tougher Than Dodgers," *Cleveland News*, March 13, 1953, 13.

4. David Bohmer, "Cleveland Indians Team Ownership History," Society for American Baseball Research website, https://sabr.org/bioproj/topic/cleveland-indians-team-ownership-history/, Accessed June 27, 2020.

5. "A Kind and Gentle Man," *Cleveland Plain Dealer*, March 31, 1953, 12.

6. Harry Jones, "Don't Pick A.L. Winner Too Soon," *Cleveland Plain Dealer*, April 12, 1953, 3-C.

7. Ed McAuley, "McAuley Picks Tribe for Flag," *Cleveland News*, April 6, 1953, 22.

8. "Game of 26 Walks Taken by White Sox," *New York Times*, April 19, 1953, S1.

9. Hal Lebovitz, "You'll Do OK Without Me," *Cleveland News*, April 20, 1953, 14.

10. Harry Jones, "Pitch Fractures Luke's Left Foot," *Cleveland Plain Dealer*, April 19, 1953, 1-C.

11. "5 of 13 Schools Ripped by Tornado to Reopen," *Cleveland Plain Dealer*, June 10, 1953, 1-A.

12. Chuck Heaton, "Stengel Says Yanks 'Over Hump' Now," *Cleveland Plain Dealer*, June 15, 1953, 27.

13. Harry Jones, "Yanks Reach 18, Rip Indians, 6–2, 3–0," *Cleveland Plain Dealer*, June 15, 1953, 31.

14. Cynthia J. Wilber, *For the Love of the Game: Baseball Memories From the Men Who Were There* (New York: William Morrow, 1992), 102.

15. Dana Mozley, "Tribe Sweeps Yanks 4–1, for 7 in a row," *New York Daily News*, June 29, 1953, C-1.

16. "Rommel Defends Action at Plate," *Cleveland Plain Dealer*, June 29, 1953, 23.

17. *Ibid.*

18. "Schoendienst, Musial and Slaughter Picked on NL 'Star' Team," *St. Louis Post-Dispatch*, July 6, 1953, 14.

19. J. G. Taylor Spink, "Looping the Loops," *The Sporting News*, July 15, 1953, 4.

20. *Ibid.*

21. Harold U. Ribalow and Meir Z. Ribalow, *Jewish Baseball Stars* (New York: Hippocrene Books, 1984), 124.

22. Bob Dolgan, "Close But No Cigar: When Al Rosen Nearly Won the Triple Crown," *Baseball Digest*, March 2002, 77.

23. Hal Lebovitz, "'Umpire Right,' Says Al After Near Miss of the Triple Crown," *The Sporting News*, October 7, 1953, 16.

24. Dolgan, "Close But No Cigar," 77.

25. Herb Heft, "His Nat Buddies Ganged Up to Help Vernon to Top Spot," *The Sporting News*, October 7, 1953, 16.

26. "Melon Slices," *The Sporting News*, October 14, 1953, 8.

27. Hal Lebovitz, "Landslide MVP Vote 'Brought Tears' to Al and Mrs. Rosen," *The Sporting News*, December 9, 1953, 22.

Chapter 5

1. Hal Lebovitz, "Rosen, New Pop at Noon, Is 'Man of Year' at Night," *The Sporting News*, January 27, 1954, 17.

2. Hal Lebovitz, "Birth of Son to Net Al Rosen $750 in Teammates' Wagers," *The Sporting News*, January 27, 1954, 17.

3. Some sources such as Retrosheet and Baseball-Reference have the Indians sending Philadelphia $15,000.

4. John Webster, "Athletics Trade Balky Philley for 2 Indians' Rookie Hurlers," *Philadelphia Inquirer*, February 20, 1954, 15.

5. Hal Lebovitz, "Tribe Doesn't Have Desire, Says Philley," *Cleveland News*, March 11, 1954, 27.

6. Lyall Smith, "As of Today: Even Hal Wonders What Future Holds," *Detroit Free Press*, July 23, 1953, 23.

7. Chuck Heaton, "Avila Signs: Newhouser Gets Tryout," *Cleveland Plain Dealer*, February 16, 1954, 21.

8. Ed McAuley, "Ruth's Record is Safe, Says Slugger Rosen," *Cleveland News*, March 4, 1954, 26.

9. Howard Preston, "Man in the Grandstand," *Cleveland News*, March 12, 1954, 28.

10. "Indians Final Spring Averages," *Cleveland Plain Dealer*, April 12, 1954, 29.

11. Frank Gibbons, "Indian Items," *Cleveland Press*, April 1, 1954, 40.

12. Staff, "Simpson's Arm is Broken Again," *Cleveland Plain Dealer*, March 26, 1954, 27.

13. Gordon Cobbledick, "Veteran Hurlers, Rizzuto, Coleman and Mantle Hold Key to New York Flag Hopes," *Cleveland Plain Dealer*, April 11, 1954, 2-C.

14. Harry Jones, "Sees Tribe

Improvement Not Enough, Picks Yanks," *Cleveland Plain Dealer*, April 11, 1954, 2-C.

15. "Yanks, White Sox, Indians, Say Scripps-Howard Writers," *Cleveland Press*, April 9, 1954, 50.

16. "Regalado Goes to Third, Rosen to First Today," *Cleveland Plain Dealer*, April 25, 1954, C1.

17. *Ibid.*

18. Bud Shaw, "Ex-Tribe great Rosen has finally seen it all," *Cleveland Plain Dealer*, July 13, 2003, C3.

19. Harry Jones, "Indians Pick Up Confidence on Road, Believe They Can Go on to Pennant," *Cleveland Plain Dealer*, March 8, 1954, 28.

20. Hal Lebovitz, "It's Batter, Not the Bat, Declares Rosen After Red Sox Try to 'Nail' His Secret," *The Sporting News*, June 2, 1954, 7.

21. Ed McAuley, "Williams Still Reigns, but Rosen Tries Crown for Size," Cleveland News, May 19, 1954, 17.

22. Bob Dolgan, "Close But No Cigar: When Al Rosen Nearly Won the Triple Crown," *Baseball Digest*, March 2000, 78.

23. Hal Lebovitz, "New Pepper Spices Avila's Red-Hot Start," *The Sporting News*, June 16, 1954, 3.

24. Harry Jones, "Indians Trade Chakales for Wertz," *Cleveland Plain Dealer*, June 2, 1954, 25.

25. Frank Gibbons, "Help Needed in RBI Dept. Against Yankees with Rosen Ailing," *Cleveland Press*, June 1, 1954, 24.

26. Frank Gibbons, "Our Greatest Victory in Yankee Stadium—Lopez," *Cleveland Press*, June 3, 1954, 22.

27. *Ibid.*

28. Ed Chay, "Injured Rosen Hopes to Play Against Red Sox," *Cleveland Plain Dealer*, June 6, 1954, C-1.

29. Frank Gibbons, "Time (Not Rest) to Heal Rosen, Avila Hand," *Cleveland Press*, June 4, 1954, 37.

30. Dolgan, "Close But No Cigar," 78.

31. Ray De Crane, "Doctor's Wife Murdered in Bay Village," *Cleveland Press*, July 5, 1954,: A-1.

32. "All Star Baseball Poll," *Chicago Tribune*, July 5, 1954: 4–1.

33. Hal Lebovitz, "Hero Rosen Gives Williams 'Assist,'" *Cleveland News*, July 14, 1954, 18.

34. *Ibid.*

35. Dan Taylor "All Star Game 2d to debut," *Cleveland Press*, July 14, 1954, 54.

36. *Ibid.*

37. Harry Jones, "Batting Around," *Cleveland Plain Dealer*, May 27, 1954, 27.

38. Dan Cordtz, "Doby's Home Run Larceny Becomes Routine Chore," *Cleveland Plain Dealer*, August 9, 1954, 25.

39. James Doyle, "The Sport Trail," *Cleveland Plain Dealer*, August 13, 1954, 21.

40. Harry Jones, "Batting Around," *Cleveland Plain Dealer*, August 18, 1954, 25.

41. *Ibid.*

42. Dan Daniel, "Casey Willing to Stick at Yanks Helm?—He's Willing," *The Sporting News*, September 22, 1954, 2.

43. Hal Lebovitz, "'Choke-Up' Critics of Tribe Eat Crow," *The Sporting News*, September 22, 1954, 4.

44. Lebovitz, "Choke-Up Critics," 8.

45. Bill James, *The New Bill James Historical Baseball Abstract* (New York: Free Press Publishing, 2003), 509.

46. "Yanks, White Sox, Indians, Say Scripps-Howard Writers," *Cleveland Press*, April 9, 1954, 50.

47. The Polo Grounds, New York, New York, https://www.ballparksof baseball.com/ballparks/polo-grounds/, Accessed September 15, 2019.

48. Cleveland Stadium, Cleveland, Ohio, https://www.ballparksofbaseball. com/ballparks/cleveland-municipal-stadium/, Accessed September 15, 2019.

49. Joseph Wancho, ed., *Pitching to the Pennant* (Lincoln: University of Nebraska Press, 2014), 287.

50. Chuck Heaton, "Dente Goes to Short, Rosen Returns as Indians Battle to End Slump," *Cleveland Plain Dealer*, October 2, 1954, 25.

51. Peter Ephross, with Martin Abramowitz, *Jewish Major Leaguers in Their Own Words* (Jefferson, NC: McFarland, 2012), 82.

52. Shirley Povich, "Why the Indians Looked So Bad?" *Baseball Digest*, November 1954, 35.

53. Povich, "Why the Indians Looked So Bad?" 33–34.

54. *Ibid.*, 31.

55. Ruttman, *American Jews & America's Game*, 74.

Chapter 6

1. Chuck Heaton, "Kiner Gives Indians Extra Siege Gun," *Cleveland Plain Dealer*, November 17, 1954, 29.

2. *Ibid.*

3. *Ibid.*, 30.

4. "Yogi Says Kiner Should Hit Well," *Cleveland Plain Dealer*, November 17, 1954, 29.

5. Hal Lebovitz, "Frick Calls Balk as Kiner Takes Big Cut at Own Pay," *The Sporting News*, December 22, 1954, 9.

6. Harry Jones, "Rosen Signs For Estimated $40,000," *Cleveland Plain Dealer*, January 12, 1955, 27.

7. Harry Jones, "Batting Around," *Cleveland Plain Dealer*, March 5, 1955, 23.

8. Hank Greenberg, with Ira Berkow, *Hank Greenberg: The Story of My Life* (New York: Random House, 1989), 221.

9. James E. Doyle, "The Sport Trail," *Cleveland Plain Dealer*, March 11, 1955, 27.

10. Edgar G. Brands, "Major Citations Swept by Giants," *The Sporting News*, January 5, 1955, 1.

11. *Ibid.*, 2.

12. Dan Parker, "Baseball Forecast 1955," *American Weekly*, April 10, 1955, 10.

13. Harry Jones, "Jones Picks Tribe to Make Runaway of Pennant Race," *Cleveland Plain Dealer*, April 10, 1955, 2-C.

14. Gordon Cobbledick, "Indians Good Pitching-Long Ball Formula Will Win Pennant--Cobbledick," *Cleveland Plain Dealer*, April 10, 1955, 2-C.

15. Red Smith, "They All Put Kansas City Last," *Sports Illustrated*, April 18, 1955, https://www.si.com/vault/1955/04/18/621613/they-all-put-kansas-city-last, Accessed January 26, 2020.

16. Frank Gibbons, "Feller Was Better Than I Was—Score," *Cleveland Press*, May 2, 1955, 44.

17. Chuck Heaton, "Rosen Asks for Chance After Wertz Is Sidelined," *Cleveland Plain Dealer*, May 9, 1955, 31.

18. "Al Credits About Everybody on Club for Helping Him," *The Sporting News*, September 7, 1955, 3.

19. Hal Lebovitz, "Al Smith Keeping Indians in Race-Lopez," *The Sporting News*, September 7, 1955, 3.

20. Associated Press, "Williams Will Rejoin Red Sox; Newhouser, Simpson Leave Tribe," *Cleveland Plain Dealer*, May 12, 1955, 27.

21. Lou Hatter, "Orioles Beat Indians' Lemon, 4–1, Bow to Garcia, 5–0," *Baltimore Sun*, May 16, 1955, 16.

22. Hal Lebovitz, "Senor Playing Put-and-Take with Indians," *The Sporting News*, June 1, 1955, 7.

23. Chuck Heaton, "Nieman Sees No Need to Change Specs, Now," *Cleveland Plain Dealer*, May 25, 1955, 33.

24. Bob Maisel, "Kansas City Gets Runs on Wind-Blown Double by Demaestri in Fourth," *Baltimore Sun*, June 12, 1955, 41.

25. Harry Jones, "Batting Around," *Cleveland Plain Dealer*, June 21, 1955, 23.

26. "Orioles Pay Cash to Wind Up Indian Deal," *Cleveland Plain Dealer*, June 23, 1955, 23.

27. Jim Schlemmer, "Even Scorer Helps Slump-Ridden Rosen," *Akron Beacon Journal*, June 29, 1955, 25.

28. "Fans Name Only Five Repeaters in Balloting for Starting Lineup," *The Sporting News*, July 13, 1955, 9.

29. Gordon Cobbledick, "Indians Can't Hope to Overhaul Yankees Unless Rosen and Avila Regain Batting Eyes," *Cleveland Plain Dealer*, July 14, 1955, 25.

30. Harry Jones. "Failure on Mound Puts Tribe Down," *Cleveland Plain Dealer*, August 18, 1955, 23–34.

31. Harry Jones, "No disgrace to Lose Flag, says Lopez," *Cleveland Plain Dealer*, September 24, 1955, 29.

32. Harry Jones, "Yankees Deserve to Win—Lopez," Cleveland Plain Dealer, September 24, 1955, 32.

33. "Rosen Riled by Fans 'Boos'—But I'll Make 'Em Cheer,'" *The Sporting News*, September 28, 1955, 19.

34. *Ibid.*

35. Harry Jones, "Indians Trade Doby to Chicago," *Cleveland Plain Dealer*, October 26, 1955, 1.

36. *Ibid.*

37. Hal Lebovitz, "Cut to 30 Grand, Rosen Admits He 'Had It Coming,'" *The Sporting News*, January 25, 1956, 4.

38. *Ibid.*

39. Hal Lebovitz, "Neck Injury Puts Rosen in 'Collar,'" Baseball Hall of Fame Player Clip File of Al Rosen.

40. Hal Lebovitz, "Rosen's Raps Raise Hope of Comeback," *The Sporting News*, April 11, 1956, 22.

41. *Ibid.*

42. Harry Jones, "Batting Around," *Cleveland Plain Dealer*, April 16, 1956, 31.

43. Harry Jones, "Yanks to Win, Tribe to Place," *Cleveland Plain Dealer*, April 15, 1956, 2-C.

44. Jim Schlemmer, "Lopez Is No Casey," *Akron Beacon Journal*, May 19, 1956, 12.

45. *Ibid.*

46. Hal Lebovitz, "Rosen Rappers Reddened by Senor's Scorching Blast," *The Sporting News*, May 30, 1956, 9.

47. Hal Lebovitz, "TV Viewing Shows Al Rosen 'Why Fans Get Burned Up,'" *The Sporting News*, June 6, 1956, 8.

48. Hal Lebovitz, "Rosen to Be Traded Hank Hints: 'I'll Quit First,' Flip Indicates," *The Sporting News*, September 26, 1956,11.

49. *Ibid.*

50. *Ibid.*

51. "Spoils of the Series," *The Sporting News*, October 24, 1956, 14.

52. Doby was traded back to the Indians from Chicago in 1958 and smacked 13 home runs that year for a career total of 215 as a Cleveland Indian.

53. *2019 Cleveland Indians Information & Record Book.*

54. United Press International, "Rosen of Indians Quits Baseball; Infielder 'Can't Do Job Anymore,'" January 31, 1957, Baseball Hall of Fame Player Clip File of Al Rosen.

55. *Ibid.*

56. Associated Press, "'Boos Didn't End Career'-Rosen," February 12, 1957, Baseball Hall of Fame Player Clip File of Al Rosen.

57. *Ibid.*

58. "Hank Still Hasn't Given Up on Rosen," *Cleveland Plain Dealer*, March 16, 1957, 26.

59. Chuck Heaton, "Greenberg Says 'No' to Big Rosen Boost," *Cleveland Plain Dealer*, April 2, 1957: 29.

60. *Ibid.*, 30.

61. Gordon Cobbledick, "Indians Do Not Believe Rosen Can Help Team; Many Don't Want Him to Return," *Cleveland Plain Dealer*, April 2, 1957, 29.

62. "Anticlimax—or Al Rosen's Fall from Grace," *Cleveland Plain Dealer*, April 3, 1957, 14.

63. Chuck Heaton, "Sports Scene on TV," *Cleveland Plain Dealer*, July 30, 1960, 25.

64. Cleveland Indians 2019 Information & Record Book, Attendance History, 324.

65. Wahoo Club, https://wahooclub.org/our-history, Accessed February 14, 2020.

66. *Ibid.*

67. "Baseball Backers Led by Al Rosen," *Cleveland Plain Dealer*, March 18, 1962, 2-C.

68. Wahoo Club, Official Booster Club of the Cleveland Indians, https://wahooclub.org/our-history, Accessed July 5, 2020.

69. "Group 66-New Force in City," *Cleveland Plain Dealer*, April 6, 1966, 14.

70. "Group 66 to Launch Massive Program to Revitalize Stadium," *Cleveland Plain Dealer*, May 20, 1966, 1.

71. *Ibid.*, 4.

72. Al Rosen, *Baseball and Your Boy* (Cleveland, OH: World Publishing, 1967), ix–x.

73. Gene L. Maeroff, "Al Rosen ... A Growth Story," 13.

74. History Channel, https://www.history.com/topics/middle-east/six-day-war, Accessed February 17, 2020.

75. Patricia M. Mote, "An Unlikely Pair—Dorothy Fuldheim and Al Rosen," April 4, 2015, https://www.cleveland.com/opinion/2015/04/an_unlikely_pair_--_dorothy_fu.html, Accessed February 17, 2020.

76. *Ibid.*

77. *Ibid.*

78. "Al Rosen Reports on Israeli Spirit," *Cleveland Jewish News*, June 30, 1967, 5.

79. Baseball Hall of Fame Player's Clip File of Al Rosen.

80. Gene L. Maeroff, "Al Rosen ... A Growth Story," *Cleveland Plain Dealer Sunday Magazine*, September 8, 1968, 14.

81. Burr Snider, "Al Rosen's Giant Steps," *San Francisco Examiner*, September 29, 1987, E-4.

82. Earl Wilson, "Ex-Cleveland Indian Al Rosen to Marry July 24," *Cleveland Plain Dealer*, July 9, 1971, 11.

83. Stephanie Storm, "Competitive streak still burning in Al Rosen," *Akron Beacon Journal*, February 29, 2004, C4.

84. Russell Schneider, "Stouffer Halts Switch Talk by Buying Indians," *The Sporting News*, August 27, 1966, 5.

85. Russell Schneider, "Five Changes in Indians' Top Command since '46," *The Sporting News*, August 27, 1966, 5.

86. Bill Madden, *Steinbrenner: The Last Lion of Baseball* (New York: Harper Collins, 2010), 4.

87. Madden, *Steinbrenner: The Last Lion of Baseball*, 5.

88. *Ibid.*, 6.

89. *Ibid.*

90. *Ibid.*, 7.

91. Russell Schneider, "Director Convinced Tribe Will Stay," *Cleveland Plain Dealer*, December 8, 1971, 1-E.

92. *Ibid.*, 4-E.

Chapter 7

1. Bill Lubinger, "Indians great Rosen endured, prevailed in face of bigotry," *Cleveland Plain Dealer*, October 11, 2010, D1.

2. Bill Madden, *Steinbrenner: The Last Lion of Baseball* (New York: Harper-Collins, 2010), 8.

3. *Ibid.*

4. Ibid., 12.

5. *Ibid.*

6. "Former AL MVP Joins Caesars Staff," *Las Vegas Review Journal*, May 15, 1975, 67.

7. *Ibid.*

8. Madden, *Steinbrenner: The Last Lion of Baseball*, 132.

9. Murray Chass, "Paul Resigns from Yankees; Rallis, Rosen to Replace Him," *New York Times*, December 2, 1977, A23.

10. Steve Cady, "Rosen is Named President of the Yankees," *New York Times*, March 28, 1978, 44–48.

11. Peter Golenbock, *Wild, High and Tight: The Life and Death of Billy Martin* (New York: St. Martin's, 1994), 267.

12. Cady, "Rosen is Named President of the Yankees," 48.

13. "Yanks Battery Makes Pitch to Owner," *New York Times*, March 7, 1978, 29, 36.

14. Phil Pepe, "Blair's 3-Run HR Trips Mets in 9th," *New York Daily News*, March 27, 1978, 44.

15. Murray Chass, "Doctor Doubts Diabetes Will Curb Hunter Career." *New York Times*, March 3, 1978, A19.

16. Murray Chass, "Yankee Day: Absentee and an Ailment," *New York Times*, March 4, 1978, 15.

17. Murray Chass, "Blomberg on White Sox: A Less-Humorous Player," *New York Times*, March 19, 1978, S4.

18. Phil: Pepe, "Martin Says Yankees Will Win in Tough Race," *The Sporting News*, April 22, 1978, 21.

19. *Ibid.*

20. Roger Kahn, *October Men: Reggie Jackson, George Steinbrenner, Billy Martin, and the Yankees' Miraculous* Finish *in 1978* (Orlando, FL: Harcourt, 2003), 221.

21. *Ibid.*

22. Steve Cady, "5 Fined, but Yankees Triumph, 3–2; Expos Beat Mets on Homer in 11th," *New York Times*, April 16, 1978, 1, 6.

23. *Ibid.*

24. Kahn, *October Men*, 225.

25. Joe Flaherty, "Yankees: 'More Than Players,'" *New York Daily News*, April 23, 1978, 87.

26. *Ibid.*

27. *Ibid.*

28. *Ibid.*

29. "Munson Object of Fan Complaint," *New York Times*, May 1, 1978, C4.

30. "Munson Extra Touchy," *The Sporting News*, May 20, 1978, 14.

205

31. Dave Anderson, "Thurman Munson's Isolation," *New York Times*, May 9, 1978, 14.
32. "Figgy: Use Me More or Trade Me," *New York Daily News*, May 27, 1978, 160.
33. *Ibid.*
34. Red Foley, "Andy, Rawley: 1-Hitter, Nettles' HR in 7th Beats Tribe, 2–0," *New York Daily News*, May 30, 1978, 49.
35. Phil Pepe, "Flanagan 4-Hits Ailing Yanks, 3–2," *New York Daily News*, June 1, 1978, 84.
36. *Ibid.*
37. Murray Chass, "Yankees' Hassles Resurfacing," *New York Times*, June 3, 1978, 13.
38. *Ibid.*
39. Gerald Eskenazi, "Twins Take Carew Off Trade Mart," *New York Times*, June 15, 1978, B21.
40. Dick Young, "Yanks: No Rod Deal; Twins Also Nix Royals, Rangers," *New York Daily News*, June 15, 1978, 64.
41. Dick Young, "Billy Near Ax Again," *New York Daily News*, June 7, 1978, 96.
42. *Ibid.*
43. Murray Chass, "Guidry Fans 18 Angels for Yank Mark, Wins No. 11 Without Loss, 4–0," *New York Times*, June 18, 1978, S1.
44. "Martin Seething as Criticism Mounts," *New York Times*, June 23, 1978, A17.
45. Murray Chass, "Yanks Weigh Shift of Martin's Aide," *New York Times*, June 26, 1978, C1.
46. "Martin Seething as Criticism Mounts," New York Times, June 23, 1978, A17.
47. Red Smith, "Slowly in the Wind," *New York Times*, June 25, 1978, S3.
48. Phil Pepe, "Peace, It's Wonderful," *New York Daily News*, June 28, 1978, 109.
49. Kahn, *October Men*, 281.
50. Murray Chass, "Yankees Change, But Still Lose, 6–1," *New York Times*, July 14, 1978, A14.
51. Kahn, *October Men*, 285.
52. *Ibid.*
53. Murray Chass, "Reggie Jackson Penalized: 5 Days, $9,000," *New York Times*, July 19, 1978, A15.
54. *Ibid.*

55. Murray Chass, "Jackson's 'Differences' Stir Turmoil," *New York Times*, July 20, 1978.
56. Murray Chass, "Owner Stunned by Manager's Outburst," *New York Times*, July 24, 1978, C6.
57. Madden, *Steinbrenner: The Last Lion of Baseball*, 144.
58. Chass, "Owner Stunned by Manager's Outburst," C1.
59. Madden, *Steinbrenner: The Last Lion of Baseball*, 64.
60. Murray Chass, "Martin Resigns, Bob Lemon to Manage Yankees," *New York Times*, July 24, 1978, B11.
61. Madden, *Steinbrenner: The Last Lion of Baseball*, 146.
62. Chass, "Martin Resigns; Bob Lemon to Manage Yankees," B11.
63. Dave Nightingale, "Sox fire Bob Lemon, name Doby," *Chicago Tribune*, July 1, 1978, 2–2.
64. Al Harvin, "Lemon Is Classified as a Disciplinarian," *New York Times*, July 25, 1978, B12.
65. "Optimistic Lemon Takes Yanks' Helm," *New York Times*, July 26, 1978, B7.
66. Madden, *Steinbrenner: The Last Lion of Baseball*, 147.
67. Kahn, *October Men*, 313.
68. Madden, *Steinbrenner: The Last Lion of Baseball*, 149.
69. Kahn, *October Men*, 315.
70. *Ibid.*
71. Madden, *Steinbrenner: The Last Lion of Baseball*, 243.
72. Dick Young, "Young Ideas," *New York Daily News*, August 6, 1978, 88.
73. https://www.si.com/mlb/2018/09/19/14-back-documentary-yankees-red-sox-1978-pennant-race, Sports Illustrated.com, Tom Verduci September 19, 2018, accessed on March 20, 2020.
74. Madden, *Steinbrenner: The Last Lion of Baseball*, 153.
75. Francis Rosa, "The Power of Positive Thinking," *Boston Globe*, September 11, 1978, 28.
76. *Ibid.*
77. Madden, *Steinbrenner: The Last Lion of Baseball*, 154.
78. Dan Coughlin "Spoiler Tribe Wins, Ties Up East; N.Y., Boston Battle for Title

Today," *Cleveland Plain Dealer*, October 2, 1978, 1-C.

79. Larry Ruttman, *American Jews & America's Game: Voices of a Growing Legacy in Baseball* (Lincoln: University of Nebraska Press, 2013), 76.

80. Bill Madden, "Proud Record: Yanks Never Fold in Stretch," *The Sporting News*, October 14, 1978, 23.

81. Melissa Isaacson, *Sweet Lou, Lou Piniella: A Life in Baseball* (Chicago: Triumph Books, 2009), 75.

82. *Ibid.*

83. Ross Newhan, "Team October KOS Dodgers Again," *Los Angeles Times*, October 18, 1978, III-1, III-10.

84. "Crash kills Lemon's son," *Arizona Republic*, November 1, 1978, 17.

85. Phil Pepe, "Bob Lemon's sweet and sour times," *New York Daily News*, February 18, 1979, 15.

86. Jack Lang, "Yankees Sign Tiant: Two years at 200G, 10 years as a scout," *New York Daily News*, November 14, 1978, 92.

87. *Ibid.*

88. Murray Chass, "Yankees Sign John for $1.4 Million," *New York Times*, November 23, 1978, D13.

89. Joseph Durso, "Stage Set for 3 Major League Divisions; Carew, Lee Trades Expected at Meeting," *New York Times*, December 3, 1978, S1.

90. Phil Pepe, "Carew $ jackpot has Phils leading," *New York Daily News*, December 7, 1978, 112, 131.

91. Phil Pepe, "Rules on Carew: Yankees," *New York Daily News*, January 24, 1979, 48.

92. Phil Pepe, "Clubhouse Scuffle Puts Goose in Drydock," *The Sporting News*, May 5, 1979, 9.

93. Phil Pepe, "Guidry Relief Gesture Hailed by Yankees," *The Sporting News*, May 19, 1979, 25.

94. Dave Anderson, "Yankees Gamble With Guidry," *New York Times*, May 23, 1979, B12.

95. Madden, *Steinbrenner: The Last Lion of Baseball,* 164.

96. *Ibid.*

97. Murray Chass, "Steinbrenner Hails Martin as Man for Job; New Manager Calls Jackson's Role Crucial," *New York Times*, June 19, 1979, B17,

98. Malcolm Moran, "Lemon Backs Move 'To Get Club Going,'" *New York Times*, June 19, 1979, B17.

99. Murray Chass, "Yankees Explore Trading of Jackson," *New York Times*, June 24, 1979, S1.

100. *Ibid.*, S4.

101. Phil Pepe, "Jax Wants Out, Murcer Glad for Yank Return," *The Sporting News*, July 14, 1979, 29.

102. Madden, *Steinbrenner: The Last Lion of Baseball,* 165.

103. Madden, *Steinbrenner: The Last Lion of Baseball,* 166.

104. *Ibid.*

105. *Ibid.*

106. Rich Chere, "Rosen Makes It Official," *Newark Star-Ledger*, July 20, 1979, 39, 44.

107. Dave Sims, "Reggie Hits 17th; Blasts George," *New York Daily News*, July 20, 1979, 45.

108. Dave Anderson, "Martin's Power," *New York Times*, July 22, 1979, S3.

109. Dave Anderson, "Face on the Scoreboard," *New York Times*, August 4, 1979, 13.

Chapter 8

1. Dick Young, "Rosen to Run Padres," *New York Daily News*, August 7, 1980, 28C.

2. Phil Collier, "Smith Denies Report that Rosen, Lemon To Be Hired," *San Diego Union*, August 7, 1980, C-1.

3. Harry Shattuck, "Rosen won't shake Astro foundation,'" *Houston Chronicle*, October 29, 1980, 2–4.

4. Clark Nealon, "Astros' New Home Dubbed Astrodome," *The Sporting News*, December 26, 1964, 12.

5. *Ibid.*

6. *Ibid.*

7. Linda Gillan, "Astrodomain, an aging $2-billion plus for Houston's economy," *Houston Chronicle*, November 23, 1979, 2–3.

8. Tal Smith, "Reflections on the Opening of the Astrodome," *Dome Sweet Dome*, Society for American Baseball Research, 2017, 4.

9. Baseball Reference Bullpen Page:

Notes—Chapter 8

Tal Smith, https://www.baseball-reference.com/bullpen/Tal_Smith, Accessed October 15, 2019.

10. Jack Lang, "Fabled Yanks Sold for Cut-Rate $10 Million," *The Sporting News*, January 20, 1973, 39.

11. Harry Shattuck, "Astros Ask Tal Smith To Get Them Off Pad," *The Sporting News*, August 23, 1975, 6.

12. *Ibid.*

13. Peter Golenbock, *Wild, High and Tight: The Life and Death of Billy Martin* (New York: St. Martin's Press, 1994), 246.

14. Houston Astros Attendance, 1965–2012, https://www.baseball-almanac.com/teams/housattn.shtml, Accessed on October 16, 2019.

15. Ed Fowler, "His ship came in," *Houston Chronicle*, May 17, 1979, 3–1.

16. Murray Chass, "McMullen's Goal: Astros Champs in 3–5 Years," *The Sporting News*, June 9, 1979, 11.

17. Nolan Ryan's Contract.

18. Ed Fowler, "Who Shot J.R.?" *Houston Chronicle*, July 15, 1980, 1–1.

19. Jeff Katz, *Split Season 1981* (New York: St. Martin's Press, 2015), 28–29.

20. Houston Astros Attendance, 1965–2012, https://www.baseball-almanac.com/teams/housattn.shtml, Accessed on October 19, 2019.

21. Harry Shattuck, "Nothing Detracts From Job Tal Smith Did," *The Sporting News*, December 20, 1980, 42.

22. Harry Shattuck, "Virdon Voted Best Manager," *The Sporting News*, November 1, 1980, 7.

23. Harry Shattuck, "Firing of Smith Stirs Houston Hornet Nest," *The Sporting News*, November 15, 1980, 56.

24. Chronicle News Services, "Smith: McMullen wants the Astros to be his team," *Houston Chronicle*, October 29, 1980, 2–1.

25. Harry Shattuck, "Don't Say Goodbye ... Yet," *Houston Chronicle*, October 28, 1980, 1–1.

26. "Here's reaction to firing," *Houston Chronicle*, October 28, 1980, 2–1.

27. John Wilson, "McMullen Challenge is studied," *Houston Chronicle*, October 29, 1980, 2–4.

28. Harry Shattuck, "Rosen won't

shake Astro foundation,'" *Houston Chronicle*, October 29, 1980, 2–4.

29. *Ibid.*

30. Neil Hohlfeld, "Astros must honor pacts if receiver takes control," *Houston Chronicle*, November 21, 1980, 2–1.

31. Associated Press, "Bilk Jersey casinos in $3M credit scam," *Herald-News*, November 16, 1980, A-1, A-13.

32. Harry Shattuck, "Astros' Big Playing Field Lures Sutton," *The Sporting News*, December 20, 1980, 47.

33. *Ibid.*

34. Harry Shattuck, "Smith won't be back as Astros' GM," *Houston Chronicle*, January 28, 1981, 2–1.

35. *Ibid.*

36. Harry Shattuck, "Decision not to bring Smith back great relief to Rosen," *Houston Chronicle*, January 28, 1981, 2–7.

37. Harry Shattuck, "Rough Going: Rosen's position with Astros solidifies," *Houston Chronicle*, April 26, 1981, 3–1.

38. *Ibid.*, 3–6.

39. *Ibid.*

40. Katz, *Split Season 1981*, 17–18.

41. Eddie Sefko, "Andujar traded to Cards for Scott," *Houston Chronicle*, June 7, 1981, 3–6.

42. Katz, *Split Season 1981*, 180.

43. Ibid., 238.

44. Neil Hohlfeld, "Ryan claims record with 5th no-hitter," *Houston Chronicle*, September 27, 1981, 3–1.

45. Katz, *Split Season 1981*, 240.

46. Harry Shattuck, "Astros Cite Knight's Hustle, Endurance," *The Sporting News*, January 2, 1982, 40.

47. Harry Shattuck, "Howe Uneasy Over Possible Job Loss," *The Sporting News*, February 13, 1982, 39.

48. George White, "Sutton brought his glove to Houston, but left his heart at home," *Houston Chronicle*, March 12, 1982, 2–2.

49. Associated Press, "Sutton comment may be probed," Houston *Chronicle*, February 19, 1982, 2–2.

50. Ed Fowler, "Final accounting to be Sutton's won-loss record," *Houston Chronicle*, March 18, 1982, 2–2.

51. Neil Hohlfeld, "Rosen meets with

Sutton," *Houston Chronicle*, March 18, 1982, 2–8.

52. Harry Shattuck, "Astros Stand Pat Despite Skid," *The Sporting News*, June 28, 1982, 22.

53. Harry Shattuck, "Everybody Lauds Departed Virdon," *The Sporting News*, August 23, 1982, 20.

54. Harry Shattuck, "Lillis debut a success: Astros win," *Houston Chronicle*, August 11, 1982, 2–1.

55. "Sutton dealt to Brewers," *Houston Chronicle*, August 31, 1982, 2–5.

56. Harry Shattuck, "Astros Debate Moving In Fences," *The Sporting News*, January 17, 1983, 40.

57. Harry Shattuck, "Free-agent Moreno new Astro," *Houston Chronicle*, December 11, 1982, 3–1.

58. Harry Shattuck, "Sambito Cautious In Comeback Bid," *The Sporting News*, February 21, 1983, 36.

59. Harry Shattuck, "Astros unload Moreno," *Houston Chronicle*, August 11, 1983, 2–16.

60. Harry Shattuck, "Rosen signs new pact," *Houston Chronicle*, October 21, 1983, 2–1, 2–5.

61. Harry Shattuck, "Walling Becomes a Millionaire," *The Sporting News*, January 2, 1984, 40.

62. *Ibid.*

63. Harry Shattuck, "Ryan Rejects Cut, Cites Principle," *The Sporting News*, February 14, 1983, 43.

64. Dave Nightingale, "Baseball's Drug Policy: Still Piecemeal," *The Sporting News*, April 9, 1984, 31.

65. Harry Shattuck, "Astros fall short again, despite bullpen," *Houston Chronicle*, April 25, 1984, 2–5.

66. Harry Shattuck, "Injuries Enervate Astros Offense," *The Sporting News*, May 14, 1984, 20.

67. *Ibid.*

68. Harry Shattuck, "Inability to Score Is Dooming Astros," *The Sporting News*, May 21, 1984, 18.

69. Harry Shattuck, "Dark Season for Knight," *The Sporting News*, September 3, 1984, 34.

70. Harry Shattuck, "Was Houston in '84 Success or Failure?" *The Sporting News*, October 15, 1984, 21.

71. *Ibid.*

72. Harry Shattuck, "Dome fences returning to '72 distances," *Houston Chronicle*, December 3, 1984, 3–1.

73. Harry Shattuck, "New Spring Complex a Smash Hit," *The Sporting News*, February 25, 1985, 39.

74. Neil Hohlfeld, "Astros plan change at the top," *Houston Chronicle*, September 13, 1985, 2–1.

75. Ed Fowler, "Another tack, another blunder," *Houston Chronicle*, September 14, 1985, 2–1.

Chapter 9

1. David Bush, "Rosen, Craig: A Turning Point," *San Francisco Chronicle*, September 19, 1985, 71.

2. *Ibid.*

3. *Ibid.*

4. Lowell Cohn, "Give and Take with Al Rosen," *San Francisco Chronicle*, September 19, 1985, 71.

5. *Ibid.*

6. Glenn Dickey, "The Giants Finally Make a Good Move," *San Francisco Chronicle*, September 19, 1985, 73.

7. Voice of the Fan, "Another Bad Deal for Giants," *The Sporting News*, October 28, 1985, 8.

8. Tom Flaherty, "Deer's Year: Promise Fulfilled," *The Sporting News*, September 15, 1986, 12.

9. Robert F. Garratt, *Home Team: The Turbulent History of the San Francisco Giants* (Lincoln: University of Nebraska Press, 2017), 127.

10. San Francisco Attendance Records, https://www.baseball-almanac.com/teams/sfatte.shtml, Accessed December 17, 2019.

11. Rob Garratt, "San Francisco Giants Team Ownership History," Society for American Baseball Research website, https://sabr.org/research/san-francisco-giants-team-ownership-history, Accessed December 1, 2019.

12. *Ibid.*

13. *Ibid.*

14. "How to Get to the Stadium," *San Francisco Chronicle*, April 11, 1960, 4C.

15. Nick Peters, "Giants' Brass Visits

Notes—Chapter 9

Denver," *The Sporting News*, November 18, 1985, 53.

16. Bill Conlin, "'86 Giants Seem Doomed to Fail," *The Sporting News*, February 3, 1986, 31.

17. *Ibid.*

18. Glenn Schwarz, "Giants Notebook," *San Francisco Examiner*, May 1, 1986, F-4.

19. Nick Peters, "Clark Feeds on his flair for the dramatic," *The Sporting News*, April 21, 1986, 12.

20. Ed Fowler, "Wagnerian theme fills air at Dome," *Houston Chronicle*, April 9, 1986, 2–1.

21. Stan Isle, "Baseball-Mad Dominicans Catch Mets Fever," *The Sporting News*, September 29, 1986, 10.

22. "Jose, Robby, Top Rookies," *San Francisco Chronicle*, October 15, 1986, 57.

23. Frank Blackman, "Giants, A's take cautious approach," *San Francisco Chronicle*, October 19, 1986, C-3.

24. *Ibid.*

25. "Giants," *The Sporting News*, January 5, 1987, 62.

26. Bruce Jenkins, "Brown: I'm Out for the Season," *San Francisco Chronicle*, September 2, 1986, 55.

27. *Ibid.*

28. Bill Conlin, "Critics Owe San Francisco's Brown An Apology," *The Sporting News*, November 24, 1986, 45.

29. Glenn Schwarz, "Trade means Rosen isn't waiting," *San Francisco Examiner*, "July 6, 1987, F-3.

30. Ray Ratto, "Mitchell Can't Understand Deal," *San Francisco Chronicle*, July 6, 1987, 61.

31. Glenn Schwarz, "How Reuschel Cleared Waivers," *San Francisco Examiner*, August 22, 1987, C-7.

32. Glenn Schwarz, "Trader Al's Best Deal?" *San Francisco Examiner*, August 22, 1987, C-7.

33. Nick Peters, "Some Gigantic Strides in 'Frisco," *The Sporting News*, October 5, 1987, 14.

34. *Ibid.*

35. Peter Pascarelli, "Zimmer Thinks Parity Gives Everyone Help," *The Sporting News*, October 26, 1987, 21.

36. Ray Ratto, "Dravecky Two-Hits

Cards," *San Francisco Chronicle*, October 8, 1987, D-1.

37. Steve Wiegand and Carl Nolte, "Record Crowd Sees 6–3 Win," *San Francisco Chronicle*, October 12, 1987, A-1.

38. *Ibid.*

39. *Ibid.*

40. Marc Sandalour, "A Giant Welcome Home," *San Francisco Chronicle*, October 16, 1987, A-1.

41. Art Spander, "There's No Joy in Mudville—Or San Francisco," *The Sporting News*, October 26, 1987, 12.

42. Nick Peters, "Shopper Al Rosen Bags Exec Award," *The Sporting News*, December 14, 1987, 48.

43. Larry Stone and Eric Brazil. "Al Rosen bows out as boss of Giants," *San Francisco Examiner*, November 20, 1992, A-22.

44. Nick Peters, "Shopper Al Rosen Bags Exec Award," *The Sporting News*, December 14, 1987, 49.

45. *Ibid.*

46. Rob Garratt, "San Francisco Giants Team Ownership History," Society for American Baseball Research website, https://sabr.org/research/san-francisco-giants-team-ownership-history, Accessed December 8, 2019.

47. Ray Ratto, "Giants Sign Butler; Chili Goes to Angels," *San Francisco Chronicle*, December 2, 1987, D-4.

48. Edvins Beitiks, "Aldrete Keyed Hac Man Trade," *San Francisco Examiner*, June 9, 1988, B-1.

49. *Ibid.*

50. *Ibid.*, B-5.

51. Nick Peters, "'Take a Hike,' Giants Tell Leonard," *The Sporting News*, June 20, 1988, 10.

52. Art Spander, "A Bad Trade," *San Francisco Examiner*, June 10, 1988, D-1.

53. Mark Camps "Krukow Stays Off Disabled—For Now," *San Francisco Chronicle*, July 2, 1988, D-3.

54. Ray Ratto, "Reds Beat Giants ,5–1—Reuschel Is Denied 20th Victory," *San Francisco Chronicle*, September 22, 1988, D-7.

55. David Perlman and Ray Ratto, "Giants' Dravecky Has Cancer in Pitching Arm," *San Francisco Chronicle*, October 1, 1988, A—16.

56. Ross McKeon, "Gossage is looking for help," *San Francisco Examiner*, April 15, 1989, C-4.

57. Bill Madden, "Yankees Hope Goose Can Pitch Again," *The Sporting News*, August 28, 1989, 21.

58. Ray Ratto, "Giants Get Bedrosian From Phils," *San Francisco Chronicle*, June 19, 1989, D-1.

59. Lisa M. Krieger, "Pitcher's cancer weakened the arm," *San Francisco Examiner*, August 17, 1989, A-22.

60. Casey Tefertiller, "Storybook Comeback Halted by Broken Arm," *San Francisco Examiner*, August 16, 1989, A-24.

61. Garratt, *Home Team: The Turbulent History of the San Francisco Giants*, 128.

62. J. McCarthy, "The Latest Line," *San Francisco Examiner*, October 13, 1989, B-16.

63. Art Spander, "G.M. Story: Best of Two Worlds," *The Sporting News*, October 23, 1989, 36.

64. Peter Pascarelli, "Rosen Deserves Plaudits for Rebirth of Giants," *The Sporting News*, October 23, 1989, 37.

65. Lance Williams, "After Quake, a New World," *San Francisco Examiner*, October 19, 1989, A-1.

66. Damage Assessment, County by County, *San Francisco Examiner*, October 19, 1989, A-9.

67. Paul Attner, "Series Diminishes in Wake of Quake," *The Sporting News*, October 30, 1989, 17.

68. Casey Tefertiller, "Odd injury scratches Reuschel's start," *San Francisco Examiner*, October 27, 1989, D-6.

69. Attner, 19.

70. Nick Peters, "Giants," *The Sporting News*, November 13, 1989, 51.

71. Ray Ratto, "Giants Gamble on Gary Carter," *San Francisco Chronicle*, January 20, 1990, D-7.

72. Nick Peters, "Bottom Line on Clark Contract: $20,000 a Hit!" *The Sporting News*, February 5, 1990, 32.

73. Ray Ratto, "Injured Quisenberry Retires From Game," *San Francisco Chronicle*, April 30, 1990, D-1.

74. Nick Peters, "Giants," *The Sporting News*, June 11, 1990, 18.

75. Nick Peters, "Giants," *The Sporting News*, September 10, 1990,: 28.

76. *Ibid.*, 18.

77. C. W. Nevius, "Giants Sign Lefty Starter," *San Francisco Chronicle*, November 10, 1990, D-1.

78. Peter Pascarelli, "Rival GM's rap Giants' Rosen for large Black contract," *The National Sports Daily*, November 14, 1990, 44.

79. Ray Ratto, "Giants Sign McGee, Give Up on Butler," *San Francisco Chronicle*, December 4, 1990, D-1.

80. Nick Peters, "Butler Says Giants Acted Too Hastily," *The Sporting News*, December 17, 1990, 38.

81. *Ibid.*

82. Ratto, "Giants Sign McGee, Give Up on Butler," D-1.

83. Larry Stone, "Early Christmas for Giants," *San Francisco Examiner*, December 5, 1990, D-9.

84. Bob Hertzel, "Giants Set Pace in Latest California Gold Rush," *The Sporting News*, December 17, 1990, 37.

85. Mark Camps, "LaCoss, Reuschel Survive in Giants' War of Attrition," *San Francisco Chronicle*, April 6, 1991, D-4.

86. Bob Nightengale, "Swift changes in order for Giants, Expos," *The Sporting News*, May 13, 1991, 39.

87. Mark Newman, "San Francisco Giants," *The Sporting News*, May 20, 1991, 15.

88. Larry Stone, "Rangers willing to listen to talks about Mitchell," *San Francisco Examiner*, December 10, 1991, C-3.

89. Bruce Jenkins, "Giants Case Against Mitchell," *San Francisco Chronicle*, December 18, 1991, D-1.

90. *Ibid.*, D-7.

91. *Ibid.*

92. *Ibid.*

93. "Letters to the Green," *San Francisco Chronicle*, December 14, 1991, D-6.

94. Garratt, *Home Team: The Turbulent History of the San Francisco Giants*, 155.

95. *Ibid.*

96. Rob Garratt, "San Francisco Giants Team Ownership History," Society for American Baseball Research website, https://sabr.org/research/san-francisco-giants-team-ownership-history, Accessed

December 17, 2019.

97. Stephen Nohlgren, "What might still go wrong," *Tampa Bay Times, August 8*, 1992, 1A.

98. Marc Topkin, "Deal set to Bring Giants to Dome," *Tampa Bay Times, August 8*, 1992, 1A.

99. *Ibid.*

100. Rob Garratt, "San Francisco Giants Team Ownership History," Society for American Baseball Research website, https://sabr.org/research/san-francisco-giants-team-ownership-history, Accessed December 17, 2019.

101. *Ibid.*

102. *Ibid.*

103. Glenn Dickey, "Baker as Manager is Right Move," *San Francisco Chronicle,* December 2, 1992, E-3.

104. Larry Stone and Eric Brazil. "Al Rosen bows out as boss of Giants," *San Francisco Examiner,* November 20, 1992, A-22.

105. Glenn Dickey, "Rosen Wasn't Afraid to Act Quickly," *San Francisco Chronicle,* November 21, 1992, D-2.

Epilogue

1. Mike Pettica, "Crowd roars for Rocky: Fans and former players cherish chance to relive the past," *Cleveland Plain Dealer,* July 22, 2001: C8.

2. Interview, November 2, 2019, Cleveland Public Library.

3. "Hall of Fame Inducts Star Al Rosen," *Cleveland Jewish News*, August 8, 1980: 6.

4. "A Pitcher First: Ronald Reagan's body double had one of the best arms of an era rich in hurlers," *Sports Illustrated,* January 24, 2000: 32.

5. Bill Lubinger, "Indians great Rosen enduered, prevailed in the face of bigotry," *Cleveland Plain Dealer,* October 12, 2010: D1.

6. Bill Lubinger, "Indians great Rosen endured, prevailed in the face of bigotry," *Cleveland Plain Dealer,* October 12, 2010: D1.

7. Steve Marconi, "Al Rosen: Short but Great Year," *Las Vegas Sun,* June 8, 1975: 29.

8. Larry Ruttman, *American Jews & America's Game: Voices of a Growing Legacy in Baseball* (Nebraska: University of Nebraska Press, 2013), 78.

9. Tom Withers, "Rosen, AL MVP with Indians, recalled as Hebrew Hammer,'" *Cleveland Jewish News,* March 20, 2015: 50.

10. Tom Withers, "Tribe great, 1953 MVP, MLB leader is dead at 91," Associated Press, March 14, 2015: C1.

Bibliography

Newspapers

Akron Beacon Journal
American Weekly
Arizona Republic
Baltimore Sun
Berkshire Eagle
Berkshire Evening Eagle
Boston Globe
Chicago Tribune
Cleveland Jewish News
Cleveland News
Cleveland Plain Dealer
Cleveland Press
Daily Oklahoman
Detroit Free Press
Dothan Eagle
Herald News
Houston Chronicle
Jewish Independent

Las Vegas Review Journal
Las Vegas Sun
Los Angeles Times
Miami Herald
Miami News
New York Daily News
New York Times
Newark Star-Ledger
Philadelphia Inquirer
St. Louis Post-Dispatch
St. Petersburg Times
San Diego Union
San Francisco Chronicle
San Francisco Examiner
Springfield Union
Star Tribune (Minneapolis)
Tampa Bay Times

Magazines

Baseball Digest
The National Sports Daily
Saturday Evening Post

SPORT Magazine
The Sporting News
Sports Illustrated

Books

2019 Cleveland Indians Information & Record Book.

Ephross, Peter, with Martin Abramowitz. Jewish Major Leaguers in Their Own Words. Jefferson, NC: McFarland, 2012.

Garratt, Robert F. Home Team: The Turbulent History of the San Francisco Giants. Lincoln: University of Nebraska Press, 2017.

Golenbock, Peter. Wild, High and Tight: The Life and Death of Billy Martin. New York: St. Martin's Press, 1994.

Greenberg, Hank, with Ira Berkow. Hank Greenberg: The Story of My Life. New York: Random House, 1989.

Isaacson, Melissa. Sweet Lou, Lou Piniella: A Life in Baseball. Chicago: Triumph Books, 2009.

Bibliography

James, Bill. *The New Bill James Historical Baseball Abstract*. New York: Free Press Publishing, 2003.

Kahn, Roger. *How the Weather Was*. New York: Harper & Row, 1973.

_____. *October Men: Reggie Jackson, George Steinbrenner, Billy Martin, and the Yankees' Miraculous Finish in 1978*. Orlando, FL: Harcourt Books, 2003.

Katz, Jeff. *Split Season 1981*. New York: St. Martin's Press, 2015.

Madden, Bill. *Steinbrenner: The Last Lion of Baseball*. New York: HarperCollins, 2010.

Moore, Joseph Thomas. *Larry Doby: The Struggle of American League's First Black Player*. Mineola, NY: Dover Publications, 2012.

Peary, Danny. *We Played the Game*. New York: Hyperion, 1994.

Ribalow, Harold U., and Meir Z. Ribalow. *Jewish Baseball Stars*. New York: Hippocrene Books, 1984.

Rosen, Al. *Baseball and Your Boy*. Cleveland: World Publishing Company, 1967.

Ruttman, Larry. *American Jews & Americas Game: Voices of a Growing Legacy in Baseball*. Lincoln: University of Nebraska Press, 2013.

Wancho, Joseph. *Pitching to the Pennant*. Lincoln: University of Nebraska Press, 2014.

Wilber, Cynthia J. *For the Love of the Game: Baseball Memories from the Men Who Were There*. New York: William Morrow, 1992.

Websites

https://www.mlb.com/indians
https://www.mlb.com/yankees
https://www.mlb.com/astros
https://www.mlb.com/giants
https://sabr.org/
https://www.baseball-reference.com/
https://www.retrosheet.org/
https://www.baseball-almanac.com/

https://www.spartanburg.com/
https://www.history.com/
http://www.umsportshalloffame.com/
https://www.ballparksofbaseball.com/
https://www.cleveland.com/
https://wahooclub.org/
https://wahooclub.org/our-history
https://www.si.com/

Other Sources

Al Rosen's Clip File, Courtesy of the National Baseball Hall of Fame.
Interview with Robert Rosen, August 18, 2020.
United States Census Bureau—1920, 1930, 1940, 2000, 2010.

Index

215

Index

216

Index

217

Index

Index

Index

Index

Index